SEVEN ECUMENICAL COUNCILS OF THE CATHOLIC CHURCH

Translated by: Henry Percival
Forward by: D.P. Curtin

Dalcassian Publishing Company
PHILADELPHIA, PA

SEVEN ECUMENICAL COUNCILS OF THE CHURCH

All rights reserved. No part of the material protected by this copyright may be reproduced or utilized in any form, electronic or mechanical, including photocopying, recording or by any information storage and retrieval system, without written permission from the copyright owner.

Library of Congress Cataloging-in-Publication Data

Copyright © 2021 Dalcassian Publishing Co.
In association with St. Macartan Press
All rights reserved.

SEVEN ECUMENICAL COUNCILS OF THE CHURCH

COUNCIL OF FIRST NICAEA

The Nicene Creed
The Synod at Nice set forth this Creed.

The Ecthesis of the Synod at Nice.

We believe in one God, the Father Almighty, maker of all things visible and invisible; and in one Lord Jesus Christ, the Son of God, the only-begotten of his Father, of the substance of the Father, God of God, Light of Light, very God of very God, begotten (γεννηθέντα), not made, being of one substance (ὁμοούσιον, consubstantialem) with the Father. By whom all things were made, both which be in heaven and in earth. Who for us men and for our salvation came down [from heaven] and was incarnate and was made man. He suffered and the third day he rose again, and ascended into heaven. And he shall come again to judge both the quick and the dead. And [we believe] in the Holy Ghost. And whosoever shall say that there was a time when the Son of God was not (ἤν ποτε ὅτε οὐκ ἦν), or that before he was begotten he was not, or that he was made of things that were not, or that he is of a different substance or essence [from the Father] or that he is a creature, or subject to change or conversion — all that so say, the Catholic and Apostolic Church anathematizes them.

The Canons

Canon 1
If any one in sickness has been subjected by physicians to a surgical operation, or if he has been castrated by barbarians, let him remain among the clergy; but, if any one in sound health has castrated himself, it behooves that such an one, if [already] enrolled among the clergy, should cease [from his ministry], and that from henceforth no such person should be promoted. But, as it is evident that this is said of those who wilfully do the thing and presume to castrate themselves, so if any have been made eunuchs by barbarians, or by their masters, and should otherwise be found worthy, such men the Canon admits to the clergy.

Canon 2
Forasmuch as, either from necessity, or through the urgency of individuals, many things have been done contrary to the Ecclesiastical canon, so that men just converted from heathenism to the faith, and who have been instructed but a little while, are straightway brought to the spiritual laver, and as soon as they have been baptized, are advanced to the episcopate or the presbyterate, it has seemed right to us that for the time to come no such thing shall be done. For to the catechumen himself there is need of time and of a longer trial after baptism. For the saying is clear, "Not a novice; lest, being lifted up with "pride, he fall into condemnation and the snare of the devil. But if, as time goes on, any sensual sin should be found out about the person, and he should be convicted by two or three witnesses, let him cease from the clerical office. And whoso shall transgress these [enactments] will imperil his own clerical position, as a person who presumes to disobey the great Synod.

Canon 3

The great Synod has stringently forbidden any bishop, presbyter, deacon, or any one of the clergy whatever, to have a subintroducta dwelling with him, except only a mother, or sister, or aunt, or such persons only as are beyond all suspicion.

Canon 4

It is by all means proper that a bishop should be appointed by all the bishops in the province; but should this be difficult, either on account of urgent necessity or because of distance, three at least should meet together, and the suffrages of the absent [bishops] also being given and communicated in writing, then the ordination should take place. But in every province the ratification of what is done should be left to the Metropolitan.

Canon 5

Concerning those, whether of the clergy or of the laity, who have been excommunicated in the several provinces, let the provision of the canon be observed by the bishops which provides that persons cast out by some be not readmitted by others. Nevertheless, inquiry should be made whether they have been excommunicated through captiousness, or contentiousness, or any such like ungracious disposition in the bishop. And, that this matter may have due investigation, it is decreed that in every province synods shall be held twice a year, in order that when all the bishops of the province are assembled together, such questions may by them be thoroughly examined, that so those who have confessedly offended against their bishop, may be seen by all to be for just cause excommunicated, until it shall seem fit to a general meeting of the bishops to pronounce a milder sentence upon them. And let these synods be held, the one before Lent, (that the pure Gift may be offered to God after all bitterness has been put away), and let the second be held about autumn.

Canon 6

Let the ancient customs in Egypt, Libya and Pentapolis prevail, that the Bishop of Alexandria have jurisdiction in all these, since the like is customary for the Bishop of Rome also. Likewise in Antioch and the other provinces, let the Churches retain their privileges. And this is to be universally understood, that if any one be made bishop without the consent of the Metropolitan, the great Synod has declared that such a man ought not to be a bishop. If, however, two or three bishops shall from natural love of contradiction, oppose the common suffrage of the rest, it being reasonable and in accordance with the ecclesiastical law, then let the choice of the majority prevail.

Canon 7

Since custom and ancient tradition have prevailed that the Bishop of Ælia [i.e., Jerusalem] should be honoured, let him, saving its due dignity to the Metropolis, have the next place of honour.

Canon 8
Concerning those who call themselves Cathari, if they come over to the Catholic and Apostolic Church, the great and holy Synod decrees that they who are ordained shall continue as they are in the clergy. But it is before all things necessary that they should profess in writing that they will observe and follow the dogmas of the Catholic and Apostolic Church; in particular that they will communicate with persons who have been twice married, and with those who having lapsed in persecution have had a period [of penance] laid upon them, and a time [of restoration] fixed so that in all things they will follow the dogmas of the Catholic Church. Wheresoever, then, whether in villages or in cities, all of the ordained are found to be of these only, let them remain in the clergy, and in the same rank in which they are found. But if they come over where there is a bishop or presbyter of the Catholic Church, it is manifest that the Bishop of the Church must have the bishop's dignity; and he who was named bishop by those who are called Cathari shall have the rank of presbyter, unless it shall seem fit to the Bishop to admit him to partake in the honour of the title. Or, if this should not be satisfactory, then shall the bishop provide for him a place as Chorepiscopus, or presbyter, in order that he may be evidently seen to be of the clergy, and that there may not be two bishops in the city.

Canon 9
If any presbyters have been advanced without examination, or if upon examination they have made confession of crime, and men acting in violation of the canon have laid hands upon them, notwithstanding their confession, such the canon does not admit; for the Catholic Church requires that [only] which is blameless.

Canon 10
If any who have lapsed have been ordained through the ignorance, or even with the previous knowledge of the ordainers, this shall not prejudice the canon of the Church; for when they are discovered they shall be deposed.

Canon 11
Concerning those who have fallen without compulsion, without the spoiling of their property, without danger or the like, as happened during the tyranny of Licinius, the Synod declares that, though they have deserved no clemency, they shall be dealt with mercifully. As many as were communicants, if they heartily repent, shall pass three years among the hearers; for seven years they shall be prostrators; and for two years they shall communicate with the people in prayers, but without oblation.

Canon 12
As many as were called by grace, and displayed the first zeal, having cast aside their military girdles, but afterwards returned, like dogs, to their own vomit, (so that some spent money and by means of gifts regained their military stations); let these, after they have passed the space of three years as hearers, be for ten years prostrators. But in all these cases it is necessary to examine well into their purpose and what their repentance appears to be like. For as many as give evidence of their conversions by

deeds, and not pretence, with fear, and tears, and perseverance, and good works, when they have fulfilled their appointed time as hearers, may properly communicate in prayers; and after that the bishop may determine yet more favourably concerning them. But those who take [the matter] with indifference, and who think the form of [not] entering the Church is sufficient for their conversion, must fulfil the whole time.

Canon 13

Concerning the departing, the ancient canonical law is still to be maintained, to wit, that, if any man be at the point of death, he must not be deprived of the last and most indispensable Viaticum. But, if any one should be restored to health again who has received the communion when his life was despaired of, let him remain among those who communicate in prayers only. But in general, and in the case of any dying person whatsoever asking to receive the Eucharist, let the Bishop, after examination made, give it him.

Canon 14

Concerning catechumens who have lapsed, the holy and great Synod has decreed that, after they have passed three years only as hearers, they shall pray with the catechumens.

Canon 15

On account of the great disturbance and discords that occur, it is decreed that the custom prevailing in certain places contrary to the Canon, must wholly be done away; so that neither bishop, presbyter, nor deacon shall pass from city to city. And if any one, after this decree of the holy and great Synod, shall attempt any such thing, or continue in any such course, his proceedings shall be utterly void, and he shall be restored to the Church for which he was ordained bishop or presbyter.

Canon 16

Neither presbyters, nor deacons, nor any others enrolled among the clergy, who, not having the fear of God before their eyes, nor regarding the ecclesiastical Canon, shall recklessly remove from their own church, ought by any means to be received by another church; but every constraint should be applied to restore them to their own parishes; and, if they will not go, they must be excommunicated. And if anyone shall dare surreptitiously to carry off and in his own Church ordain a man belonging to another, without the consent of his own proper bishop, from whom although he was enrolled in the clergy list he has seceded, let the ordination be void.

Canon 17

Forasmuch as many enrolled among the Clergy, following covetousness and lust of gain, have forgotten the divine Scripture, which says, "He has not given his money upon usury," and in lending money ask the hundredth of the sum [as monthly interest], the holy and great Synod thinks it just that if after this decree any one be found to receive usury, whether he accomplish it by secret transaction or otherwise, as by demanding the whole and one half, or by using any other contrivance whatever for filthy lucre's sake, he shall be deposed from the clergy and his name stricken from the list.

Canon 18

It has come to the knowledge of the holy and great Synod that, in some districts and cities, the deacons administer the Eucharist to the presbyters, whereas neither canon nor custom permits that they who have no right to offer should give the Body of Christ to them that do offer. And this also has been made known, that certain deacons now touch the Eucharist even before the bishops. Let all such practices be utterly done away, and let the deacons remain within their own bounds, knowing that they are the ministers of the bishop and the inferiors of the presbyters. Let them receive the Eucharist according to their order, after the presbyters, and let either the bishop or the presbyter administer to them. Furthermore, let not the deacons sit among the presbyters, for that is contrary to canon and order. And if, after this decree, any one shall refuse to obey, let him be deposed from the diaconate.

Canon 19

Concerning the Paulianists who have flown for refuge to the Catholic Church, it has been decreed that they must by all means be rebaptized; and if any of them who in past time have been numbered among their clergy should be found blameless and without reproach, let them be rebaptized and ordained by the Bishop of the Catholic Church; but if the examination should discover them to be unfit, they ought to be deposed. Likewise in the case of their deaconesses, and generally in the case of those who have been enrolled among their clergy, let the same form be observed. And we mean by deaconesses such as have assumed the habit, but who, since they have no imposition of hands, are to be numbered only among the laity.

Canon 20

Forasmuch as there are certain persons who kneel on the Lord's Day and in the days of Pentecost, therefore, to the intent that all things may be uniformly observed everywhere (in every parish), it seems good to the holy Synod that prayer be made to God standing.

The Synodal Letter

To the Church of Alexandria, by the grace of God, holy and great; and to our well-beloved brethren, the orthodox clergy and laity throughout Egypt, and Pentapolis, and Lybia, and every nation under heaven, the holy and great synod, the bishops assembled at Nicea, wish health in the Lord .

Forasmuch as the great and holy Synod, which was assembled at Niece through the grace of Christ and our most religious Sovereign Constantine, who brought us together from our several provinces and cities, has considered matters which concern the faith of the Church, it seemed to us to be necessary that certain things should be communicated from us to you in writing, so that you might have the means of knowing what has been mooted and investigated, and also what has been decreed and confirmed.

First of all, then, in the presence of our most religious Sovereign Constantine, investigation was made of matters concerning the impiety and transgression of Arius and his adherents; and it was unanimously decreed that he and his impious opinion should be anathematized, together with the blasphemous words and speculations in which he indulged, blaspheming the Son of God, and saying that he is from things that are not, and that before he was begotten he was not, and that there was a time when he was not, and that the Son of God is by his free will capable of vice and virtue; saying also that he is a creature. All these things the holy Synod has anathematized, not even enduring to hear his impious doctrine and madness and blasphemous words. And of the charges against him and of the results they had, you have either already heard or will hear the particulars, lest we should seem to be oppressing a man who has in fact received a fitting recompense for his own sin. So far indeed has his impiety prevailed, that he has even destroyed Theonas of Marmorica and Secundes of Ptolemais; for they also have received the same sentence as the rest.

But when the grace of God had delivered Egypt from that heresy and blasphemy, and from the persons who have dared to make disturbance and division among a people heretofore at peace, there remained the matter of the insolence of Meletius and those who have been ordained by him; and concerning this part of our work we now, beloved brethren, proceed to inform you of the decrees of the Synod. The Synod, then, being disposed to deal gently with Meletius (for in strict justice he deserved no leniency), decreed that he should remain in his own city, but have no authority either to ordain, or to administer affairs, or to make appointments; and that he should not appear in the country or in any other city for this purpose, but should enjoy the bare title of his rank; but that those who have been placed by him, after they have been confirmed by a more sacred laying on of hands, shall on these conditions be admitted to communion: that they shall both have their rank and the right to officiate, but that they shall be altogether the inferiors of all those who are enrolled in any church or parish, and have been appointed by our most honourable colleague Alexander. So that these men are to have no authority to make appointments of persons who may be pleasing to them, nor to suggest names, nor to do anything whatever, without the consent of the bishops of the Catholic and Apostolic Church, who are serving under our most holy colleague Alexander; while those who, by the grace of God and through your prayers, have been found in no schism, but on the contrary are without spot in the Catholic and Apostolic Church, are to have authority to make appointments and nominations of worthy persons among the clergy, and in short to do all things according to the law and ordinance of the Church. But, if it happen that any of the clergy who are now in the Church should die, then those who have been lately received are to succeed to the office of the deceased; always provided that they shall appear to be worthy, and that the people elect them, and that the bishop of Alexandria shall concur in the election and ratify it. This concession has been made to all the rest; but, on account of his disorderly conduct from the first, and the rashness and precipitation of his character, the same decree was not made concerning Meletius himself, but that, inasmuch as he is a man capable of committing again the same disorders, no authority nor privilege should be conceded to him.

These are the particulars, which are of special interest to Egypt and to the most holy Church of Alexandria; but if in the presence of our most honoured lord, our colleague and brother Alexander, anything else has been enacted by canon or other decree, he will himself convey it to you in greater detail, he having been both a guide and fellow-worker in what has been done.

We further proclaim to you the good news of the agreement concerning the holy Easter, that this particular also has through your prayers been rightly settled; so that all our brethren in the East who formerly followed the custom of the Jews are henceforth to celebrate the said most sacred feast of Easter at the same time with the Romans and yourselves and all those who have observed Easter from the beginning.

Wherefore, rejoicing in these wholesome results, and in our common peace and harmony, and in the cutting off of every heresy, receive with the greater honour and with increased love, our colleague your Bishop Alexander, who has gladdened us by his presence, and who at so great an age has undergone so great fatigue that peace might be established among you and all of us. Pray also for us all, that the things which have been deemed advisable may stand fast; for they have been done, as we believe, to the well-pleasing of Almighty God and of his only Begotten Son, our Lord Jesus Christ, and of the Holy Ghost, to whom be glory for ever. Amen.

SEVEN ECUMENICAL COUNCILS OF THE CHURCH

Letter of Eusebius of Cæsarea to the people of his Diocese.

1. What was transacted concerning ecclesiastical faith at the Great Council assembled at Nicæa, you have probably learned, Beloved, from other sources, rumour being wont to precede the accurate account of what is doing. But lest in such reports the circumstances of the case have been misrepresented, we have been obliged to transmit to you, first, the formula of faith presented by ourselves, and next, the second, which [the Fathers] put forth with some additions to our words. Our own paper, then, which was read in the presence of our most pious Emperor, and declared to be good and unexceptionable, ran thus:—

2. "As we have received from the Bishops who preceded us, and in our first catechisings, and when we received the Holy Laver, and as we have learned from the divine Scriptures, and as we believed and taught in the presbytery, and in the Episcopate itself, so believing also at the time present, we report to you our faith, and it is this :"—

3. "We believe in One God, the Father Almighty, the Maker of all things visible and invisible. And in One Lord Jesus Christ, the Word of God, God from God, Light from Light, Life from Life, Son Only-begotten, first-born of every creature, before all the ages, begotten from the Father, by Whom also all things were made; Who for our salvation was made flesh, and lived among men, and suffered, and rose again the third day, and ascended to the Father, and will come again in glory to judge the quick and dead. And we believe also in One Holy Ghost:"

believing each of these to be and to exist, the Father truly Father, and the Son truly Son, and the Holy Ghost truly Holy Ghost, as also our Lord, sending forth His disciples for the preaching, said, "Go teach all nations, baptizing them in the Name of the Father and of the Son, and of the Holy Ghost Matthew 28:19 ." Concerning Whom we confidently affirm that so we hold, and so we think, and so we have held aforetime, and we maintain this faith unto the death, anathematizing every godless heresy. That this we have ever thought from our heart and soul, from the time we recollect ourselves, and now think and say in truth, before God Almighty and our Lord Jesus Christ do we witness, being able by proofs to show and to convince you, that, even in times past, such has been our belief and preaching.

4. On this faith being publicly put forth by us, no room for contradiction appeared; but our most pious Emperor, before any one else, testified that it comprised most orthodox statements. He confessed moreover that such were his own sentiments, and he advised all present to agree to it, and to subscribe its articles and to assent to them, with the insertion of the single word, One-in-essence, which moreover he interpreted as not in the sense of the affections of bodies, nor as if the Son subsisted from the Father in the way of division, or any severance; for that the immaterial, and intellectual, and incorporeal nature could not be the subject of any corporeal affection, but that it became us to conceive of such things in a divine and ineffable

SEVEN ECUMENICAL COUNCILS OF THE CHURCH

manner. And such were the theological remarks of our most wise and most religious Emperor; but they, with a view to the addition of One in essence, drew up the following formula:—

The Faith dictated in the Council.

"We believe in One God, the Father Almighty, Maker of all things visible and invisible:"—

"And in One Lord Jesus Christ, the Son of God, begotten of the Father, Only-begotten, that is, from the essence of the Father; God from God, Light from Light, Very God from Very God, begotten not made, One in essence with the Father, by Whom all things were made, both things in heaven and things in earth; Who for us men and for our salvation came down and was made flesh, was made man, suffered, and rose again the third day, ascended into heaven, and comes to judge quick and dead."

"And in the Holy Ghost."

"And those who say, 'Once He was not,' and 'Before His generation He was not,' and 'He came to be from nothing,' or those who pretend that the Son of God is 'Of other subsistence or essence ,' or 'created' or 'alterable,' or 'mutable,' the Catholic Church anathematizes."

5. On their dictating this formula, we did not let it pass without inquiry in what sense they introduced "of the essence of the Father," and "one in essence with the Father." Accordingly questions and explanations took place, and the meaning of the words underwent the scrutiny of reason. And they professed, that the phrase "of the essence" was indicative of the Son's being indeed from the Father, yet without being as if a part of Him. And with this understanding we thought good to assent to the sense of such religious doctrine, teaching, as it did, that the Son was from the Father, not however a part of His essence. On this account we assented to the sense ourselves, without declining even the term "One in essence," peace being the object which we set before us, and steadfastness in the orthodox view.

6. In the same way we also admitted "begotten, not made;" since the Council alleged that "made" was an appellative common to the other creatures which came to be through the Son, to whom the Son had no likeness. Wherefore, say they, He was not a work resembling the things which through Him came to be , but was of an essence which is too high for the level of any work; and which the Divine oracles teach to have been generated from the Father , the mode of generation being inscrutable and incalculable to every originated nature.

7. And so too on examination there are grounds for saying that the Son is "one in essence" with the Father; not in the way of bodies, nor like mortal beings, for He is not such by division of essence, or by severance, no, nor by any affection, or alteration, or changing of the Father's essence and power (since from all such the unoriginate nature of the Father is alien), but because "one in essence with the

SEVEN ECUMENICAL COUNCILS OF THE CHURCH

Father" suggests that the Son of God bears no resemblance to the originated creatures, but that to His Father alone Who begot Him is He in every way assimilated, and that He is not of any other subsistence and essence, but from the Father. To which term also, thus interpreted, it appeared well to assent; since we were aware that even among the ancients, some learned and illustrious Bishops and writers have used the term "one in essence," in their theological teaching concerning the Father and Son.

8. So much then be said concerning the faith which was published; to which all of us assented, not without inquiry, but according to the specified senses, mentioned before the most religious Emperor himself, and justified by the forementioned considerations. And as to the anathematism published by them at the end of the Faith, it did not pain us, because it forbade to use words not in Scripture, from which almost all the confusion and disorder of the Church have come. Since then no divinely inspired Scripture has used the phrases, "out of nothing," and "once He was not," and the rest which follow, there appeared no ground for using or teaching them; to which also we assented as a good decision, since it had not been our custom hitherto to use these terms.

9. Moreover to anathematize "Before His generation He was not," did not seem preposterous, in that it is confessed by all, that the Son of God was before the generation according to the flesh.

10. Nay, our most religious Emperor did at the time prove, in a speech, that He was in being even according to His divine generation which is before all ages, since even before He was generated in energy, He was in virtue with the Father ingenerately, the Father being always Father, as King always, and Saviour always, being all things in virtue, and being always in the same respects and in the same way.

11. This we have been forced to transmit to you, Beloved, as making clear to you the deliberation of our inquiry and assent, and how reasonably we resisted even to the last minute as long as we were offended at statements which differed from our own, but received without contention what no longer pained us, as soon as, on a candid examination of the sense of the words, they appeared to us to coincide with what we ourselves have professed in the faith which we have already published.

Canons of the Synod of Neocaeserea
315 Anno Domini

Canon 1
If a presbyter marry, let him be removed from his order; but if he commit fornication or adultery, let him be altogether cast out [i.e. of communion] and put to penance.

Canon 2
If a woman shall have married two brothers, let her be cast out [i.e. of communion] until her death. Nevertheless, at the hour of death she may, as an act of mercy, be received to penance, provided she declare that she will break the marriage, should she recover. But if the woman in such a marriage, or the man, die, penance for the survivor shall be very difficult.

Canon 3
Concerning those who fall into many marriages, the appointed time of penance is well known; but their manner of living and faith shortens the time.

Canon 4
If any man lusting after a woman purposes to lie with her, and his design does not come to effect, it is evident that he has been saved by grace.

Canon 5
If a catechumen coming into the Church have taken his place in the order of catechumens, and fall into sin, let him, if a kneeler, become a hearer and sin no more. But should he again sin while a hearer, let him be cast out.

John Zonaras: "There are two sorts of catechumens. For some have only just come in and these, as still imperfect, go out immediately after the reading of the scriptures and of the Gospels. But there are others who have been for some time in preparation and have attained some perfection; these wait after the Gospel for the prayers for the catechumens, and when they hear the words "Catechumens, bow down your heads to the Lord," they kneel down. These, as being more perfect, having tasted the good words of God, if they fall, are removed from their position; and are placed with the "hearers"; but if any happen to sin while "hearers" they are cast out of the Church altogether."

Canon 6
Concerning a woman with child, it is determined that she ought to be baptized whenever she will; for in this the woman communicates nothing to the child, since the bringing forward to profession is evidently the individual [privilege] of every single person.

Canon 7

A presbyter shall not be a guest at the nuptials of persons contracting a second marriage; for, since the digamist is worthy of penance, what kind of a presbyter shall he be, who, by being present at the feast, sanctioned the marriage?

Canon 8

If the wife of a layman has committed adultery and been clearly convicted, such [a husband] cannot enter the ministry; and if she commit adultery after his ordination, he must put her away; but if he retain her, he can have no part in the ministry committed to him.

Canon 9

A presbyter who has been promoted after having committed carnal sin, and who shall confess that he had sinned before his ordination, shall not make the oblation, though he may remain in his other functions on account of his zeal in other respects; for the majority have affirmed that ordination blots out other kinds of sins. But if he do not confess and cannot be openly convicted, the decision shall depend upon himself.

Canon 10

Likewise, if a deacon have fallen into the same sin, let him have the rank of a minister.

Canon 11

Let not a presbyter be ordained before he is thirty years of age, even though he be in all respects a worthy man, but let him be made to wait. For our Lord Jesus Christ was baptized and began to teach in his thirtieth year.

Canon 12

If any one be baptized when he is ill, forasmuch as his [profession of] faith was not voluntary, but of necessity [i.e. though fear of death] he cannot be promoted to the presbyterate, unless on account of his subsequent [display of] zeal and faith, and because of a lack of men.

The word used in the Greek for "baptized" is "illuminated" (φωτισθῇ), a very common expression among the ancients.

Zonaras explains that the reason for this prohibition was the well-known fact that in those ages baptism was put off so as the longer to be free from the restraints which baptism was considered to impose.

Canon 13

Country presbyters may not make the oblation in the church of the city when the bishop or presbyters of the city are present; nor may they give the Bread or the Cup with prayer. If, however, they be absent, and he [i.e., a country presbyter] alone be called to prayer, he may give them.

Many scholars, including Dionysius Exiguus and Isidore, read the last clause in the plural. In many manuscripts this canon is united with the following and the whole number given as 14.

Canon 14

The chorepiscopi, however, are indeed after the pattern of the Seventy; and as fellow-servants, on account of their devotion to the poor, they have the honour of making the oblation.

See the note under the previous canon, as in many manuscripts the two canons are united in the Ancient Epitome.

Canon 15

The deacons ought to be seven in number, according to the canon, even if the city be great. Of this you will be persuaded from the Book of the Acts.

Canons of the Synod of Ancyra
314 Anno Domini

Soon after the death of the Emperor Maximin, a council was held at Ancyra, the capital of Galatia. Only about a dozen bishops were present, and the lists of subscriptions which are found appended to the canons are not to be depended on, being evidently in their present form of later authorship; as has been shown by the Ballerini. If we may at all trust the lists, it would seem that nearly every part of Syria and Asia Minor was represented, and that therefore the council while small in numbers was of considerable weight. It is not certain whether Vitalis, (bishop of Antioch,) presided or Marcellus, who was at the time bishop of Ancyra. The honour is by the Libellus Synodicus assigned to the latter.

The disciplinary decrees of this council possess a singular interest as being the first enacted after the ceasing of the persecution of the Christians and as providing for the proper treatment of the lapsed. Recently two papyri have been recovered, containing the official certificates granted by the Roman government to those who had lapsed and offered sacrifice. These apostates were obliged to acknowledge in public their adhesion to the national religion of the empire, and then were provided with a document certifying to this fact to keep them from further trouble. Dr. Harnack (Preussische Jahrbücher) writing of the yielding of the lapsed says:

"The Church condemned this as lying and denial of the faith, and after the termination of the persecution, these unhappy people were partly excommunicated, partly obliged to submit to severe discipline. Who would ever suppose that the records of their shame would come doom to our time?— and yet it has actually happened. Two of these papers have been preserved, contrary to all likelihood, by the sands of Egypt which so carefully keep what has been entrusted to them. The first was found by Krebs in a heap of papyrus, that had come to Berlin; the other was found by Wessely in the papyrus collection of Archduke Rainer. 'I, Diogenes, have constantly sacrificed and made offerings, and have eaten in your presence the sacrificial meat, and I petition you to give me a certificate.' Who today, without deep emotion, can read this paper and measure the trouble and terror of heart under which the Christians of that day collapsed?"

Canon 1
With regard to those presbyters who have offered sacrifices and afterwards returned to the conflict, not with hypocrisy, but in sincerity, it has seemed good that they may retain the honour of their chair; provided they had not used management, arrangement, or persuasion, so as to appear to be subjected to the torture, when it was applied only in seeming and pretence. Nevertheless it is not lawful for them to make the oblation, nor to preach, nor in short to perform any act of sacerdotal function.

John Zonaras writes: Of those that yielded to the tyrants in the persecution, and offered sacrifice, some, after having been subjected to torture, being unable to withstand to the end its force and intensity, were conquered, and denied the faith; some, through effeminacy, before they experienced any suffering, gave way, and lest they should seem to sacrifice voluntarily they persuaded the executioners, either by bribes or entreaties, to manifest perhaps a greater degree of severity against them, and seemingly to apply the torture to them, in order that sacrificing under these circumstances they might seem to have denied Christ, conquered by force, and not through effeminacy.

Canon 2

It is likewise decreed that deacons who have sacrificed and afterwards resumed the conflict, shall enjoy their other honours, but shall abstain from every sacred ministry, neither bringing forth the bread and the cup, nor making proclamations. Nevertheless, if any of the bishops shall observe in them distress of mind and meek humiliation, it shall be lawful to the bishops to grant more indulgence, or to take away [what has been granted].

Canon 3

Those who have fled and been apprehended, or have been betrayed by their servants; or those who have been otherwise despoiled of their goods, or have endured tortures, or have been imprisoned and abused, declaring themselves to be Christians; or who have been forced to receive something which their persecutors violently thrust into their hands, or meat [offered to idols], continually professing that they were Christians; and who, by their whole apparel, and demeanour, and humility of life, always give evidence of grief at what has happened; these persons, inasmuch as they are free from sin, are not to be repelled from the communion; and if, through an extreme strictness or ignorance of some things, they have been repelled, let them immediately be re-admitted. This shall hold good alike of clergy and laity. It has also been considered whether laymen who have fallen under the same compulsion may be admitted to orders, and we have decreed that, since they have in no respect been guilty, they may be ordained; provided their past course of life be found to have been upright.

In the translation the word "abused" is given as the equivalent of περισχισθέντας, which Zonaras translated, "if their clothes have been torn from their bodies," and this is quite accurate if the reading is correct, but Routh has found in the Bodleian several mss. which had περισχεθέντας . Hefele adopts this reading and translates "declaring themselves to be Christians but who have subsequently been vanquished, whether their oppressors have by force put incense into their hands or have compelled them, etc." Hammond translates "and have been harassed by their persecutors forcibly putting something into their hands or who have been compelled, etc." The phrase is obscure at best with either reading.

Canon 4

Concerning those who have been forced to sacrifice, and who, in addition, have partaken of feasts in honour of the idols; as many as were haled away, but afterwards went up with a cheerful countenance, and wore their costliest apparel, and partook with indifference of the feast provided; it is decreed that all such be hearers for one year, and prostrators for three years, and that they communicate in prayers only for two years, and then return to full communion.

In the Greek the word for "full communion" is τὸ τέλειον ("the perfection"), an expression frequently used by early writers to denote the Holy Communion. Vide Suicer, Thesaurus ad h. v.

Canon 5

As many, however, as went up in mourning attire and sat down and ate, weeping throughout the whole entertainment, if they have fulfilled the three years as prostrators, let them be received without oblation; and if they did not eat, let them be prostrators two years, and in the third year let them communicate without oblation, so that in the fourth year they may be received into full communion. But the bishops have the right, after considering the character of their conversion, either to deal with them more leniently, or to extend the time. But, first of all, let their life before and since be thoroughly examined, and let the indulgence be determined accordingly.

Canon 6

Concerning those who have yielded merely upon threat of penalties and of the confiscation of their goods, or of banishment, and have sacrificed, and who till this present time have not repented nor been converted, but who now, at the time of this synod, have approached with a purpose of conversion, it is decreed that they be received as hearers till the Great Day, and that after the Great Day they be prostrators for three years, and for two years more communicate without oblation, and then come to full communion, so as to complete the period of six full years. And if any have been admitted to penance before this synod, let the beginning of the six years be reckoned to them from that time. Nevertheless, if there should be any danger or prospect of death whether from disease or any other cause, let them be received, but under limitation.

John Zonaras: But should any of those debarred from communion as penitents be seized with illness or in any other way be brought near to death, they may be received to communion; but in accordance with this law or distinction, that if they escape death and recover their health, they shall be altogether deprived again of communion until they have finished their six years penance.

Canon 7

Concerning those who have partaken at a heathen feast in a place appointed for heathens, but who have brought and eaten their own meats, it is decreed that they be received after they have been prostrators two years; but whether with oblation, every bishop must determine after he has made examination into the rest of their life.

Hefele: Several Christians tried with worldly prudence, to take a middle course. On the one hand, hoping to escape persecution, they were present at the feasts of the heathen sacrifices, which were held in the buildings adjoining the temples; and on the other, in order to appease their consciences, they took their own food, and touched nothing that had been offered to the gods. These Christians forgot that St. Paul had ordered that meats sacrificed to the gods should be avoided, not because they were tainted in themselves, as the idols were nothing, but from another, and in fact a twofold reason: first, Because, in partaking of them, some had still the idols in their hearts, that is to say, were still attached to the worship of idols, and thereby sinned; and secondly, Because others scandalized their brethren, and sinned in that way. To these two reasons a third may be added, namely, the hypocrisy and the duplicity of those Christians who wished to appear heathens, and nevertheless to remain Christians. The Synod punished them with two years of penance in the third degree, and gave to each bishop the right, at the expiration of this time, either to admit them to communion, or to make them remain some time longer in the fourth degree.

Canon 8
Let those who have twice or thrice sacrificed under compulsion, be prostrators four years, and communicate without oblation two years, and the seventh year they shall be received to full communion.

Canon 9
As many as have not merely apostatized, but have risen against their brethren and forced them [to apostatize], and have been guilty of their being forced, let these for three years take the place of hearers, and for another term of six years that of prostrators, and for another year let them communicate without oblation, in order that, when they have fulfilled the space of ten years, they may partake of the communion; but during this time the rest of their life must also be enquired into.

Canon 10
They who have been made deacons, declaring when they were ordained that they must marry, because they were not able to abide so, and who afterwards have married, shall continue in their ministry, because it was conceded to them by the bishop. But if any were silent on this matter, undertaking at their ordination to abide as they were, and afterwards proceeded to marriage, these shall cease from the diaconate.

Van Espen comments: "The case proposed to the synod and decided in this canon was as follows: When the bishop was willing to ordain two to the diaconate, one of them declared that he did not intend to bind himself to preserving perpetual continence, but intended to get married, because he had not the power to remain continent. The other said nothing. The bishop laid his hands on each and conferred the diaconate."

After the ordination it fell out that both got married, the question propounded is, What must be done in each case? The synod ruled that he who had made protestation at his ordination should remain in his ministry, "because of the license of the bishop," that is that he might contract matrimony after the reception of the diaconate. With regard to him who kept silence the synod declares that he should cease from his ministry.

The resolution of the synod to the first question shows that there was a general law which bound the deacons to continence; but this synod judged it meet that the bishops for just cause might dispense with this law, and this license or dispensation was deemed to have been given by the bishop if he ordained him after his protestation at the time of his ordination that he intended to be married, because he could not remain as he was; giving by the act of ordination his tacit approbation. Moreover from this decision it is also evident that not only was the ordained deacon allowed to enter but also to use matrimony after his ordination. Moreover the deacon who after this protestation entered and used matrimony, not only remained a deacon, but continued in the exercise of his ministry.

Canon 11
It is decreed that virgins who have been betrothed, and who have afterwards been carried off by others, shall be restored to those to whom they had formerly been betrothed, even though they may have suffered violence from the ravisher.

Compare St. Basil's twenty-second canon in his letter to Amphilochius, where it is so ruled.

Canon 12
It is decreed that they who have offered sacrifice before their baptism, and were afterwards baptized, may be promoted to orders, inasmuch as they have been cleansed.

Canon 13
It is not lawful for Chorepiscopi to ordain presbyters or deacons, and most assuredly not presbyters of a city, without the commission of the bishop given in writing, in another parish.

If the first part of the thirteenth canon is easy to understand, the second, on the contrary, presents a great difficulty; for a priest of a town could not in any case have the power of consecrating priests and deacons, least of all in a strange diocese. Many of the most learned men have, for this reason, supposed that the Greek text of the second half of the canon, as we have read it, is incorrect or defective. It wants, say they, ποιεῖν τι, or aliquid agere, i.e., to complete a religious function. To confirm this supposition, they have appealed to several ancient versions, especially to that of Isidore: sed nec presbyteris civitatis sine episcopi præcepto amplius aliquid imperare, vel sine auctoritate literarum ejus in unaquaque (some read ἐν ἑκάστῃ instead of ἐν ἑτέρᾳ) parochia aliquid agere. The ancient Roman ms. of the canons, Codex Canonum, has the same reading, only that it has provincia instead of parochia. Fulgentius Ferrandus, deacon of Carthage, who long ago made a collection of canons, translates in the same way in his Breviatio Canonum: Ut presbyteri civitatis sine jussu episcopi nihil jubeant, nec in unaquaque parochia aliquid agant. Van Espen has explained this canon in the same way.

Routh has given another interpretation. He maintained that there was not a word missing in this canon, but that at the commencement one ought to read, according to several mss. χωρεπισκόποις in the dative, and further down ἀλλὰ μὴν μηδὲ instead of ἀλλα μηδὲ then πρεσβυτέρους (in the accusative) πόλεως and finally ἑκάστῃ instead of ἑτέρᾳ, and that we must therefore translate, " Chorepiscopi are not permitted to consecrate priests and deacons (for the country) still less (ἀλλὰ μὴν μηδὲ) can they consecrate priests for the town without the consent of the bishop of the place." The Greek text, thus modified according to some mss., especially those in the Bodleian Library, certainly gives a good meaning. Still ἀλλὰ μὴν μηδὲ does not mean, but still less: it means, but certainly not, which makes a considerable difference.

Besides this, it can very seldom have happened that the chorepiscopi ordained presbyters or deacons for a town; and if so, they were already forbidden, at least implicitly, in the first part of the canon.

Canon 14
It is decreed that among the clergy, presbyters and deacons who abstain from flesh shall taste of it, and afterwards, if they shall so please, may abstain. But if they disdain it, and will not even eat herbs served with flesh, but disobey the canon, let them be removed from their order.

There is a serious dispute about the reading of the Greek text. I have followed Routh, who, relying on three mss. the Collectio of John of Antioch and the Latin versions, reads εἰ δὲ βδελύσσοιντο instead of the εἰ δὲ βούλοιντο of the ordinary text, which as Bp. Beveridge had pointed out before has no meaning unless a μὴ be introduced.

Zonaras points out that the canon chiefly refers to the Love feasts.

I cannot agree with Hefele in his translation of the last clause. He makes the reference to "this present canon," I think it is clearly to the 53 (52) of the so-called Canons of the Apostles, τῷ κανόνι "the well-known Canon."

Canon 15
Concerning things belonging to the church, which presbyters may have sold when there was no bishop, it is decreed that the Church property shall be reclaimed; and it shall be in the discretion of the bishop whether it is better to receive the purchase price, or not; for oftentimes the revenue of the things sold might yield them the greater value.

Hefele: "If the purchaser of ecclesiastical properties has realized more by the temporary revenue of such properties than the price of the purchase, the Synod thinks there is no occasion to restore him this price, as he has already received a sufficient indemnity from the revenue, and as, according to the rules then in force, interest drawn from the purchase money was not permitted. Besides, the purchaser had done wrong in buying ecclesiastical property during the vacancy of a see (sede vacante). Beveridge and Routh have shown that in the text ἀνακαλεῖσθαι and πρόσοδον must be read."

Canon 16
Let those who have been or who are guilty of bestial lusts, if they have sinned while under twenty years of age, be prostrators fifteen years, and afterwards communicate in prayers; then, having passed five years in this communion, let them have a share in the oblation. But let their life as prostrators be examined, and so let them receive indulgence; and if any have been insatiable in their crimes, then let their time of prostration be prolonged. And if any who have passed this age and had wives, have fallen into this sin, let them be prostrators twenty-five years, and then communicate in prayers; and, after they have been five years in the communion of prayers, let them share the oblation. And if any married men of more than fifty years of age have so sinned, let them be admitted to communion only at the point of death.

Canon 17
Defilers of themselves with beasts, being also leprous, who have infected others [with the leprosy of this crime], the holy Synod commands to pray among the hiemantes.

Canon 18
If any who have been constituted bishops, but have not been received by the parish to which they were designated, shall invade other parishes and wrong the constituted [bishops] there, stirring up seditions against them, let such persons be suspended from office and communion. But if they are willing to accept a seat among the presbyterate, where they formerly were presbyters, let them not be deprived of that honour. But if they shall act seditiously against the bishops established there, the honour of the presbyterate also shall be taken from them and themselves expelled.

Canon 19
If any persons who profess virginity shall disregard their profession, let them fulfil the term of digamists. And, moreover, we prohibit women who are virgins from living with men as sisters.

Canon 20
If the wife of anyone has committed adultery or if any man commit adultery it seems fit that he shall be restored to full communion after seven years passed in the prescribed degrees [of penance].

Canon 21
Concerning women who commit fornication, and destroy that which they have conceived, or who are employed in making drugs for abortion, a former decree excluded them until the hour of death, and to this some have assented. Nevertheless, being desirous to use somewhat greater lenity, we have ordained that they fulfil ten years [of penance], according to the prescribed degrees.

Canon 22
Concerning wilful murderers let them remain prostrators; but at the end of life let them be indulged with full communion.

Canon 23
Concerning involuntary homicides, a former decree directs that they be received to full communion after seven years [of penance], according to the prescribed degrees; but this second one, that they fulfil a term of five years.

Canon 24
They who practice divination, and follow the customs of the heathen, or who take men to their houses for the invention of sorceries, or for lustrations, fall under the canon of five years' [penance], according to the prescribed degrees; that is, three years as prostrators, and two of prayer without oblation.

I read ἐθνῶν for χρόνων and accordingly translate "of the heathen."

Canon 25
One who had betrothed a maiden, corrupted her sister, so that she conceived. After that he married his betrothed, but she who had been corrupted hanged herself. The parties to this affair were ordered to be received among the co-standers after ten years [of penance] according to the prescribed degrees.

SEVEN ECUMENICAL COUNCILS OF THE CHURCH

The Synod held at Carthage over which presided the Great and Holy Martyr Cyprian, Bishop of Carthage- 257 Anno Domini

When very many bishops were met together at Carthage on the Calends of September from the province of Africa, Numidia and Mauritania, with the presbyters and deacons (the greater part of the people being likewise present) and when the holy letters of Jubaianus to Cyprian had been read, and Cyprian's answers to Jubaianus, concerning heretical baptisms, as well as what the same Jubaianus afterwards wrote to Cyprian,

Cyprian said: You have heard, my dearly beloved colleagues, what our fellow bishop Jubaianus has written to me, taking counsel of my littleness concerning the illicit and profane baptisms of heretics, and the answer which I made him; being of the same opinion as we have been on former occasions, that heretics coming to the Church should be baptized and sanctified with the Church's baptism. Moreover there has been read to you also the other letter of Jubaianus, in which answering for his sincere and pious devotion to our letter, not only he agrees therewith but offered thanks that he has been so instructed by it. It only remains therefore that we, each one of us, one by one, say what our mind is in this matter, without condemning any one or removing any one from the right of communion who does not agree with us.

For no one [of us] has set himself up [to be] bishop [of bishops], or attempted with tyrannical dread to force his colleagues to obedience to him, since every bishop has, for the license of liberty and power, his own will, and as he cannot be judged by another, so neither can he judge another. But we await the judgment of our universal Lord, our Lord Jesus Christ, who one and alone has the power, both of advancing us in the governance of his Church, and of judging of our actions [in that position].

The bishops then one by one declared against heretical baptism. Last of all:

Cyprian, the Confessor and Martyr of Carthage, said: The letter which was written to Jubaianus, my colleague, most fully set forth my opinion, that heretics who, according to the evangelical and apostolic witness, are called adversaries of Christ's and anti-Christs, when they come to the Church, should be baptized with the one (unico) baptism of the Church, that they may become instead of adversaries friends, and Christians instead of Antichrists.

Alexander's Deposition of Arius and his companions, and Encyclical Letter on the subject.

Alexander, being assembled with his beloved brethren, the Presbyters and Deacons of Alexandria, and the Mareotis, greets them in the Lord.

Although you have already subscribed to the letter I addressed to Arius and his fellows, exhorting them to renounce his impiety, and to submit themselves to the sound Catholic Faith, and have shown your right-mindedness and agreement in the doctrines of the Catholic Church: yet forasmuch as I have written also to our fellow-ministers in every place concerning Arius and his fellows, and especially since some of you, as the Presbyters Chares and Pistus, and the Deacons Serapion, Parammon, Zosimus, and Irenæus, have joined Arius and his fellows, and been content to suffer deposition with them, I thought it needful to assemble together you, the Clergy of the city, and to send for you the Clergy of the Mareotis, in order that you may learn what I am now writing, and may testify your agreement thereto, and give your concurrence in the deposition of Arius, Pistus, and their fellows. For it is desirable that you should be made acquainted with what I write, and that each of you should heartily embrace it, as though he had written it himself.

A Copy.

To his dearly beloved and most honoured fellow-ministers of the Catholic Church in every place, Alexander sends health in the Lord.

1. As there is one body of the Catholic Church, and a command is given us in the sacred Scriptures to preserve the bond of unity and peace, it is agreeable thereto that we should write and signify to one another whatever is done by each of us individually; so that whether one member suffer or rejoice, we may either suffer or rejoice with one another. Now there are gone forth in this diocese, at this time, certain lawless men, enemies of Christ, teaching an apostasy, which one may justly suspect and designate as a forerunner of Antichrist. I was desirous to pass such a matter by without notice, in the hope that perhaps the evil would spend itself among its supporters, and not extend to other places to defile the ears of the simple. But seeing that Eusebius, now of Nicomedia, who thinks that the government of the Church rests with him, because retribution has not come upon him for his desertion of Berytus, when he had cast an eye of desire on the Church of the Nicomedians, begins to support these apostates, and has taken upon him to write letters every where in their behalf, if by any means he may draw in certain ignorant persons to this most base and antichristian heresy; I am therefore constrained, knowing what is written in the law, no longer to hold my peace, but to make it known to you all; that you may understand who the apostates are, and the cavils which their heresy has adopted, and that, should Eusebius write to you, you may pay no attention to him, for he now desires by means of these men to exhibit anew his old malevolence, which has so long been concealed, pretending to write in their favour, while in truth it

clearly appears, that he does it to forward his own interests.

2. Now those who became apostates are these, Arius, Achilles, Aeithales, Carpones, another Arius, and Sarmates, sometime Presbyters: Euzoïus, Lucius, Julius, Menas, Helladius, and Gaius, sometime Deacons: and with them Secundus and Theonas, sometime called Bishops. And the novelties they have invented and put forth contrary to the Scriptures are these following:— God was not always a Father , but there was a time when God was not a Father. The Word of God was not always, but originated from things that were not; for God that is, has made him that was not, of that which was not; wherefore there was a time when He was not; for the Son is a creature and a work. Neither is He like in essence to the Father; neither is He the true and natural Word of the Father; neither is He His true Wisdom; but He is one of the things made and created, and is called the Word and Wisdom by an abuse of terms, since He Himself originated by the proper Word of God, and by the Wisdom that is in God, by which God has made not only all other things but Him also. Wherefore He is by nature subject to change and variation as are all rational creatures. And the Word is foreign from the essence of the Father, and is alien and separated therefrom. And the Father cannot be described by the Son, for the Word does not know the Father perfectly and accurately, neither can He see Him perfectly. Moreover, the Son knows not His own essence as it really is; for He is made for us, that God might create us by Him, as by an instrument; and He would not have existed, had not God wished to create us. Accordingly, when some one asked them, whether the Word of God can possibly change as the devil changed, they were not afraid to say that He can; for being something made and created, His nature is subject to change.

3. Now when Arius and his fellows made these assertions, and shamelessly avowed them, we being assembled with the Bishops of Egypt and Libya, nearly a hundred in number, anathematized both them and their followers. But Eusebius and his fellows admitted them to communion, being desirous to mingle falsehood with the truth, and impiety with piety. But they will not be able to do so, for the truth must prevail; neither is there any "communion of light with darkness," nor any "concord of Christ with Belial. " For who ever heard such assertions before? Or who that hears them now is not astonished and does not stop his ears lest they should be defiled with such language? Who that has heard the words of John, "In the beginning was the Word (John 1:1)," will not denounce the saying of these men, that "there was a time when He was not?" Or who that has heard in the Gospel, "the Only-begotten Son," and "by Him were all things made," will not detest their declaration that He is "one of the things that were made." For how can He be one of those things which were made by Himself? Or how can He be the Only-begotten, when, according to them, He is counted as one among the rest, since He is Himself a creature and a work? And how can He be "made of things that were not," when the Father says, "My heart has uttered a good Word," and "Out of the womb I have begotten You before the morning star?" Or again, how is He "unlike in substance to the Father," seeing He is the perfect "image" and "brightness (Hebrews 1:3) " of the Father, and that He says, "He that has seen Me has seen the Father?" And if the Son is the "Word" and "Wisdom" of God, how was there "a time when He was not?" It is the same as if they should say that God was once without Word and without Wisdom. And how is He "subject to change and variation," Who says, by Himself, "I am in the Father, and the

SEVEN ECUMENICAL COUNCILS OF THE CHURCH

Father in Me," and "I and the Father are One ;" and by the Prophet, "Behold Me, for I am, and I change not ?" For although one may refer this expression to the Father, yet it may now be more aptly spoken of the Word, viz., that though He has been made man, He has not changed; but as the Apostle has said, "Jesus Christ is the same yesterday, today, and for ever." And who can have persuaded them to say, that He was made for us, whereas Paul writes, "for Whom are all things, and by Whom are all things?"

4. As to their blasphemous position that "the Son knows not the Father perfectly," we ought not to wonder at it; for having once set themselves to fight against Christ, they contradict even His express words, since He says, "As the Father knows Me, even so know I the Father (John 10:15)." Now if the Father knows the Son but in part, then it is evident that the Son does not know the Father perfectly; but if it is not lawful to say this, but the Father does know the Son perfectly, then it is evident that as the Father knows His own Word, so also the Word knows His own Father Whose Word He is.

5. By these arguments and references to the sacred Scriptures we frequently overthrew them; but they changed like chameleons, and again shifted their ground, striving to bring upon themselves that sentence, "when the wicked falls into the depth of evils, he despises. " There have been many heresies before them, which, venturing further than they ought, have fallen into folly; but these men by endeavouring in all their cavils to overthrow the Divinity of the Word, have justified the other in comparison of themselves, as approaching nearer to Antichrist. Wherefore they have been excommunicated and anathematized by the Church. We grieve for their destruction, and especially because, having once been instructed in the doctrines of the Church, they have now sprung away. Yet we are not greatly surprised, for Hymenæus and Philetus (2 Timothy 2:17) did the same, and before them Judas, who followed the Saviour, but afterwards became a traitor and an apostate. And concerning these same persons, we have not been left without instruction; for our Lord has forewarned us; "Take heed lest any man deceive you: for many shall come in My name, saying, I am Christ, and the time draws near, and they shall deceive many: go ye not after them (Luke 21:8);" while Paul, who was taught these things by our Saviour, wrote that "in the latter times some shall depart from the sound faith, giving heed to seducing spirits and doctrines of devils, which reject the truth. "

6. Since then our Lord and Saviour Jesus Christ has instructed us by His own mouth, and also has signified to us by the Apostle concerning such men, we accordingly being personal witnesses of their impiety, have anathematized, as we said, all such, and declared them to be alien from the Catholic Faith and Church. And we have made this known to your piety, dearly beloved and most honoured fellow-ministers, in order that should any of them have the boldness to come unto you, you may not receive them, nor comply with the desire of Eusebius, or any other person writing in their behalf. For it becomes us who are Christians to turn away from all who speak or think any thing against Christ, as being enemies of God, and destroyers of souls; and not even to "bid such God speed (2 John 10)," lest we become partakers of their sins, as the blessed John has charged us. Salute the brethren that are with you. They that are with me salute you.

SEVEN ECUMENICAL COUNCILS OF THE CHURCH

Presbyters of Alexandria.

7. I, Colluthus, Presbyter, agree with what is here written, and give my assent to the deposition of Arius and his associates in impiety.

    Alexander , Presbyter, likewise
    Dioscorus , Presbyter, likewise
    Dionysius , Presbyter, likewise
    Eusebius, Presbyter, likewise
    Alexander, Presbyter, likewise
    Nilaras , Presbyter, likewise
    Arpocration, Presbyter, likewise
    Agathus, Presbyter
    Nemesius, Presbyter
    Longus , Presbyter
    Silvanus, Presbyter
    Peroys, Presbyter
    Apis, Presbyter
    Proterius, Presbyter
    Paulus, Presbyter
    Cyrus, Presbyter, likewise

Deacons
Ammonius , Deacon, likewise
Macarius, Deacon
Pistus , Deacon, likewise
Athanasius, Deacon
Eumenes, Deacon
Apollonius , Deacon
Olympius, Deacon
Aphthonius , Deacon
Athanasius , Deacon
Macarius, Deacon, likewise
Paulus, Deacon
Petrus, Deacon
Ambytianus, Deacon
Gaius , Deacon, likewise
Alexander, Deacon
Dionysius, Deacon
Agathon, Deacon
Polybius, Deacon, likewise
Theonas, Deacon
Marcus, Deacon
Comodus, Deacon
Serapion , Deacon
Nilon, Deacon
Romanus, Deacon, likewise

SEVEN ECUMENICAL COUNCILS OF THE CHURCH

Presbyters of the Mareotis.

I, Apollonius, Presbyter, agree with what is here written, and give my assent to the deposition of Arius and his associates in impiety.

Ingenius , Presbyter, likewise
Ammonius, Presbyter
Dioscorus , Presbyter
Sostras, Presbyter
Theon , Presbyter
Tyrannus, Presbyter
Copres, Presbyter
Ammonas , Presbyter
Orion, Presbyter
Serenus, Presbyter
Didymus, Presbyter
Heracles , Presbyter
Boccon , Presbyter
Agathus, Presbyter
Achillas, Presbyter
Paulus, Presbyter
Thalelæus, Presbyter
Dionysius, Presbyter, likewise
Deacons
Sarapion , Deacon, likewise
Justus, Deacon, likewise
Didymus, Deacon
Demetrius , Deacon
Maurus , Deacon
Alexander, Deacon
Marcus , Deacon
Comon, Deacon
Tryphon , Deacon
Ammonius , Deacon
Didymus, Deacon
Ptollarion , Deacon
Seras, Deacon
Gaius , Deacon
Hierax , Deacon
Marcus, Deacon
Theonas, Deacon
Sarmaton, Deacon
Carpon, Deacon
Zoilus, Deacon, likewise

COUNCIL OF FIRST CONSTANTINOPLE

Creed

We believe in one God, the Father Almighty, maker of heaven and earth and of all things visible and invisible. And in one Lord Jesus Christ, the only begotten Son of God, begotten of his Father before all worlds, Light of Light, very God of very God, begotten not made, being of one substance with the Father, by whom all things were made. Who for us men and for our salvation came down from heaven and was incarnate by the Holy Ghost and the Virgin Mary, and was made man, and was crucified also for us under Pontius Pilate. He suffered and was buried, and the third day he rose again according to the Scriptures, and ascended into heaven, and sits at the Right Hand of the Father. And he shall come again with glory to judge both the quick and the dead. Whose kingdom shall have no end. (*I*)

And [we believe] in the Holy Ghost, the Lord and Giver-of-Life, who proceeds from the Father, who with the Father and the Son together is worshipped and glorified, who spoke by the prophets. And [we believe] in one, holy, (*II*) Catholic and Apostolic Church. We acknowledge one Baptism for the remission of sins, [and] we look for the resurrection of the dead and the life of the world to come. Amen.

Letter of the Same Holy Synod to the Most Pious Emperor Theodosius the Great, to Which are Appended the Canons Enacted by Them

To the most religious Emperor Theodosius, the Holy Synod of Bishops assembled in Constantinople out of different Provinces.

We begin our letter to your Piety with thanks to God, who has established the empire of your Piety for the common peace of the Churches and for the support of the true Faith. And, after rendering due thanks unto God, as in duty bound we lay before your Piety the things which have been done in the Holy Synod. When, then, we had assembled in Constantinople, according to the letter of your Piety, we first of all renewed our unity of heart each with the other, and then we pronounced some concise definitions, ratifying the Faith of the Nicene Fathers, and anathematizing the heresies which have sprung up, contrary thereto. Besides these things, we also framed certain Canons for the better ordering of the Churches, all which we have subjoined to this our letter. Wherefore we beseech your Piety that the decree of the Synod may be ratified, to the end that, as you have honoured the Church by your letter of citation, so you should set your seal to the conclusion of what has been decreed. May the Lord establish your empire in peace and righteousness, and prolong it from generation to generation; and may he add unto your earthly power the fruition of the heavenly kingdom also. May God by the prayers (εὐχαῖς τῶν ἁγίων) of the Saints, show favour to the world, that you may be strong and eminent in all good things as an Emperor most truly pious and beloved of God.

Canons of the One Hundred and Fifty Fathers who assembled at Constantinople during the Consulate of those Illustrious Men, Flavius Eucherius and Flavius Evagrius on the VII of the Ides of July.

The Bishops out of different provinces assembled by the grace of God in Constantinople, on the summons of the most religious Emperor Theodosius, have decreed as follows:

Canon 1

The Faith of the Three Hundred and Eighteen Fathers assembled at Nice in Bithynia shall not be set aside, but shall remain firm. And every heresy shall be anathematized, particularly that of the Eunomians or [*Anomœans, the Arians or*] Eudoxians, and that of the Semi-Arians or Pneumatomachi, and that of the Sabellians, and that of the Marcellians, and that of the Photinians, and that of the Apollinarians.

Canon 2

The bishops are not to go beyond their dioceses to churches lying outside of their bounds, nor bring confusion on the churches; but let the Bishop of Alexandria, according to the canons, alone administer the affairs of Egypt; and let the bishops of the East manage the East alone, the privileges of the Church in Antioch, which are mentioned in the canons of Nice, being preserved; and let the bishops of the Asian Diocese administer the Asian affairs only; and the Pontic bishops only Pontic matters; and the Thracian bishops only Thracian affairs. And let not bishops go beyond their dioceses for ordination or any other ecclesiastical ministrations, unless they be invited. And the aforesaid canon concerning dioceses being observed, it is evident that the synod of every province will administer the affairs of that particular province as was decreed at Nice. But the Churches of God in heathen nations must be governed according to the custom which has prevailed from the times of the Fathers.

Canon 3

Concerning Maximus the Cynic and the disorder which has happened in Constantinople on his account, it is decreed that Maximus never was and is not now a Bishop; that those who have been ordained by him are in no order whatever of the clergy; since all which has been done concerning him or by him, is declared to be invalid.

Canon 4

(Probably adopted at a Council held in Constantinople the next year, 382. *Vide.* Introduction on the number of the Canons.)

In regard to the tome of the Western [Bishops], we receive those in Antioch also who confess the unity of the Godhead of the Father, and of the Son, and of the Holy Ghost.

Canon 5

Those who from heresy turn to orthodoxy, and to the portion of those who are being saved, we receive according to the following method and custom: Arians, and Macedonians, and Sabbatians, and Novatians, who call themselves Cathari or Aristori, and Quarto-decimans or Tetradites, and Apollinarians, we receive, upon their giving a written renunciation [of their errors] and anathematize every heresy which is not in accordance with the Holy, Catholic, and Apostolic Church of God. Thereupon, they are first sealed or anointed with the holy oil upon the forehead, eyes, nostrils, mouth, and ears; and when we seal them, we say, The Seal of the gift of the Holy Ghost. But Eunomians, who are baptized with only one immersion, and Montanists, who are here called Phrygians, and Sabellians, who teach the identity of Father and Son, and do sundry other mischievous things, and [the partisans of] all other heresies— for there are many such here, particularly among those who come from the country of the Galatians:— all these, when they desire to turn to orthodoxy, we receive as heathen. On the first day we make them Christians; on the second, catechumens; on the third, we exorcise them by breathing thrice in their face and ears; and thus we instruct them and oblige them to spend some time in the Church, and to hear the Scriptures; and then we baptize them.

COUNCIL OF EPHESUS

Session I

Extracts from the Acts

[*Before the arrival of the Papal Legates.*]

The Nicene Synod set forth this faith:

We believe in one God, etc.

When this creed had been recited, Peter the Presbyter of Alexandria, and primicerius of the notaries said:

We have in our hands the letter of the most holy and most reverend archbishop Cyril, which he wrote to the most reverend Nestorius, filled with counsel and advice, on account of his aberration from the right faith. I will read this if your holiness [i.e., the holy Synod] so orders....The letter began as follows:

Καταφλυαροῦσι μὲν, ὡς ἀκούω, κ.τ.λ .

The Epistle of Cyril to Nestorius("Intelligo quosdam meæ")

To the most religious and beloved of God, fellow minister Nestorius, Cyril sends greeting in the Lord.

I hear that some are rashly talking of the estimation in which I hold your holiness, and that this is frequently the case especially at the times that meetings are held of those in authority. And perchance they think in so doing to say something agreeable to you, but they speak senselessly, for they have suffered no injustice at my hands, but have been exposed by me only to their profit; this man as an oppressor of the blind and needy, and that as one who wounded his mother with a sword. Another because he stole, in collusion with his waiting maid, another's money, and had always laboured under the imputation of such like crimes as no one would wish even one of his bitterest enemies to be laden with. I take little reckoning of the words of such people, for the disciple is not above his Master, nor would I stretch the measure of my narrow brain above the Fathers, for no matter what path of life one pursues it is hardly possible to escape the smirching of the wicked, whose mouths are full of cursing and bitterness, and who at the last must give an account to the Judge of all.

But I return to the point which especially I had in mind. And now I urge you, as a brother in the Lord, to propose the word of teaching and the doctrine of the faith with all accuracy to the people, and to consider that the giving of scandal to one even of the least of those who believe in Christ, exposes a body to the unbearable indignation of God. And of how great diligence and skill there is need when the multitude of those grieved is so great, so that we may administer the healing word of truth to them that seek it. But this we shall accomplish most excellently if we shall turn over the words of the holy Fathers, and are zealous to obey their commands, proving ourselves, whether we be in the faith according to that which is written, and conform our thoughts to their upright and irreprehensible teaching.

The holy and great Synod therefore says, that the only begotten Son, born according to nature of God the Father, very God of very God, Light of Light, by whom the Father made all things, came down, and was incarnate, and was made man, suffered, and rose again the third day, and ascended into heaven. These words and these decrees we ought to follow, considering what is meant by the Word of God being incarnate and made man. For we do not say that the nature of the Word was changed and became flesh, or that it was converted into a whole man consisting of soul and body; but rather that the Word having personally united to himself flesh animated by a rational soul, did in an ineffable and inconceivable manner become man, and was called the Son of Man, not merely as willing or being pleased to be so called, neither on account of taking to himself a person, but because the two natures being brought together in a true union, there is of both one Christ and one Son; for the difference of the natures is not taken away by the union, but rather the divinity and the humanity make perfect for us the one Lord Jesus Christ by their ineffable and inexpressible union. So then he who had an existence before all ages and was born of the Father, is said to have been born according to the flesh of a woman, not as though his divine nature received its beginning of existence in the holy Virgin, for it needed not any second generation after that of the Father (for it would be absurd and foolish to say that he who existed before all ages, coeternal with the Father, needed any second beginning of existence), but since, for us and for our salvation, he personally united to himself an human body, and came forth of a woman, he is in this way said to be born after the flesh; for he was not first born a common man of the Holy Virgin, and then the Word came down and entered into him, but the union being made in the womb itself, he is said to endure a birth after the flesh, ascribing to himself the birth of his own flesh. On this account we say that he suffered and rose again; not as if God the Word suffered in his own nature stripes, or the piercing of the nails, or any other wounds, for the Divine nature is incapable of suffering, inasmuch as it is incorporeal, but since that which had become his own body suffered in this way, he is also said to suffer for us; for he who is in himself incapable of suffering was in a suffering body. In the same manner also we conceive respecting his dying; for the Word of God is by nature immortal and incorruptible, and life and life-giving; since, however, his own body did, as Paul says, by the grace of God taste death for every man, he himself is said to have suffered death for us, not as if he had any experience of death in his own nature (for it would be madness to say or think this), but because, as I have just said, his flesh tasted death. In like manner his flesh being raised again, it is spoken of as his resurrection, not as if he had fallen into corruption (God forbid), but because his own body was raised again. We, therefore, confess one Christ and Lord, not as worshipping. a man with the Word (lest this expression with the Word should suggest to the mind the idea of division), but worshipping him as one and the same, forasmuch as the body of the Word, with which he sits with the Father, is not separated from the Word himself, not as if two sons were sitting with him, but one by the union with the flesh. If, however, we reject the personal union as impossible or unbecoming, we fall into the error of speaking of two sons, for it will be necessary to distinguish, and to say, that he who was properly man was honoured with the appellation of Son, and that he who is properly the Word of God, has by nature both the name and the reality of Sonship. We must not, therefore, divide the one Lord Jesus Christ into two Sons. Neither will it at all avail to a sound faith to hold, as some do, an union of persons; for the Scripture has not said that the Word united to himself the person of man, but that he was made flesh. This expression, however, the Word was made flesh, can mean nothing else but that he partook of flesh and blood like to us; he made our body his own, and came forth man from a woman, not casting off his existence as God, or his generation of God the Father, but even in taking to himself flesh remaining what he was. This the declaration of the correct faith proclaims everywhere. This was the sentiment of the holy Fathers; therefore they ventured to call the Holy Virgin, the Mother of God, not as if the nature of the Word or his divinity had its beginning from the Holy Virgin, but because of her was born that holy body with a rational soul, to which the Word being personally united is said to be born according to the flesh. These things, therefore, I now write unto you for the love of Christ, beseeching you as a brother, and testifying to you before Christ and the elect angels, that you would both think and teach these things with us, that the peace of the Churches may be preserved and the bond of concord and love continue unbroken among the Priests of God.

Extracts from the Acts (Continued)

And after the letter was read, Cyril, the bishop of Alexandria, said: This holy and great Synod has heard what I wrote to the most religious Nestorius, defending the right faith. I think that I have in no respect departed from the true statement of the faith, that is from the creed set forth by the holy and great synod formerly assembled at Nice. Wherefore I desire your holiness [i.e. the Council] to say whether rightly and blamelessly and in accordance with that holy synod I have written these things or no.

[*A number of bishops then gave their opinion, all favourable to Cyril; after these individual opinions the Acts continue* (col. 491):]

And all the rest of the bishops in the order of their rank deposed to the same things, and so believed, according as the Fathers had set forth, and as the Epistle of the most holy Archbishop Cyril to Nestorius the bishop declared.

Palladius, the bishop of Amasea, said, The next thing to be done is to read the letter of the most reverend Nestorius, of which the most religious presbyter Peter made mention; so that we may understand whether or no it agrees with the exposition of the Nicene fathers.

And after this letter was read, Cyril, the bishop of Alexandria, said, What seems good to this holy and great synod with regard to the letter just read? Does it also seem to be consonant to the faith set forth by the holy Synod assembled in the city of Nice?

[*The bishops, then as before, individually express their opinion, and at last the Acts continue* (col. 502):]

All the bishops cried out together: Whoever does not anathematize Nestorius let him be anathema. Such an one the right faith anathematizes; such an one the holy Synod anathematizes. Whoever communicates with Nestorius let him be anathema! We anathematize all the apostles of Nestorius: we all anathematize Nestorius as a heretic: let all such as communicate with Nestorius be anathema, etc., etc.

Juvenal, the bishop of Jerusalem said: Let the letter of the most holy and reverend Cælestine, archbishop of the Church of Rome, be read, which he wrote concerning the faith.

[*The letter of Cælestine was read and no opinion expressed.*]

Peter the presbyter of Alexandria, and primicerius of the notaries said: Altogether in agreement with the things just read are those which his holiness Cyril our most pious bishop wrote, which I now have at hand, and will read if your piety so shall order.

[*The letter was read which begins thus*:]

Τοῦ Σωτῆρος ἡμῶν λέγοντος ἐναργῶς, κ.τ.λ.

The Epistle of Cyril to Nestorius("Cum salvator noster")

To the most reverend and God-loving fellow-minister Nestorius, Cyril and the synod assembled in Alexandria, of the Egyptian Province, Greeting in the Lord.

When our Saviour says clearly: He that loves father or mother more than me is not worthy of me: and he that loves son or daughter more than me is not worthy of me, what is to become of us, from whom your Holiness requires that we love you more than Christ the Saviour of us all? Who can help us in the day of judgment, or what kind of excuse shall we find for thus keeping silence so long, with regard to the blasphemies made by you against him? If you injured yourself alone, by teaching and holding such things, perhaps it would be less matter; but you have greatly scandalized the whole Church, and have cast among the people the leaven of a strange and new heresy. And not to those there [i.e. at Constantinople] only; but also to those everywhere [the books of your explanation were sent]. How can we any longer, under these circumstances, make a defense for our silence, or how shall we not be forced to remember that Christ said: Think not that I have come to send peace on earth: I came not to send peace, but a sword. For I have come to set a man at variance against his father, and the daughter against her mother. For if faith be injured, let there be lost the honour due to parents, as stale and tottering, let even the law of tender love towards children and brothers be silenced, let death be better to the pious than living; that they might obtain a better resurrection, as it is written.

Behold, therefore, how we, together with the holy synod which met in great Rome, presided over by the most holy and most reverend brother and fellow-minister, Celestine the Bishop, also testify by this third letter to you, and counsel you to abstain from these mischievous and distorted dogmas, which you hold and teach, and to receive the right faith, handed down to the churches from the beginning through the holy Apostles and Evangelists, who were eye-witnesses, and ministers of the Word. And if your holiness have not a mind to this according to the limits defined in the writings of our brother of blessed memory and most reverend fellow-minister Celestine, Bishop of the Church of Rome, be well assured then that you have no lot with us, nor place or standing (λόγον) among the priests and bishops of God. For it is not possible for us to overlook the churches thus troubled, and the people scandalized, and the right faith set aside, and the sheep scattered by you, who ought to save them, if indeed we are ourselves adherents of the right faith, and followers of the devotion of the holy fathers. And we are in communion with all those laymen and clergymen cast out or deposed by your holiness on account of the faith; for it is not right that those, who resolved to believe rightly, should suffer by your choice; for they do well in opposing you. This very thing you have mentioned in your epistle written to our most holy and fellow bishop Celestine of great Rome.

But it would not be sufficient for your reverence to confess with us only the symbol of the faith set out some time ago by the Holy Ghost at the great and holy synod convened in Nice: for you have not held and interpreted it rightly, but rather perversely; even though you confess with your voice the form of words. But in addition, in writing and by oath, you must confess that you also anathematize those polluted and unholy dogmas of yours, and that you will hold and teach that which we all, bishops, teachers, and leaders of the people both East and West, hold. The holy synod of Rome and we all agreed on the epistle written to your Holiness from the Alexandrian Church as being right and blameless. We have added to these our own letters and that which it is necessary for you to hold and teach, and what you should be careful to avoid. Now this is the Faith of the Catholic and Apostolic Church to which all Orthodox Bishops, both East and West, agree:

We believe in one God, the Father Almighty, Maker of all things visible and invisible, and in one Lord Jesus Christ, the Only-begotten Son of God, begotten of his Father, that is, of the substance of the Father; God of God, Light of Light, Very God of very God, begotten, not made, being of one substance with the Father, by whom all things were made, both those in heaven and those in the earth. Who for us men and for our salvation, came down, and was incarnate, and was made man. He suffered, and rose again the third day. He ascended into the heavens, from thence he shall come to judge both the quick and the dead. And in the Holy Ghost: But those that say, There was a time when he was not, and, before he was begotten he was not, and that he was made of that which previously was not, or that he was of some other substance or essence; and that the Son of God was capable of change or alteration; those the Catholic and Apostolic Church anathematizes.

Following in all points the confessions of the Holy Fathers which they made (the Holy Ghost speaking in them), and following the scope of their opinions, and going, as it were, in the royal way, we confess that the Only begotten Word of God, begotten of the same substance of the Father, True God from True God, Light from Light, through Whom all things were made, the things in heaven and the things in the earth, coming down for our salvation, making himself of no reputation (καθεὶς ἑαυτὸν εἰς κένωσιν), was incarnate and made man; that is, taking flesh of the Holy Virgin, and having made it his own from the womb, he subjected himself to birth for us, and came forth man from a woman, without casting off that which he was; but although he assumed flesh and blood, he remained what he was, God in essence and in truth. Neither do we say that his flesh was changed into the nature of divinity, nor that the ineffable nature of the Word of God was laid aside for the nature of flesh; for he is unchanged and absolutely unchangeable, being the same always, according to the Scriptures. For although visible and a child in swaddling clothes, and even in the bosom of his Virgin Mother, he filled all creation as God, and was a fellow-ruler with him who begot him, for the Godhead is without quantity and dimension, and cannot have limits.

Confessing the Word to be made one with the flesh according to substance, we adore one Son and Lord Jesus Christ: we do not divide the God from the man, nor separate him into parts, as though the two natures were mutually united in him only through a sharing of dignity and authority (for that is a novelty and nothing else), neither do we give separately to the Word of God the name Christ and the same name separately to a different one born of a woman; but we know only one Christ, the Word from God the Father with his own Flesh. For as man he was anointed with us, although it is he himself who gives the Spirit to those who are worthy and not in measure, according to the saying of the blessed Evangelist John.

But we do not say that the Word of God dwelt in him as in a common man born of the Holy Virgin, lest Christ be thought of as a God-bearing man; for although the Word tabernacled among us, it is also said that in Christ dwelt all the fullness of the Godhead bodily; but we understand that he became flesh, not just as he is said to dwell in the saints, but we define that that tabernacling in him was according to equality (κατὰ τον ἴσον ἐν αὐτῷ τρόπον). But being made one κατὰ φύσιν, and not converted into flesh, he made his indwelling in such a way, as we may say that the soul of man does in his own body.

One therefore is Christ both Son and Lord, not as if a man had attained only such a conjunction with God as consists in a unity of dignity alone or of authority. For it is not equality of honour which unites natures; for then Peter and John, who were of equal honour with each other, being both Apostles and holy disciples [would have been one, and], yet the two are not one. Neither do we understand the manner of conjunction to be apposition, for this does not suffice for natural oneness (πρὸς ἕνωσον φυσικήν). Nor yet according to relative participation, as we are also joined to the Lord, as it is written we are one Spirit in him. Rather we deprecate the term of junction (συναφείας) as not having sufficiently signified the oneness. But we do not call the Word of God the Father, the God nor the Lord of Christ, lest we openly cut in two the one Christ, the Son and Lord, and fall under the charge of blasphemy, making him the God and Lord of himself. For the Word of God, as we have said already, was made hypostatically one in flesh, yet he is God of all and he rules all; but he is not the slave of himself, nor his own Lord. For it is foolish, or rather impious, to think or teach thus. For he said that God was his Father, although he was God by nature, and of his substance. Yet we are not ignorant that while he remained God, he also became man and subject to God, according to the law suitable to the nature of the manhood. But how could he become the God or Lord of himself? Consequently as man, and with regard to the measure of his humiliation, it is said that he is equally with us subject to God; thus he became under the Law, although as God he spoke the Law and was the Law-giver.

We are careful also how we say about Christ: I worship the One clothed on account of the One clothing him, and on account of the Unseen, I worship the Seen. It is horrible to say in this connection as follows: The assumed as well as the assuming have the name of God. For the saying of this divides again Christ into two, and puts the man separately by himself and God also by himself. For this saying denies openly the Unity according to which one is not worshipped in the other, nor does God exist together with the other; but Jesus Christ is considered as One, the Only-begotten Son, to be honoured with one adoration together with his own flesh.

We confess that he is the Son, begotten of God the Father, and Only-begotten God; and although according to his own nature he was not subject to suffering, yet he suffered for us in the flesh according to the Scriptures, and although impassible, yet in his Crucified Body he made his own the sufferings of his own flesh; and by the grace of God he tasted death for all: he gave his own Body thereto, although he was by nature himself the life and the resurrection, in order that, having trodden down death by his unspeakable power, first in his own flesh, he might become the first born from the dead, and the first-fruits of them that slept. And that he might make a way for the nature of man to attain incorruption, by the grace of God (as we just now said), he tasted death for every man, and after three days rose again, having despoiled hell. So although it is said that the resurrection of the dead was through man, yet we understand that man to have been the Word of God, and the power of death was loosed through him, and he shall come in the fullness of time as the One Son and Lord, in the glory of the Father, in order to judge the world in righteousness, as it is written.

For when as God he speaks about himself: He who has seen me has seen the Father, and I and my Father are one, we consider his ineffable divine nature according to which he is One with his Father through the identity of essence— The image and impress and brightness of his glory. But when not scorning the measure of his humanity, he said to the Jews: But now you seek to kill me, a man that has told you the truth. Again no less than before we recognize that he is the Word of God from his identity and likeness to the Father and from the circumstances of his humanity. For if it is necessary to believe that being by nature God, he became flesh, that is, a man endowed with a reasonable soul, what reason can certain ones have to be ashamed of this language about him, which is suitable to him as man? For if he should reject the words suitable to him as man, who compelled him to become man like us? And as he humbled himself to a voluntary abasement (κένωσιν) for us, for what cause can any one reject the words suitable to such abasement? Therefore all the words which are read in the Gospels are to be applied to One Person, to One hypostasis of the Word Incarnate. For the Lord Jesus Christ is One, according to the Scriptures, although he is called the Apostle and High Priest of our profession, as offering to God and the Father the confession of faith which we make to him, and through him to God even the Father and also to the Holy Spirit; yet we say he is, according to nature, the Only-begotten of God. And not to any man different from him do we assign the name of priesthood, and the thing, for he became the Mediator between God and men, and a Reconciler unto peace, having offered himself as a sweet smelling savour to God and the Father. Therefore also he said: Sacrifice and offering you would not; but a body have you prepared me: In burnt offerings and sacrifices for sin you have had no pleasure. Then said I, Lo, I come (in the volume of the book it is written of me) to do your will, O God. For on account of us he offered his body as a sweet smelling savour, and not for himself; for what offering or sacrifice was needed for himself, who as God existed above all sins? For all have sinned and come short of the glory of God, so that we became prone to fall, and the nature of man has fallen into sin, yet not so he (and therefore we fall short of his glory). How then can there be further doubt that the true Lamb died for us and on our account? And to say that he offered himself for himself and us, could in no way escape the charge of impiety. For he never committed a fault at all, neither did he sin. What offering then did he need, not having sin for which sacrifices are rightly offered? But when he spoke about the Spirit, he said: He shall glorify me. If we think rightly, we do not say that the One Christ and Son as needing glory from another received glory from the Holy Spirit; for neither greater than he nor above him is his Spirit, but because he used the Holy Spirit to show forth his own divinity in his mighty works, therefore he is said to have been glorified by him just as if any one of us should say concerning his inherent strength for example, or his knowledge of anything, They glorified me. For although the Spirit is the same essence, yet we think of him by himself, as he is the Spirit and not the Son; but he is not different from him; for he is called the Spirit of truth and Christ is the Truth, and he is sent by him, just as, moreover, he is from God and the Father. When then the Spirit worked miracles through the hands of the holy apostles after the Ascension of Our Lord Jesus Christ into heaven, he glorified him. For it is believed that he who works through his own Spirit is God according to nature. Therefore he said: He shall receive of mine, and shall show it unto you. But we do not say this as if the Spirit is wise and powerful through some sharing with another; for he is all perfect and in need of no good thing. Since, therefore, he is the Spirit of the Power and Wisdom of the Father (that is, of the Son), he is evidently Wisdom and Power.

And since the holy Virgin brought forth corporally God made one with flesh according to nature, for this reason we also call her Mother of God, not as if the nature of the Word had the beginning of its existence from the flesh.

For In the beginning was the Word, and the Word was God, and the Word was with God, and he is the Maker of the ages, coeternal with the Father, and Creator of all; but, as we have already said, since he united to himself hypostatically human nature from her womb, also he subjected himself to birth as man, not as needing necessarily in his own nature birth in time and in these last times of the world, but in order that he might bless the beginning of our existence, and that that which sent the earthly bodies of our whole race to death, might lose its power for the future by his being born of a woman in the flesh. And this: In sorrow you shall bring forth children, being removed through him, he showed the truth of that spoken by the prophet, Strong death swallowed them up, and again God has wiped away every tear from off all faces. For this cause also we say that he attended, having been called, and also blessed, the marriage in Cana of Galilee, with his holy Apostles in accordance with the economy. We have been taught to hold these things by the holy Apostles and Evangelists, and all the God-inspired Scriptures, and in the true confessions of the blessed Fathers.

To all these your reverence also should agree, and give heed, without any guile. And what it is necessary your reverence should anathematize we have subjoined to our epistle.

The Twelve Anathemas of St. Cyril Against Nestorius

1

If anyone will not confess that the Emmanuel is very God, and that therefore the Holy Virgin is the Mother of God (Θεοτόκος), inasmuch as in the flesh she bore the Word of God made flesh [as it is written, The Word was made flesh] let him be anathema.

Nestorius: If anyone says that the Emmanuel is true God, and not rather God with us, that is, that he has united himself to a like nature with ours, which he assumed from the Virgin Mary, and dwelt in it; and if anyone calls Mary the mother of God the Word, and not rather mother of him who is Emmanuel; and if he maintains that God the Word has changed himself into the flesh, which he only assumed in order to make his Godhead visible, and to be found in form as a man, let him be anathema.

2

If anyone shall not confess that the Word of God the Father is united hypostatically to flesh, and that with that flesh of his own, he is one only Christ both God and man at the same time: let him be anathema.

Nestorius: If any one asserts that, at the union of the Logos with the flesh, the divine Essence moved from one place to another; or says that the flesh is capable of receiving the divine nature, and that it has been partially united with the flesh; or ascribes to the flesh, by reason of its reception of God, an extension to the infinite and boundless, and says that God and man are one and the same in nature; let him be anathema.

3

If anyone shall after the [hypostatic] union divide the hypostases in the one Christ, joining them by that connection alone, which happens according to worthiness, or even authority and power, and not rather by a coming together (συνόδῳ), which is made by natural union (ἕνωσιν φυσικὴν): let him be anathema.

Nestorius: If any one says that Christ, who is also Emmanuel, is One, not [merely] in consequence of *connection*, but [also] in *nature*, and does not acknowledge the *connection* (συνάφεια) of the two natures, that of the Logos and of the assumed manhood, in one Son, as still continuing without mingling; let him be anathema.

4

If anyone shall divide between two persons or subsistences those expressions (φωνάς) which are contained in the Evangelical and Apostolical writings, or which have been said concerning Christ by the Saints, or by himself, and shall apply some to him as to a man separate from the Word of God, and shall apply others to the only Word of God the Father, on the ground that they are fit to be applied to God: let him be anathema.

Nestorius: If any one assigns the expressions of the Gospels and Apostolic letters, which refer to the two natures of Christ, to one only of those natures, and even ascribes suffering to the divine Word, both in the flesh and in the Godhead; let him be anathema.

5

If anyone shall dare to say that the Christ is a Theophorus [that is, God-bearing] man and not rather that he is very God, as an only Son through nature, because the Word was made flesh, and has a share in flesh and blood as we do: let him be anathema.

Nestorius: If any one ventures to say that, even after the assumption of human nature, there is only one Son of God, namely, he who is so in nature (*naturaliter filius* = Logos), while he (since the assumption of the flesh) is certainly Emmanuel; let him be anathema.

6

If anyone shall dare say that the Word of God the Father is the God of Christ or the Lord of Christ, and shall not rather confess him as at the same time both God and Man, since according to the Scriptures, The Word was made flesh: let him be anathema.

Nestorius: "If anyone, after the Incarnation calls another than Christ the Word, and ventures to say that the form of a servant is equally with the Word of God, without beginning and uncreated, and not rather that it is made by him as its natural Lord and Creator and God, and that he has promised to raise it again in the words: Destroy this temple, and in three days I will build it up again; let him be anathema."

7

If anyone shall say that Jesus as man is only energized by the Word of God, and that the glory of the Only-begotten is attributed to him as something not properly his: let him be anathema.

Nestorius: If any one says that the man who was formed of the Virgin is the Only-begotten, who was born from the bosom of the Father, before the morning star was Psalm 108:3 , and does not rather confess that he has obtained the designation of Only-begotten on account of his connection with him who in nature is the Only-begotten of the Father; and besides, if any one calls another than the Emmanuel Christ let him be anathema.

8

If anyone shall dare to say that the assumed man (ἀναληφθέντα) ought to be worshipped together with God the Word, and glorified together with him, and recognised together with him as God, and yet as two different things, the one with the other (for this Together with is added [*i.e.*, by the Nestorians] to convey this meaning); and shall not rather with one adoration worship the Emmanuel and pay to him one glorification, as [it is written] The Word was made flesh: let him be anathema.

Nestorius: If any one says that the form of a servant should, for its own sake, that is, in reference to its own nature, be reverenced, and that it is the ruler of all things, and not rather, that [merely] on account of its connection with the holy and in itself universally-ruling nature of the Only-begotten, it is to be reverenced; let him be anathema.

9

If any man shall say that the one Lord Jesus Christ was glorified by the Holy Ghost, so that he used through him a power not his own and from him received power against unclean spirits and power to work miracles before men and shall not rather confess that it was his own Spirit through which he worked these divine signs; let him be anathema.

Nestorius: If anyone says that the form of a servant is of like nature with the Holy Ghost, and not rather that it owes its union with the Word which has existed since the conception, to his mediation, by which it works miraculous healings among men, and possesses the power of expelling demons; let him be anathema.

10

Whosoever shall say that it is not the divine Word himself, when he was made flesh and had become man as we are, but another than he, a man born of a woman, yet different from him (ἰδικῶς ἄνθρωπον), who has become our Great High Priest and Apostle; or if any man shall say that he offered himself in sacrifice for himself and not rather for us, whereas, being without sin, he had no need of offering or sacrifice: let him be anathema.

Nestorius: If any one maintains that the Word, who is from the beginning, has become the high priest and apostle of our confession, and has offered himself for us, and does not rather say that it is the work of Emmanuel to be an apostle; and if any one in such a manner divides the sacrifice between him who united [the Word] and him who was united [the manhood] referring it to a common sonship, that is, not giving to God that which is God's, and to man that which is man's; let him be anathema.

11

Whosoever shall not confess that the flesh of the Lord gives life and that it pertains to the Word of God the Father as his very own, but shall pretend that it belongs to another person who is united to him [i.e., the Word] only according to honour, and who has served as a dwelling for the divinity; and shall not rather confess, as we say, that that flesh gives life because it is that of the Word who gives life to all: let him be anathema.

Nestorius: "If any one maintains that the flesh which is united with God the Word is by the power of its own nature life-giving, whereas the Lord himself says, It is the Spirit that quickens; the flesh profits nothing John 6:61, let him be anathema. [He adds, God is a Spirit John 4:24. If, then, any one maintains that God the Logos has in a carnal manner, in his substance, become flesh, and persists in this with reference to the Lord Christ; who himself after his resurrection said to his disciples, Handle me and see; for a spirit has not flesh and bones, as you behold me having Luke 24:39; let him be anathema.]"

12

Whosoever shall not recognize that the Word of God suffered in the flesh, that he was crucified in the flesh, and that likewise in that same flesh he tasted death and that he has become the first-begotten of the dead, for, as he is God, he is the life and it is he that gives life: let him be anathema.

Nestorius: If any one, in confessing the sufferings of the flesh, ascribes these also to the Word of God as to the flesh in which he appeared, and thus does not distinguish the dignity of the natures; let him be anathema.

Extracts from the Acts (Continued)

[No action is recorded in the Acts as having been taken. A verbal report was made by certain who had seen Nestorius during the past three days, that they were hopeless of any repentance on his part. On the motion of Flavian, bishop of Philippi, a number of passages from the Fathers were read; and after that some selections from the writings of Nestorius. A letter from Capreolus, Archbishop of Carthage, was next read, excusing his absence; after the reading of the letter, which makes no direct reference to Nestorius whatever, but prays the Synod to see to it that no novelties be tolerated, the Acts proceed. (Col. 534).]

Cyril, the bishop of the Church of Alexandria, said: As this letter of the most reverend and pious Capreolus, bishop of Carthage, which has been read, contains a most lucid expression of opinion, let it be inserted in the Acts. For it wishes that the ancient dogmas of the faith should be confirmed, and that novelties, absurdly conceived and impiously brought forth, should be reprobated and proscribed.

All the bishops at the same time cried out: These are the sentiments (φωναί) of all of us, these are the things we all say — the accomplishment of this is the desire of us all.

[Immediately follows the sentence of deposition and the subscriptions. It seems almost certain that something has dropped out here, most probably the whole discussion of Cyril's XII. Anathematisms.]

Decree of the Council Against Nestorius

(*Found in all the* Concilia *in Greek with Latin Versions.*)

As, in addition to other things, the impious Nestorius has not obeyed our citation, and did not receive the holy bishops who were sent by us to him, we were compelled to examine his ungodly doctrines. We discovered that he had held and published impious doctrines in his letters and treatises, as well as in discourses which he delivered in this city, and which have been testified to. Compelled thereto by the canons and by the letter (ἀναγκαίως κατεπειχθέντες ἀπό τε τῶν κανόνων, καὶ ἐκ τῆς ἐπιστολῆς, κ.τ.λ.) of our most holy father and fellow-servant Cœlestine, the Roman bishop, we have come, with many tears, to this sorrowful sentence against him, namely, that our Lord Jesus Christ, whom he has blasphemed, decrees by the holy Synod that Nestorius be excluded from the episcopal dignity, and from all priestly communion.

Session II

Extracts from the Acts

The most pious and God-beloved bishops, Arcadius and Projectus, as also the most beloved-of-God Philip, a presbyter and legate of the Apostolic See, then entered and took their seats.

Philip the presbyter and legate of the Apostolic See said: We bless the holy and adorable Trinity that our lowliness has been deemed worthy to attend your holy Synod. For a long time ago (πάλαι) our most holy and blessed pope Cœlestine, bishop of the Apostolic See, through his letters to that holy and most pious man Cyril, bishop of Alexandria, gave judgment concerning the present cause and affair (ὥρισεν) which letters have been shown to your holy assembly. And now again for the corroboration of the Catholic (καθολικῆς) faith, he has sent through us letters to all your holinesses, which you will bid (κελούσατε) to be read with becoming reverence (πρεπόντως) and to be entered on the ecclesiastical minutes.

Arcadius, a bishop and legate of the Roman Church said: May it please your blessedness to give order that the letters of the holy and ever-to-be-mentioned-with-veneration Pope Cœlestine, bishop of the Apostolic See, which have been brought by us, be read, from which your reverence will be able to see what care he has for all the Churches.

Projectus, a bishop and legate of the Roman Church said, May it please, etc. [*The same as Arcadius had said* verbatim!]

And afterwards the most holy and beloved-of-God Cyril, bishop of the Church of Alexandria, spoke as is next in order contained; Siricius, notary of the holy Catholic (καθολικῆς) Church of Rome read it.

Cyril, the bishop of Alexandria said: Let the letter received from the most holy and altogether most blessed Cœlestine, bishop of the Apostolic See of Rome be read to the holy Synod with fitting honour.

Siricius, notary of the holy Catholic (καθολικῆς) Church of the city of Rome read it.

And after it was read in Latin, Juvenal, the bishop of Jerusalem said: Let the writings of the most holy and blessed bishop of great Rome which have just been read, be entered on the minutes.

And all the most reverend bishops prayed that the letter might be translated and read.

Philip, the presbyter of the Apostolic See and Legate said: The custom has been sufficiently complied with, that the writings of the Apostolic See should first be read in Latin. But now since your holiness has demanded that they be read in Greek also, it is necessary that your holiness's desire should be satisfied; We have taken care that this be done, and that the Latin be turned into Greek.

Give order therefore that it be received and read in your holy hearing.

Arcadius and Projectus, bishops and legates said, As your blessedness ordered that the writings which we brought should be brought to the knowledge of all, for of our holy brethren bishops there are not a few who do not understand Latin, therefore the letter has been translated into Greek and if you so command let it be read.

Flavian, the bishop of Philippi said: Let the translation of the letter of the most holy and beloved of God, bishop of the Roman Church be received and read.

Peter, the presbyter of Alexandria and primicerius of the notaries read as follows:

The Letter of Pope Cœlestine to the Synod of Ephesus

Cœlestine the bishop to the holy Synod assembled at Ephesus, brethren beloved and most longed for, greeting in the Lord.

A Synod of priests gives witness to the presence of the Holy Spirit. For true is that which we read, since the Truth cannot lie, to wit, the promise of the Gospel; Where two or three are gathered together in my name, there am I in the midst of them. And since this is so, if the Holy Spirit is not absent from so small a number how much more may we believe he is present when so great a multitude of holy ones are assembled together! Every council is holy on account of a peculiar veneration which is its due; for in every such council the reverence which should be paid to that most famous council of the Apostles of which we read is to be had regard to. Never was the Master, whom they had received to preach, lacking to this, but ever was present as Lord and Master; and never were those who taught deserted by their teacher. For he that had sent them was their teacher; he who had commanded what was to be taught, was their teacher; he who affirms that he himself is heard in his Apostles, was their teacher. This duty of preaching has been entrusted to all the Lord's priests in common, for by right of inheritance we are bound to undertake this solicitude, whoever of us preach the name of the Lord in various lands in their stead for he said to them, Go, teach all nations. You, dear brethren, should observe that we have received a general command: for he wills that all of us should perform that office, which he thus entrusted in common to all the Apostles. We must needs follow our predecessors. Let us all, then, undertake their labours, since we are the successors in their honour. And we show forth our diligence in preaching the same doctrines that they taught, beside which, according to the admonition of the Apostle, we are forbidden to add anything. For the office of keeping what is committed to our trust is no less dignified than that of handing it down.

They sowed the seed of the faith. This shall be our care that the coming of our great father of the family, to whom alone assuredly this fullness of the Apostles is assigned, may find fruit uncorrupt and many fold. For the vase of election tells us that it is not sufficient to plant and to water unless God gives the increase. We must strive therefore in common to keep the faith which has come down to us today, through the Apostolic Succession. For we are expected to walk according to the Apostle. For now not our appearance (*species*) but our faith is called in question. Spiritual weapons are those we must take, because the war is one of minds, and the weapons are words; so shall we be strong in the faith of our King. Now the Blessed Apostle Paul admonishes that all should remain in that place in which he bid Timothy remain. The same place therefore, the same cause, lays upon us the same duty. Let us now also do and study that which he then commanded him to do. And let no one think otherwise, and let no one pay heed to over strange fables, as he himself ordered. Let us be unanimous, thinking the same thing, for this is expedient: let us do nothing out of contention, nothing out of vain glory: let us be in all things of one mind, of one heart, when the faith which is one, is attacked. Let the whole body grieve and mourn in common with us. He who is to judge the world is called into judgment; he who is to criticise all, is himself made the object of criticism, he who redeemed us is made to suffer calumny. Dear Brethren, gird yourselves with the armour of God. You know what helmet must protect our head, what breast-plate our breast. For this is not the first time the ecclesiastical camps have received you as their rulers. Let no one doubt that by the favour of the Lord who makes two to be one, there will be peace, and that arms will be laid aside since the very cause defends itself.

SEVEN ECUMENICAL COUNCILS OF THE CHURCH

Let us look once again at these words of our Doctor, which he uses with express reference to bishops, saying, Take heed to yourselves and to the whole flock, over which the Holy Ghost has placed you as bishop, that you rule the church of God, which he has purchased with his blood.

We read that they who heard this at Ephesus, the same place at which your holiness has come together, were called thence. To them therefore to whom this preaching of the faith was known, to them also let your defense of the same faith also be known. Let us show them the constancy of our mind with that reverence which is due to matters of great importance; which things peace has guarded for a long time with pious understanding.

Let there be announced by you what things have been preserved intact from the Apostles; for the words of tyrannical opposition are never admitted against the King of Kings, nor can the business of truth be oppressed by falsehood.

I exhort you, most blessed brethren, that love alone be regarded in which we ought to remain, according to the voice of John the Apostle whose relics we venerate in this city. Let common prayer be offered to the Lord. For we can form some idea of what will be the power of the divine presence at the united intercession of such a multitude of priests, by considering how the very place was moved where, as we read, the Twelve made together their supplication. And what was the purport of that prayer of the Apostles? It was that they might receive grace to speak the word of God with confidence, and to act through its power, both of which they received by the favour of Christ our God. And now what else is to be asked for by your holy council, except that you may speak the Word of the Lord with confidence? What else than that he would give you grace to preserve that which he has given you to preach? That being filled with the Holy Ghost, as it is written, you may set forth that one truth which the Spirit himself has taught you, although with various voices.

Animated, in brief, by all these considerations (for, as the Apostle says: I speak to them that know the law, and I speak wisdom among them that are perfect), stand fast by the Catholic faith, and defend the peace of the Churches, for so it is said, both to those past, present, and future, asking and preserving those things which belong to the peace of Jerusalem.

Out of our solicitude, we have sent our holy brethren and fellow priests, who are at one with us and are most approved men, Arcedius, and Projectus, the bishops, and our presbyter, Philip, that they may be present at what is done and may carry out what things have been already decreed be us (*quæ a nobis antea statuta sunt, exequantur*).

To the performing of which we have no doubt that your holiness will assent when it is seen that what has been decreed is for the security of the whole church. Given the viij of the Ides of May, in the consulate of Bassus and Antiochus.

Extracts from the Acts

And all the most reverend bishops at the same time cried out. This is a just judgment. To Cœlestine, a new Paul! To Cyril a new Paul! To Cœlestine the guardian of the faith! To Cœlestine of one mind with the synod! To Cœlestine the whole Synod offers its thanks! One Cœlestine! One Cyril! One faith of the Synod! One faith of the world!

Projectus, the most reverend bishop and legate, said: Let your holiness consider the form (τύπον) of the writings of the holy and venerable pope Cœlestine, the bishop, who has exhorted your holiness (not as if teaching the ignorant, but as reminding them that know) that those things which he had long ago defined, and now thought it right to remind you of, you might give command to be carried out to the uttermost, according to the canon of the common faith, and according to the use of the Catholic Church.

Firmus, the bishop of Cæsarea in Cappadocia said: The Apostolic and holy see of the most holy bishop Cœlestine, has previously given a decision and type (τύπον) in this matter, through the writings which were sent to the most God beloved bishops, to wit to Cyril of Alexandria, and to Juvenal of Jerusalem, and to Rufus of Thessalonica, and to the holy churches, both of Constantinople and of Antioch. This we have also followed and (since the limit set for Nestorius's emendation was long gone by, and much time has passed since our arrival at the city of Ephesus in accordance with the decree of the most pious emperor, and thereupon having delayed no little time so that the day fixed by the emperor was past; and since Nestorius although cited had not appeared) we carried into effect the type (τύπον) having pronounced against him a canonical and apostolic judgment.

Arcadius the most reverend bishop and legate, said: Although our sailing was slow, and contrary winds hindered us especially, so that we did not know whether we should arrive at the destined place, as we had hoped, nevertheless by God's good providence…Wherefore we desire to ask your blessedness, that you command that we be taught what has been already decreed by your holiness.

Philip, presbyter and legate of the Apostolic See said: We offer our thanks to the holy and venerable Synod, that when the writings of our holy and blessed pope had been read to you, the holy members by our [or your] holy voices, you joined yourselves to the holy head also by your holy acclamations. For your blessedness is not ignorant that the head of the whole faith, the head of the Apostles, is blessed Peter the Apostle. And since now our mediocrity, after having been tempest-tossed and much vexed, has arrived, we ask that you give order that there be laid before us what things were done in this holy Synod before our arrival; in order that according to the opinion of our blessed pope and of this present holy assembly, we likewise may ratify their determination.

Theodotus, the bishop of Ancyra said: The God of the whole world has made manifest the justice of the judgment pronounced by the holy Synod by the writings of the most religious bishop Cœlestine, and by the coming of your holiness. For you have made manifest the zeal of the most holy and reverend bishop Cœlestine, and his care for the pious faith. And since very reasonably your reverence is desirous of learning what has been done from the minutes of the acts concerning the deposition of Nestorius your reverence will be fully convinced of the justice of the sentence, and of the zeal of the holy Synod, and the symphony of the faith which the most pious and holy bishop Cœlestine has proclaimed with a great voice, of course after your full conviction, the rest shall be added to the present action.

[*In the Acts follow two short letters from Cœlestine, one to the Emperor and the other to Cyril, but nothing is said about them, or how they got there, and thus abruptly ends the account of this session.*]

Session III

Extracts from the Acts

Juvenal the bishop of Jerusalem said to Arcadius and Projectus the most reverend bishops, and to Philip the most reverend presbyter; Yesterday while this holy and great synod was in session, when your holiness was present, you demanded after the reading of the letter of the most holy and blessed bishop of Great Rome, Cœlestine, that the minutes made in the Acts with regard to the deposition of Nestorius the heretic should be read. And thereupon the Synod ordered this to be done. Your holiness will be good enough to inform us whether you have read them and understand their power.

Philip the presbyter and legate of the Apostolic See said: From reading the Acts we have found what things have been done in your holy synod with regard to Nestorius. We have found from the minutes that all things have been decided in accordance with the canons and with ecclesiastical discipline. And now also we seek from your honour, although it may be useless, that what things have been read in your synod, the same should now again be read to us also; so that we may follow the formula (τύπῳ) of the most holy pope Cœlestine (who committed this same care to us), and of your holiness also, and may be able to confirm (βεβαιῶσαι) the judgment.

[*Arcadius having seconded Philip's motion, Memnon directed the acts to be read which was done by the primicerius of the notaries.*]

Philip the presbyter and legate of the Apostolic See said: There is no doubt, and in fact it has been known in all ages, that the holy and most blessed Peter, prince (ἔξαρχος) and head of the Apostles, pillar of the faith, and foundation (θεμέλιος) of the Catholic Church, received the keys of the kingdom from our Lord Jesus Christ, the Saviour and Redeemer of the human race, and that to him was given the power of loosing and binding sins: who down even to today and forever both lives and judges in his successors. The holy and most blessed pope Cœlestine, according to due order, is his successor and holds his place, and us he sent to supply his place in this holy synod, which the most humane and Christian Emperors have commanded to assemble, bearing in mind and continually watching over the Catholic faith. For they both have kept and are now keeping intact the apostolic doctrine handed down to them from their most pious and humane grandfathers and fathers of holy memory down to the present time, etc.

[There is no further reference in the speech to the papal prerogatives.]

Arcadius the most reverend bishop and legate of the Apostolic See said: Nestorius has brought us great sorrow....And since of his own accord he has made himself an alien and an exile from us, we following the sanctions handed down from the beginning by the holy Apostles, and by the Catholic Church (for they taught what they had received from our Lord Jesus Christ), also following the types (τύποις) of Cœlestine, most holy pope of the Apostolic See, who has condescended to send us as his executors of this business, and also following the decrees of the holy Synod [we give this as our conclusion]: Let Nestorius know that he is deprived of all episcopal dignity, and is an alien from the whole Church and from the communion of all its priests.

Projectus, bishop and legate of the Roman Church said: Most clearly from the reading, etc....Moreover I also, by my authority as legate of the holy Apostolic See, define, being with my brethren an executor (ἐκβιβαστὴς) of the aforesaid sentence, that the beforenamed Nestorius is an enemy of the truth, a corrupter of the faith, and as guilty of the things of which he was accused, has been removed from the grade of Episcopal honour, and moreover from the communion of all orthodox priests.

Cyril, the bishop of Alexandria said: The professions which have been made by Arcadius and Projectus, the most holy and pious bishops, as also by Philip, the most religious presbyter of the Roman Church, stand manifest to the holy Synod. For they have made their profession in the place of the Apostolic See, and of the whole of the holy synod of the God-beloved and most holy bishops of the West. Wherefore let those things which were defined by the most holy

Cœlestine, the God-beloved bishop, be carried into effect, and the vote cast against Nestorius the heretic, by the holy Synod, which met in the metropolis of Ephesus be agreed to universally; for this purpose let there be added to the already prepared acts the proceedings of yesterday and today, and let them be shown to their holiness, so that by their subscription according to custom, their canonical agreement with all of us may be manifest.

Arcadius the most reverend bishop and legate of the Roman Church, said: According to the acts of this holy Synod, we necessarily confirm with our subscriptions their doctrines.

The Holy Synod said: Since Arcadius and Projectus the most reverend and most religious bishops and legates and Philip, the presbyter and legate of the Apostolic See, have said that they are of the same mind with us, it only remains, that they redeem their promises and confirm the acts with their signatures, and then let the minutes of the acts be shown to them.

[*The three then signed.*]

Session VII (The Canons)

The holy and ecumenical Synod, gathered together in Ephesus by the decree of our most religious Emperors, to the bishops, presbyters, deacons, and all the people in every province and city:

When we had assembled, according to the religious decree [of the Emperors], in the Metropolis of Ephesus, certain persons, a little more than thirty in number, withdrew from among us, having for the leader of their schism John, Bishop of Antioch. Their names are as follows: first, the said John of Antioch in Syria, John of Damascus, Alexander of Apamea, Alexander of Hierapolis, Himerius of Nicomedia, Fritilas of Heraclea, Helladius of Tarsus, Maximin of Anazarbus, Theodore of Marcianopolis, Peter of Trajanopolis, Paul of Emissa, Polychronius of Heracleopolis, Euthyrius of Tyana, Meletius of Neocæsarea, Theodoret of Cyrus, Apringius of Chalcedon, Macarius of Laodicea Magna, Zosys of Esbus, Sallust of Corycus in Cilicia, Hesychius of Castabala in Cilicia, Valentine of Mutloblaca, Eustathius of Parnassus, Philip of Theodosia, and Daniel, and Dexianus, and Julian, and Cyril, and Olympius, and

Diogenes, Polius, Theophanes of Philadelphia, Trajan of Augusta, Aurelius of Irenopolis, Mysæus of Aradus, Helladius of Ptolemais. These men, having no privilege of ecclesiastical communion on the ground of a priestly authority, by which they could injure or benefit any persons; since some of them had already been deposed; and since from their refusing to join in our decree against Nestorius, it was manifestly evident to all men that they were all promoting the opinions of Nestorius and Celestius; the Holy Synod, by one common decree, deposed them from all ecclesiastical communion, and deprived them of all their priestly power by which they might injure or profit any persons.

Canon 1

Whereas it is needful that they who were detained from the holy Synod and remained in their own district or city, for any reason, ecclesiastical or personal, should not be ignorant of the matters which were thereby decreed; we, therefore, notify your holiness and charity that if any Metropolitan of a Province, forsaking the holy and Ecumenical Synod, has joined the assembly of the apostates, or shall join the same hereafter; or, if he has adopted, or shall hereafter adopt, the doctrines of Celestius, he has no power in any way to do anything in opposition to the bishops of the province, since he is already cast forth from all ecclesiastical communion and made incapable of exercising his ministry; but he shall himself be subject in all things to those very bishops of the province and to the neighbouring orthodox metropolitans, and shall be degraded from his episcopal rank.

Canon 2

If any provincial bishops were not present at the holy Synod and have joined or attempted to join the apostacy; or if, after subscribing the deposition of Nestorius, they went back into the assembly of apostates; these men, according to the decree of the holy Synod, are to be deposed from the priesthood and degraded from their rank.

Canon 3

If any of the city or country clergy have been inhibited by Nestorius or his followers from the exercise of the priesthood, on account of their orthodoxy, we have declared it just that these should be restored to their proper rank. And in general we forbid all the clergy who adhere to the Orthodox and Ecumenical Synod in any way to submit to the bishops who have already apostatized or shall hereafter apostatize.

Canon 4

If any of the clergy should fall away, and publicly or privately presume to maintain the doctrines of Nestorius or Celestius, it is declared just by the holy Synod that these also should be deposed.

Canon 5

If any have been condemned for evil practices by the holy Synod, or by their own bishops; and if, with his usual lack of discrimination, Nestorius (or his followers) has attempted, or shall hereafter attempt, uncanonically to restore such persons to communion and to their former rank, we have declared that they shall not be profited thereby, but shall remain deposed nevertheless.

Canon 6

Likewise, if any should in any way attempt to set aside the orders in each case made by the holy Synod at Ephesus, the holy Synod decrees that, if they be bishops or clergymen, they shall absolutely forfeit their office; and, if laymen, that they shall be excommunicated.

Canon 7

When these things had been read, the holy Synod decreed that it is unlawful for any man to bring forward, or to write, or to compose a different (ἑτέραν) Faith as a rival to that established by the holy Fathers assembled with the Holy Ghost in Nicæa.

But those who shall dare to compose a different faith, or to introduce or offer it to persons desiring to turn to the acknowledgment of the truth, whether from Heathenism or from Judaism, or from any heresy whatsoever, shall be deposed, if they be bishops or clergymen; bishops from the episcopate and clergymen from the clergy; and if they be laymen, they shall be anathematized.

SEVEN ECUMENICAL COUNCILS OF THE CHURCH

And in like manner, if any, whether bishops, clergymen, or laymen, should be discovered to hold or teach the doctrines contained in the Exposition introduced by the Presbyter Charisius concerning the Incarnation of the Only-Begotten Son of God, or the abominable and profane doctrines of Nestorius, which are subjoined, they shall be subjected to the sentence of this holy and ecumenical Synod. So that, if it be a bishop, he shall be removed from his bishopric and degraded; if it be a clergyman, he shall likewise be stricken from the clergy; and if it be a layman, he shall be anathematized, as has been afore said.

Canon 8

Our brother bishop Rheginus, the beloved of God, and his fellow beloved of God bishops, Zeno and Evagrius, of the Province of Cyprus, have reported to us an innovation which has been introduced contrary to the ecclesiastical constitutions and the Canons of the Holy Apostles, and which touches the liberties of all. Wherefore, since injuries affecting all require the more attention, as they cause the greater damage, and particularly when they are transgressions of an ancient custom; and since those excellent men, who have petitioned the Synod, have told us in writing and by word of mouth that the Bishop of Antioch has in this way held ordinations in Cyprus; therefore the Rulers of the holy churches in Cyprus shall enjoy, without dispute or injury, according to the Canons of the blessed Fathers and ancient custom, the right of performing for themselves the ordination of their excellent Bishops. The same rule shall be observed in the other dioceses and provinces everywhere, so that none of the God beloved Bishops shall assume control of any province which has not heretofore, from the very beginning, been under his own hand or that of his predecessors. But if any one has violently taken and subjected [a Province], he shall give it up; lest the Canons of the Fathers be transgressed; or the vanities of worldly honour be brought in under pretext of sacred office; or we lose, without knowing it, little by little, the liberty which Our Lord Jesus Christ, the Deliverer of all men, has given us by his own Blood.

Wherefore, this holy and ecumenical Synod has decreed that in every province the rights which heretofore, from the beginning, have belonged to it, shall be preserved to it, according to the old prevailing custom, unchanged and uninjured: every Metropolitan having permission to take, for his own security, a copy of these acts. And if any one shall bring forward a rule contrary to what is here determined, this holy and ecumenical Synod unanimously decrees that it shall be of no effect.

The Letter of the Same Holy Synod of Ephesus, to the Sacred Synod in Pamphylia Concerning Eustathius Who Had Been Their Metropolitan

Forasmuch as the divinely inspired Scripture says, Do all things with advice, it is especially their duty who have had the priestly ministry allotted to them to examine with all diligence whatever matters are to be transacted. For to those who will so spend their lives, it comes to pass both that they are established in [the enjoyment of] an honest hope concerning what belongs to them, and that they are borne along, as by a favouring breeze, in things that they desire: so that, in truth, the saying [of the Scripture] has much reason [to commend it]. But there are times when bitter and intolerable grief swoops down upon the mind, and has the effect of cruelly beclouding it, so as to carry it away from the pursuit of what is needful, and persuade it to consider that to be of service which is in its [very] nature mischievous. Something of this kind we have seen endured by that most excellent and most religious Bishop Eustathius. For it is in evidence that he has been ordained canonically; but having been much disturbed, as he declares, by certain parties, and having entered upon circumstances he had not foreseen, therefore, though fully able to repel the slanders of his persecutors, he nevertheless, through an extraordinary inexperience of affairs, declined to battle with the difficulties which beset him, and in some way that we know not set forth an act of resignation. Yet it behooved him, when he had been once entrusted with the priestly care, to cling to it with spiritual energy, and, as it were, to strip himself to strive against the troubles and gladly to endure the sweat for which he had bargained. But inasmuch as he proved himself to be deficient in practical capacity, having met with this misfortune rather from inexperience than from cowardice and sloth, your holiness has of necessity ordained our most excellent and most religious brother and fellow bishop, Theodore, as the overseer of the Church; for it was not reasonable that it should remain in widowhood, and that the Saviour's sheep should pass their time without a shepherd. But when he came to us weeping, not contending with the aforenamed most religious Bishop Theodore for his See or Church, but in the meantime seeking only for his rank and title as a bishop, we all suffered with the old man in his grief, and considering his weeping as our own, we hastened to discover whether the aforenamed [Eustathius] had been subjected to a legal deposition, or whether, forsooth, he had been convicted on any of the absurd charges alleged by certain parties who had poured forth idle gossip against his reputation. And indeed we learned that nothing of such a kind had taken place, but rather that his resignation had been counted against the said Eustathius instead of a [regular] indictment. Wherefore, we did by no means blame your holiness for being compelled to ordain into his place the aforenamed most excellent Bishop Theodore. But forasmuch as it was not seemly to contend much against the unpractical character of the man, while it was rather necessary to have pity on the elder who, at so advanced an age, was now so far away from the city which had given him birth, and from the dwelling-places of his fathers, we have judicially pronounced and decreed without any opposition, that he shall have both the name, and the rank, and the communion of the episcopate. On this condition, however, only, that he shall not ordain, and that he shall not take and minister to a Church of his own individual authority; but that [he shall do so only] if taken as an assistant, or when appointed, if it should so chance, by a brother and fellow bishop, in accordance with the ordinance and the love which is in Christ. If, however, you shall determine anything more favourable towards him, either now or hereafter, this also will be pleasing to the Holy Synod.

The Letter of the Synod to Pope Celestine

The Holy Synod which by the grace of God was assembled at Ephesus the Metropolis to the most holy and our fellow-minister Cœlestine, health in the Lord.

The zeal of your holiness for piety, and your care for the right faith, so grateful and highly pleasing to God the Saviour of us all, are worthy of all admiration. For it is your custom in such great matters to make trial of all things, and the confirmation of the Churches you have made your own care. But since it is right that all things which have taken place should be brought to the knowledge of your holiness, we are writing of necessity [to inform you] that, by the will of Christ the Saviour of us all, and in accordance with the orders of the most pious and Christ-loving Emperors, we assembled together in the Metropolis of the Ephesians from many and far scattered regions, being in all over two hundred bishops. Then, in accordance with the decrees of the Christ-loving Emperors by whom we were assembled, we fixed the date of the meeting of the holy Synod as the Feast of the Holy Pentecost, all agreeing thereto, especially as it was contained in the letters of the Emperors that if anyone did not arrive at the appointed time, he was absent with no good conscience, and was inexcusable both before God and man. The most reverend John Bishop of Antioch stopped behind; not in singleness of heart, nor because the length of the journey made the impediment, but hiding in his mind his plan and his thought (which was so displeasing to God,) [a plan and thought] which he made clear when not long afterwards he arrived at Ephesus.

Therefore we put off the assembling [of the council] after the appointed day of the Holy Pentecost for sixteen whole days; in the meanwhile many of the bishops and clerics were overtaken with illness, and much burdened by the expense, and some even died. A great injury was thus being done to the great Synod, as your holiness easily perceives. For he used perversely such long delay that many from much greater distances arrived before him.

Nevertheless after sixteen days had passed, certain of the bishops who were with him, to wit, two Metropolitans, the one Alexander of Apamea, and the other Alexander of Hierapolis, arrived before him. And when we complained of the tardy coming of the most reverend bishop John, not once, but often, we were told, He gave us command to announce to your reverence, that if anything should happen to delay him, not to put off the Synod, but to do what was right. After having received this message — and as it was manifest, as well from his delay as from the announcements just made to us, that he refused to attend the Council, whether out of friendship to Nestorius, or because he had been a cleric of a church under his sway, or out of regard to petitions made by some in his favour — the Holy Council sat in the great church of Ephesus, which bears the name of Mary.

But when all with zeal had come together, Nestorius alone was found missing from the council, thereupon the holy Synod sent him admonition in accordance with the canons by bishops, a first, second, and third time. But he surrounding his house with soldiers, set himself up against the ecclesiastical laws, neither did he show himself, nor give any satisfaction for his iniquitous blasphemies.

After this the letters were read which were written to him by the most holy and most reverend bishop of the Church of Alexandria, Cyril, which the Holy Synod approved as being orthodox and without fault (ὀρθῶς καὶ ἀλήπτως ἔχειν), and in no point out of agreement either with the divinely inspired Scriptures, or with the faith handed down and set forth in the great synod of holy Fathers, which assembled sometime ago at Nice in Bithynia, as your holiness also rightly having examined this has given witness.

On the other hand there was read the letter of Nestorius, which was written to the already mentioned most holy and reverend brother of ours and fellow-minister, Cyril, and the Holy Synod was of opinion that those things which were taught in it were wholly alien from the Apostolic and Evangelical faith, sick with many and strange blasphemies.

His most impious expositions were likewise read, and also the letter written to him by your holiness, in which he was properly condemned as one who had written blasphemy and had inserted irreligious views (φωνᾶς) in his private exegesis, and after this a just sentence of deposition was pronounced against him; especially is this sentence just, because he is so far removed from being penitent, or from a confession of the matters in which he blasphemed, while yet he had the Church of Constantinople, that even in the very metropolis of the Ephesians, he delivered a sermon to certain of the Metropolitical bishops, men who were not ignorant, but learned and God-fearing, in which he was bold enough to say, I do not confess a two or three months old God, and he said other things more outrageous than this.

Therefore as an impious and most pestilent heresy, which perverts our most pure religion (θρησκείαν) and which overthrows from the foundation the whole economy of the mystery [i.e. the Incarnation], we cast it down, as we have said above. But it was not possible, as it seemed, that those who had the sincere love of Christ, and were zealous in the Lord should not experience many trials. For we had hoped that the most reverend John, bishop of Antioch would have praised the sedulous care and piety of the Synod, and that perchance he would have blamed the slowness of Nestorius's deposition. But all things turned out contrary to our hope. For he was found to be an enemy, and a most warlike one, to the holy Synod, and even to the orthodox faith of the churches, as these things indicate.

For as soon as he had come to Ephesus, before he had even shaken off the dust of the journey, or changed his travelling dress, he assembled those who had sided with Nestorius and who had uttered blasphemies against their head, and only not derided the glory of Christ, and gathering as a college to himself, I suppose, thirty men, having the name of bishops (some of whom were without sees, wandering about and having no dioceses, others again had for many years been deposed for serious causes from their metropolises, and with these were Pelagians and the followers of Celestius, and some of those who were turned out of Thessaly), he had the presumption to commit a piece of iniquity no man had ever done before. For all by himself he drew up a paper which he called a deposition, and reviled and reproached the most holy and reverend Cyril, bishop of Alexandria, and the most reverend Memnon, bishop of Ephesus, our brother, and fellow-minister, none of us knowing anything about it, and not even those who were thus reviling knew what was being done, nor for what reason they had presumed to do this. But ignoring the anger of God for such behaviour, and unheeding the ecclesiastical canons, and forgetting that they were hastening to destruction by such a course of action, under the name of an excommunication, they then reviled the whole Synod. And placing these acts of theirs on the public bulletin boards, they exposed them to be read by such as chose to do so, having posted them on the outside of the theatres, that they might make a spectacle of their impiety. But not even was this the limit of their audacity; but as if they had done something in accordance with the canons, they dared to bring what they had done to the ears of the most pious and Christ-loving Emperors. Things being in this condition, the most holy and reverend Cyril, bishop of Alexandria and the most reverend Memnon bishop of the city of Ephesus, offered some books composed by themselves and accusing the most reverend Bishop John and those who with him had done this thing, and conjuring our holy Synod that John and those with him should be summoned according to the canons, so that they might apologize for their daring acts, and if they had any complaints to make they might speak and prove them, for in their written deposition, or rather sheet of abuse, they made this statement as a pretext, They are Apollinarians, and Arians, and Eunomians, and therefore they have been deposed by us. When, therefore, those who had endured their reviling were present, we again necessarily assembled in the great church, being more than two hundred bishops, and by a first, second, and third call on two days, we summoned John and his companions to the Synod, in order that they might examine those who had been reviled, and might make explanations, and tell the causes which led them to draw up the sentence of deposition; but he did not dare to come.

But it was right that he, if he could truly prove the before-mentioned holy men to be heretics, both should come and prove the truth of that which, accepted as a true and indubitable crime, induced the temerarious sentence against them. But being condemned by his own conscience he did not come. Now what he had planned was this. For he thought that when that foundation-less and most unjust reviling was done away, the just vote of the Synod which it cast against the heretic Nestorius would likewise be dissolved. Being justly vexed, therefore, we determined to inflict according to law the same penalty upon him and those who were with him, which he contrary to law had pronounced against those who had been convicted of no fault. But although most justly and in accordance with law he would have suffered this punishment yet in the hope that by our patience his temerity might be conquered, we have reserved this to the decision of your holiness. In the meanwhile, we have deprived them of communion and have taken from them all priestly power, so that they may not be able to do any harm by their opinions. For those who thus ferociously, and cruelly, and uncanonically are wont to rush to such frightful and most wicked things, how was it not necessary that they should be stripped of the powers which [as a matter of fact] they did not possess, of being able to do harm.

With our brethren and fellow-ministers, both Cyril the bishop and Memnon, who had endured reproval at their hands, we are all in communion, and after the rashness [of their accusers] we both have and do perform the liturgy in common, all together celebrating the

Synaxis, having made of none effect their play in writing, and having thus shown that it lacked all validity and effect. For it was mere reviling and nothing else. For what kind of a synod could thirty men hold, some of whom were marked with the stamp of heresy, and some without sees and ejected [from their dioceses]? Or what strength could it have in opposition to a synod gathered from all the whole world? For there were sitting with us the most reverend bishops Arcadius and Projectus, and with them the most holy presbyter Philip, all of whom were sent by your holiness, who gave to us your presence and filled the place of the Apostolic See (τῆς ἀποστολικῆς καθέδρας). Let then your holiness be angered at what took place. But if license were granted to such as wished to pour reproval upon the greater sees, and thus unlawfully and uncanonically to give sentence or rather to utter revilings against those over whom they have no power, against those who for religion have endured such great conflicts, by reason of which now also piety shines forth through the prayers of your holiness [if, I say, all this should be tolerated], the affairs of the Church would fall into the greatest confusion. But when those who dare to do such things shall have been chastised aright, all disturbance will cease, and the reverence due to the canons will be observed by all.

When there had been read in the holy Synod what had been done touching the deposition of the most irreligious Pelagians and Cœlestines, of Cœlestius, and Pelagius, and Julian, and Præsidius, and Florus, and Marcellian, and Orontius, and those inclined to like errors, we also deemed it right (ἐδικαιώσαμεν) that the determinations of your holiness concerning them should stand strong and firm. And we all were of the same mind, holding them deposed. And that you may know in full all things that have been done, we have sent you a copy of the Acts, and of the subscriptions of the Synod. We pray that you, dearly beloved and most longed for, may be strong and mindful of us in the Lord.

Definition Against the Impious Messalians Who are Also Called Euchetæ and Enthusiasts

When the most pious and religious bishops, Valerian and Amphilochius had come to us, they proposed that we should consider in common the case of the Messalians, that is the Euchetes or Enthusiasts, who were flourishing in Pamphylia, or by what other name this most contaminating heresy is called. And when we were considering the question, the most pious and religious bishop Valerian, presented to us a synodical schedule which had been drawn up concerning them in the great city of Constantinople, under Sisinnius of blessed memory: What we read therein was approved by all, as well composed and as a due presentation of the case. And it seemed good to us all, and to the most pious bishops Valerian and Amphilochius and to all the most pious bishops of the provinces of Pamphylia and Lycaonia, that all things contained in that Synodical chart should be confirmed and in no way rescinded; also that the action taken at Alexandria might also be made firm, so that all those who throughout the whole province are of the Messalian or Enthusiastic heresy, or suspected of being tainted with that heresy, whether clerics or laymen, may come together; and if they shall anathematize in writing, according to the decrees pronounced in the aforesaid synod [their errors], if they are clergymen they may remain such; and if laymen they may be admitted to communion. But if they refuse to anathematize, if they were presbyters or deacons or in any other ecclesiastical grade, let them be cast out of the clergy and from their grade, and also from communion; if they be lay-men let them be anathematized.

Furthermore those convicted of this heresy are no more to be permitted to have the rule of our monasteries, lest tares be sown and increase. And we give command that the most pious bishops Valerian and Amphilochius, and the rest of the most reverend bishops of the whole province shall pay attention that this decree be carried into effect. In addition to this it seemed good that the filthy book of this heresy, which is called the Asceticon, should be anathematized, as composed by heretics, a copy of which the most religious and pious Valerian brought with him. Likewise anything savouring of their impiety which may be found among the people, let it be anathema.

Moreover when they come together, let there be commended by them in writing such things as are useful and necessary for concord, and communion, and arrangement (*dispositionem vel dispensationem*). But should any question arise in connection with the present business, and if it should prove to be difficult and ambiguous, what is not approved by the most pious bishops Valerian and Amphilochius, and the other bishops throughout the province, they ought to discuss all things by reference to what is written. And if the most pious bishops of the Lycians or of the Lycaonians shall have been passed over; nevertheless let not a Metropolitan be left out of whatever province he may be. And let these things be inserted in the Acts so that if any have need of them they would find how also to expound these things more diligently to others.

Decree of the Synod in the Matter of Euprepius and Cyril

The petition of the most pious bishops Euprepius and Cyril, which is set forth in the papers they offered, is honest. Therefore from the holy canons and the external laws, which have from ancient custom the force of law, let no innovation be made in the cities of Europa, but according to the ancient custom they shall be governed by the bishops by whom they have been formerly governed. For since there never was a metropolitan who had power otherwise, so neither hereafter shall there be any departure from the ancient custom.

Two Thracian bishops, Euprepius of Biza (Bizya) and Cyril of Cœle, gave occasion for a decree, praying for protection against their Metropolitan, Fritilas of Heraclea, who had gone over to the party of John of Antioch, and at the same time for the confirmation of the previous practice of holding two bishoprics at the same time. The Synod granted both.

SEVEN ECUMENICAL COUNCILS OF THE CHURCH

COUNCIL OF CHALCEDON

SEVEN ECUMENICAL COUNCILS OF THE CHURCH

Session I

Paschasinus, the most reverend bishop and legate of the Apostolic See, stood up in the midst with his most reverend colleagues and said: We received directions at the hands of the most blessed and apostolic bishop of the Roman city, which is the head of all the churches, which directions say that Dioscorus is not to be allowed a seat in this assembly, but that if he should attempt to take his seat he is to be cast out. This instruction we must carry out; if now your holiness so commands let him be expelled or else we leave.

The most glorious judges and the full senate said: What special charge do you prefer against the most reverend bishop Dioscorus?

Paschasinus, the most reverend bishop and legate of the Apostolic See, said: Since he has come, it is necessary that objection be made to him.

The most glorious judges and the whole senate said: In accordance with what has been said, let the charge under which he lies, be specifically made.

Lucentius, the most reverend bishop having the place of the Apostolic See, said: Let him give a reason for his judgment. For he undertook to give sentence against one over whom he had no jurisdiction. And he dared to hold a synod without the authority of the Apostolic See, a thing which had never taken place nor can take place.

Paschasinus the most reverend bishop, holding the place of the Apostolic See, said: We cannot go counter to the decrees of the most blessed and apostolic bishop ["Pope" for "bishop" in the Latin], who governs the Apostolic See, nor against the ecclesiastical canons nor the patristic traditions.

The most glorious judges and the full senate, said: It is proper that you should set forth specifically in what he has gone astray.

Lucentius, the venerable bishop and holding the place of the Apostolic See, said: We will not suffer so great a wrong to be done us and you, as that he who has come to be judged should sit down [as one to give judgment].

The glorious judges and the whole senate said: If you hold the office of judge, you ought not to defend yourself as if you were to be judged.

And when Dioscorus the most religious bishop of Alexandria at the bidding of the most glorious judges and of the sacred assembly (τῆς ἱερᾶς συγκλήτου) had sat down in the midst, and the most reverend Roman bishops also had sat down in their proper places, and kept silence, Eusebius, the most reverend bishop of the city of Dorylæum, stepping into the midst, said:

[He then presented a petition, and the Acts of the Latrocinium were read. Also the Acts of the council of Constantinople under Flavian against Eutyches (col. 175).]

And when they were read, the most glorious judges and immense assembly (ὑπερφυὴς σύγκλητος) said: What do the most reverend bishops of the present holy synod say? When he thus expounded the faith did Flavian, of holy memory, preserve the orthodox and catholic religion, or did he in any respect err concerning it?

Paschasinus the most reverend bishop, representing the Apostolic See, said; Flavian of blessed memory has most holily and perfectly expounded the faith. His faith and exposition agrees with the epistle of the most blessed and apostolic man, the bishop of Rome.

Anatolius the most reverend archbishop of Constantinople said; The blessed Flavian has beautifully and orthodoxly set forth the faith of our fathers.

Lucentius, the most reverend bishop, and legate of the Apostolic See, said; Since the faith of Flavian of blessed memory agrees with the Apostolic See and the tradition of the fathers it is just that the sentence by which he was condemned by the heretics should be turned back upon them by this most holy synod.

Maximus the most reverend bishop of Antioch in Syria, said: Archbishop Flavian of blessed memory has set forth the faith orthodoxly and in accordance with the most beloved-of-God and most holy Archbishop Leo. And this we all receive with zeal.

Thalassius, the most reverend bishop of Cæsarea in Cappadocia said; Flavian of blessed memory has spoken in accordance with Cyril of blessed memory.

[And so, one after another, the bishops expressed their opinions. The reading of the acts of the Council of Constantinople was then continued.]

And at this point of the reading, Dioscorus, the most reverend Archbishop of Alexandria said, I receive "the of two;" "the two" I do not receive (τὸ ἐκ δύο δέχομαιmatter is one which touches my soul.

SEVEN ECUMENICAL COUNCILS OF THE CHURCH

[After a few remarks the reading was continued and the rest of the acts of the Latrocinium of Ephesus completed. The judges then postponed to the morrow the setting forth a decree on the faith but intimated that Dioscorus and his associates should suffer the punishment to which they unjustly sentenced Flavian. This met with the approval of all the bishops except those of Illyrica who said: "We all have erred, let us all be pardoned." (col. 323.)]

The most glorious judges and the whole senate said; Let each one of the most reverend bishops of the present synod, hasten to set forth how he believes, writing without any fear, but placing the fear of God before his eyes; knowing that our most divine and pious lord believes according to the ecthesis of the three hundred and eighteen holy fathers at Nice, and according to the ecthesis of the one hundred and fifty after them, and according to the Canonical epistles and ectheses of the holy fathers Gregory, Basil, Athanasius, Hilary, Ambrose, and according to the two canonical epistles of Cyril, which were confirmed and published in the first Council of Ephesus, nor does he in any point depart from the faith of the same. For the most reverend archbishop of Old Rome, Leo, appears to have sent a letter to Flavian of blessed memory, with reference to Eutyches's unbelieving doubt which was springing up against the Catholic Church.

End of the first Actio.

SEVEN ECUMENICAL COUNCILS OF THE CHURCH

Session II

When all were seated before the rails of the most holy altar, the most superb and glorious judges and the great (ὑπερφυὴς) senate said; At a former meeting the question was examined of the condemnation of the most reverend bishop Flavian of blessed memory and Eusebius, and it was patent to you all with what justice and accuracy the examination was conducted: and it was proved that they had been cruelly and improperly condemned. What course we should pursue in this matter became clear after your deliberations. Now however the question to be enquired into, studied, and decided, is how the true faith is to be established, which is the chief end for which this Council has been assembled. As we know that you are to render to God a strict account not only for your own souls in particular, but as well for the souls of all of us who desire rightly to be taught all things that pertain to religion, and that all ambiguity be taken away, by the agreement and consent of all the holy fathers, and by their united exposition and doctrine; hasten therefore without any fear of pleasing or displeasing, to set forth (ἐκθέσθαι) the pure faith, so that they who do not seem to believe with all the rest, may be brought to unity through the acknowledging of the truth. For we wish you to know that the most divine and pious lord of the whole world and ourselves hold the orthodox faith set forth by the 318 and by the 150 holy fathers, and what also has been taught by the rest of the most holy and glorious fathers, and in accordance with this is our belief.

The most reverend bishops cried; Any other setting forth (ἔκθεσιν ἄλλην) no one makes, neither will we attempt it, neither will we dare to set forth [anything new] (ἐκθέσθαι). For the fathers taught, and in their writings are preserved, what things were set forth by them, and further than this we can say nothing.

Cecropius, the most reverend bishop of Sebastopol said: The matters concerning Eutyches have been examined, and the most holy archbishop of Rome has given a form (τύπον) which we follow and to his letter we all [i.e. those in his neighbourhood] have subscribed.

The most reverend bishops cried: These are the opinions of all of us. The expositions (ἐκτεθέντα) already made are quite sufficient: it is not lawful to make any other.

The most glorious judges and great senate said, If it pleases your reverence, let the most holy patriarch of each province, choosing one or two of his own province and going into the midst, and together considering the faith, make known to all what is agreed upon. So that if, as we desire, all be of one mind, all ambiguity may be removed: But if some entertain contrary opinions (which we do not believe to be the case) we may know what their opinions are.

The most reverend bishops cried out, we make no new exposition in writing. This is the law, [i.e. of the Third Synod] which teaches that what has been set forth is sufficient. The law wills that no other exposition should be made. Let the sayings of the Fathers remain fast.

Florentius, the most reverend bishop of Sardis, said, since it is not possible for those who follow the teaching of the holy Synod of Nice, which was confirmed rightly and piously at Ephesus, to draw up suddenly a declaration of faith in accordance with the faith of the holy fathers Cyril and Celestine, and of the letter of the most holy Leo, we therefore pray your magnificence to give us time, so that we may be able to arrive at the truth of the matter with a fitting document, although so far as we are concerned, who have subscribed the letter of the most holy Leo, nothing further is needed.

Cecropius, the most reverend bishop of Sebastopol, said, The faith has been well defined by the 318 holy fathers and confirmed by the holy fathers Athanasius, Cyril, Celestine, Hilary, Basil, Gregory, and now once again by the most holy Leo: and we pray that those things which were decreed by the 318 holy fathers, and by the most holy Leo be read.

The most glorious judges and great Senate said: Let there be read the expositions (ἐκτεθέντα) of the 318 fathers gathered together at Nice.

Eunomius, the most reverend bishop of Nicomedia read from a book [the Exposition of faith of the 318 fathers.]

SEVEN ECUMENICAL COUNCILS OF THE CHURCH

The Exposition of faith of the Council held at Nice.

"In the consulate of Paul and Julian" etc.

"We believe in one God," etc.

"But those who say," etc.

The most reverend bishops cried out; This is the orthodox faith; this we all believe: into this we were baptized; into this we baptize: Blessed Cyril so taught: this is the true faith: this is the holy faith: this is the everlasting faith: into this we were baptized: into this we baptize: we all so believe: so believes Leo, the Pope (ὁ πάπας): Cyril thus believed: Pope Leo so interpreted it.

The most glorious judges and great senate said, Let there be read what was set forth by the 150 holy fathers.

Aëtius, the reverend deacon of Constantinople read from a book [the creed of the 150 fathers.]

The holy faith which the 150 fathers set forth as consonant to the holy and great Synod of Nice.

"We believe in one God," etc.

All the most reverend bishops cried out: This is the faith of all of us: we all so believe.

The reverend archdeacon Aëtius said, There remains the letter of Cyril of holy and blessed memory, sometime bishop of the great city Alexandria, which he wrote to Nestorius, which was approved by all the most holy bishops assembled in the first Council at Ephesus, called to condemn the same Nestorius, and which was confirmed by the subscription of all. There is also another letter of the same Cyril, of blessed memory, which he wrote to John, of blessed memory, sometime bishop of the great city of Antioch, which likewise was confirmed. If it be so ordered, I shall read these.

The most glorious judges and great senate said, Let the letters of Cyril of blessed memory be read.

Aëtius, the Archdeacon of the imperial city Constantinople read.

To the most reverend and most religious fellow priest Nestorius, Cyril sends greeting in the Lord.

Likewise the same Archdeacon Aëtius read [the letter of the same holy Cyril of blessed memory to John of Antioch, on the peace].

[**This letter begins,** Εὐφϱαινέθωσαν οἱ οὐϱανοὶ κ.τ.λ .; **and in the Latin Lætentur cæli.**]

The Letter of Cyril to John of Antioch.

Cyril to my lord, beloved brother, and fellow minister John, greeting in the Lord.

"Let the heavens rejoice, and let the earth be glad" for the middle wall of partition has been taken away, and grief has been silenced, and all kind of difference of opinion has been removed; Christ the Saviour of us all having awarded peace to his churches, through our being called to this by our most devout and beloved of God kings, who are the best imitators of the piety of their ancestors in keeping the right faith in their souls firm and immovable, for they chiefly give their mind to the affairs of the holy Churches, in order that they may have the noted glory forever and show forth their most renowned kingdom, to whom also Christ himself the Lord of powers distributes good things with plenteous hand and gives to prevail over their enemies and grants them victory. For he does not lie in saying: "As I live says the Lord, them that honour me, I will honour." For when my lord, my most-beloved-of-God, fellow-minister and brother Paul, had arrived in Alexandria, we were filled with gladness, and most naturally at the coming of such a man as a mediator, who was ready to work beyond measure that he might overcome the envy of the devil and heal our divisions, and who by removing the offenses scattered between us, would crown your Church and ours with harmony and peace.

Of the reason of the disagreement it is superfluous to speak. I deem it more useful both to think and speak of things suitable to the time of peace. We were therefore delighted at meeting with that distinguished and most pious man, who expected perhaps to have no small struggle, persuading us that it is necessary to form an alliance for the peace of the Church, and to drive away the laughter of the heterodox, and for this end to blunt the goads of the stubbornness of the devil. He found us ready for this, so as absolutely to need no labour to be bestowed upon us. For we remembered the Saviour's saying; "My peace I give unto you, my peace I leave with you." We have been taught also to say in prayers: "O Lord our God give us peace, for you have given us all things." So that if anyone should be in the participation of the peace furnished from God, he is not lacking in any good. That as a matter of fact, the disagreement of the Churches happened altogether unnecessarily and inopportunely, we now have been fully satisfied by the document brought by my lord, the most pious bishop Paul, which contains an unimpeachable confession of faith, and this he asserted to have been prepared, by your holiness and by the God-beloved Bishops there. The document is as follows, and is set down verbatim in this our epistle.

SEVEN ECUMENICAL COUNCILS OF THE CHURCH

Concerning the Virgin Mother of God, we thus think and speak; and of the manner of the Incarnation of the Only Begotten Son of God, necessarily, not by way of addition but for the sake of certainty, as we have received from the beginning from the divine Scriptures and from the tradition of the holy fathers, we will speak briefly, adding nothing whatever to the Faith set forth by the holy Fathers in Nice. For, as we said before, it suffices for all knowledge of piety and the refutation of all false doctrine of heretics. But we speak, not presuming on the impossible; but with the confession of our own weakness, excluding those who wish us to cling to those things which transcend human consideration.

We confess, therefore, our Lord Jesus Christ, the Only Begotten Son of God, perfect God, and perfect Man of a reasonable soul and flesh consisting; begotten before the ages of the Father according to his Divinity, and in the last days, for us and for our salvation, of Mary the Virgin according to his humanity, of the same substance with his Father according to his Divinity, and of the same substance with us according to his humanity; for there became a union of two natures. Wherefore we confess one Christ, one Son, one Lord.

According to this understanding of this unmixed union, we confess the holy Virgin to be Mother of God; because God the Word was incarnate and became Man, and from this conception he united the temple taken from her with himself.

For we know the theologians make some things of the Evangelical and Apostolic teaching about the Lord common as pertaining to the one person, and other things they divide as to the two natures, and attribute the worthy ones to God on account of the Divinity of Christ, and the lowly ones on account of his humanity [to his humanity].

These being your holy voices, and finding ourselves thinking the same with them ("One Lord, One Faith, One Baptism,") we glorified God the Saviour of all, congratulating one another that our churches and yours have the Faith which agrees with the God-inspired Scriptures and the traditions of our holy Fathers.

Since I learned that certain of those accustomed to find fault were humming around like vicious wasps, and vomiting out wretched words against me, as that I say the holy Body of Christ was brought from heaven, and not of the holy Virgin, I thought it necessary to say a few words concerning this to them:

SEVEN ECUMENICAL COUNCILS OF THE CHURCH

O fools, and only knowing how to misrepresent, how have you been led to such a judgment, how have you fallen into so foolish a sickness? For it is necessary, it is undoubtedly necessary, to understand that almost all the opposition to us concerning the faith, arose from our affirming that the holy Virgin is Mother of God. But if from heaven and not from her the holy Body of the Saviour of all was born, how then is she understood to be Mother of God? What then did she bring forth except it be true that she brought forth the Emmanuel according to the flesh? They are to be laughed at who babble such things about me. For the blessed prophet Isaiah does not lie in saying "Behold the Virgin shall conceive and bear a Son, and shall call his name Emmanuel, which being interpreted is God with us." Truly also the holy Gabriel said to the Blessed Virgin: "Fear not, Mary, for you have found favour with God. And, behold, you shall conceive in your womb, and bring forth a Son, and shall call his name Jesus. He shall save his people from their sins."

For when we say our Lord Jesus Christ descended from heaven, and from above, we do not so say this as if from above and from heaven was his Holy Flesh taken, but rather by way of following the divine Paul, who distinctly declares: "the first man is of the earth, earthy; the Second Man is the Lord from heaven."

We remember too, the Saviour himself saying, "And no man has ascended up to heaven, but he that came down from heaven, even the Son of Man." Although he was born according to his flesh, as just said, of the holy Virgin, yet God the Word came down from above and from heaven. He "made himself of no reputation, and took upon him the form of a servant," and was called the Son of Man, yet remaining what he was, that is to say God. For he is unchanging and unchangeable according to nature; considered already as one with his own Flesh, he is said to have come down from heaven.

He is also called the Man from heaven, being perfect in his Divinity and perfect in his Humanity, and considered as in one Person. For one is the Lord Jesus Christ, although the difference of his natures is not unknown, from which we say the ineffable union was made.

Will your holiness vouchsafe to silence those who say that a crasis, or mingling or mixture took place between the Word of God and flesh. For it is likely that certain also gossip about me as having thought or said such things.

But I am far from any such thought as that, and I also consider them wholly to rave who think a shadow of change could occur concerning the Nature of the Word of God. For he remains that which he always was, and has not been changed, nor can he ever be changed, nor is he capable of change. For we all confess in addition to this, that the Word of God is impassible, even though when he dispenses most wisely this mystery, he appears to ascribe to himself the sufferings endured in his own flesh. To the same purpose the all-wise Peter also said when he wrote of Christ as having "suffered in the flesh," and not in the nature of his ineffable godhead. In order that he should be believed to be the Saviour of all, by an economic appropriation to himself, as just said, he assumed the sufferings of his own Flesh.

Like to this is the prophecy through the voice of the prophet, as from him, "I gave my back to the smiters, and my cheeks to them that plucked off the hair: I hid not my face from shame and spitting." Let your holiness be convinced nor let anyone else be doubtful that we altogether follow the teachings of the holy fathers, especially of our blessed and celebrated Father Athanasius, deprecating the least departure from it.

I might have added many quotations from them also establishing my words, but that it would have added to the length of my letter and it might become wearisome. And we will allow the defined Faith, the symbol of the Faith set forth by our holy Fathers who assembled some time ago at Nice, to be shaken by no one. Nor would we permit ourselves or others, to alter a single word of those set forth, or to add one syllable, remembering the saying: "Remove not the ancient landmark which your fathers have set," for it was not they who spoke but the Spirit himself of God and the Father, who proceeds also from him, and is not alien from the Son, according to his essence. And this the words of the holy initiators into mysteries confirm to us. For in the Acts of the Apostles it is written: "And after they had come to Mysia, they assayed to go into Bithynia; but the Spirit of Jesus suffered them not." And the divine Paul wrote: "So then they that are in the flesh cannot please God. But you are not in the flesh, but in the Spirit, if so be that the Spirit of God dwell in you. Now if any man have not the Spirit of Christ, he is none of his."

When some of those who are accustomed to turn from the right, twist my speech to their views, I pray your holiness not to wonder; but be well assured that the followers of every heresy gather the occasions of their error from the God-inspired Scriptures, corrupting in their evil minds the things rightly said through the Holy Spirit, and drawing down upon their own heads the unquenchable flame.

Since we have learned that certain, after having corrupted it, have set forth the orthodox epistle of our most distinguished Father Athanasius to the Blessed Epictetus, so as thereby to injure many; therefore it appeared to the brethren to be useful and necessary that we should send to your holiness a copy of it from some correct ancient transcripts which exist among us. Farewell.

Session II (Continued)

And when these letters [i.e. Cyril's letter to Nestorius Καταφλυαροῦσι and his letter to John of Antioch Εὐφραινέσθωσαν] had been read, the most reverend bishops cried out: We all so believe: Pope Leo thus believes: anathema to him who divides and to him who confounds: this is the faith of Archbishop Leo: Leo thus believes: Leo and Anatolius so believe: we all thus believe. As Cyril so believe we, all of us: eternal be the memory of Cyril: as the epistles of Cyril teach such is our mind, such has been our faith: such is our faith: this is the mind of Archbishop Leo, so he believes, so he has written.

The most glorious judges and the great senate said: Let there be read also the epistle of the most worthy Leo, Archbishop of Old Rome, the Imperial City.

Beronician, the most devout clerk of the sacred consistory, read from a book handed him by Aëtius, Archdeacon of the holy Church of Constantinople, the encyclical or synodical letter of the most holy Leo, the Archbishop, written to Flavian, Archbishop of Constantinople.

Leo [the bishop] to his [most] dear brother Flavian.

Having read your Affection's letter, the late arrival of which is matter of surprise to us, and having gone through the record of the proceedings of the bishops, we have now, at last, gained a clear view of the scandal which has risen up among you, against the integrity of the faith; and what at first seemed obscure has now been elucidated and explained. By this means Eutyches, who seemed to be deserving of honour under the title of Presbyter, is now shown to be exceedingly thoughtless and sadly inexperienced, so that to him also we may apply the prophet's words, "He refused to understand in order to act well: he meditated unrighteousness on his bed." What, indeed, is more unrighteous than to entertain ungodly thoughts, and not to yield to persons wiser and more learned? But into this folly do they fall who, when hindered by some obscurity from apprehending the truth, have recourse, not to the words of the Prophets, not to the letters of the Apostles, nor to the authority of the Gospels, but to themselves; and become teachers of error, just because they have not been disciples of the truth. For what learning has he received from the sacred pages of the New and the Old Testament, who does not so much as understand the very beginning of the Creed? And that which, all the world over, is uttered by the voices of all applicants for regeneration, is still not grasped by the mind of this aged man. If, then, he knew not what he ought to think about the Incarnation of the Word of God, and was not willing, for the sake of obtaining the light of intelligence, to make laborious search through the whole extent of the Holy Scriptures, he should at least have received with heedful attention that general Confession common to all, whereby the whole body of the faithful profess that they "believe in God the Father Almighty, and in Jesus Christ his only Son our Lord, who was born of the Holy Ghost and the Virgin Mary." By which three clauses the engines of almost all heretics are shattered. For when God is believed to be both "Almighty" and "Father," it is proved that the Son is everlasting together with himself, differing in nothing from the Father, because he was born as "God from God," Almighty from Almighty, Coeternal from Eternal; not later in time, not inferior in power, not unlike him in glory, not divided from him in essence, but the same Only-begotten and Everlasting Son of an Everlasting Parent was "born of the Holy Ghost and the Virgin Mary." This birth in time in no way detracted from, in no way added to, that divine and everlasting birth; but expended itself wholly in the work of restoring man, who had been deceived; so that it might both overcome death, and by its power "destroy the devil who had the power of death." For we could not have overcome the author of sin and of death, unless he who could neither be contaminated by sin, nor detained by death, had taken upon himself our nature, and made it his

SEVEN ECUMENICAL COUNCILS OF THE CHURCH

own. For, in fact, he was "conceived of the Holy Ghost" within the womb of a Virgin Mother, who bore him as she had conceived him, without loss of virginity. But if he (Eutyches) was not able to obtain a true conception from this pure fountain of Christian faith because by his own blindness he had darkened for himself the brightness of a truth so clear, he should have submitted himself to the Evangelist's teaching; and after reading what Matthew says, "The book of the generation of Jesus Christ, the Son of David, the Son of Abraham," he should also have sought instruction from the Apostle's preaching; and after reading in the Epistle to the Romans, "Paul, a servant of Jesus Christ, called an Apostle, separated unto the gospel of God, which he had promised before by the prophets in the Holy Scriptures, concerning his Son, who was made unto him of the seed of David according to the flesh," he should have bestowed some devout study on the pages of the Prophets; and finding that God's promise said to Abraham, "in your seed shall all nations be blessed," in order to avoid all doubt as to the proper meaning of this "seed," he should have attended to the Apostle's words, "To Abraham and to his seed were the promises made. He says not, 'and to seeds,' as in the case of many, but as in the case of one, 'and to your seed,' which is Christ." He should also have apprehended with his inward ear the declaration of Isaiah, "Behold, a Virgin shall conceive and bear a Son, and they shall call his name Emmanuel, which is, being interpreted, God with us;" and should have read with faith the words of the same prophet, "Unto us a Child has been born, unto us a Son has been given, whose power is on his shoulder; and they shall call his name Angel of great counsel, Wonderful, Counsellor, Strong God, Prince of Peace, Father of the age to come." And he should not have spoken idly to the effect that the Word was in such a sense made flesh, that the Christ who was brought forth from the Virgin's womb had the form of a man, and had not a body really derived from his Mother's body. Possibly his reason for thinking that our Lord Jesus Christ was not of our nature was this— that the Angel who was sent to the blessed and ever Virgin Mary said, "The Holy Ghost shall come upon you, and the power of the Highest shall overshadow you, and therefore also that holy thing which shall be born of you shall be called the Son of God;" as if, because the Virgin's conception was caused by a divine act, therefore the flesh of him whom she conceived was not of the nature of her who conceived him. But we are not to understand that "generation," peerlessly wonderful, and wonderfully peerless, in such a sense as that the newness of the mode of production did away with the proper character of the kind. For it was the Holy Ghost who gave fecundity to the Virgin, but it was from a body that a real body was derived; and "when Wisdom was building herself a house," the "Word was made flesh, and dwelt among us," that is, in that flesh which he assumed from a human being, and which he animated with the spirit of rational life.

Accordingly while the distinctness of both natures and substances was preserved, and both met in one Person, lowliness was assumed by majesty, weakness by power, mortality by eternity; and, in order to pay the debt of our condition, the inviolable nature was united to the passible, so that as the appropriate remedy for our ills, one and the same "Mediator between God and man, the Man Christ Jesus," might from one element be capable of dying and also from the other be incapable. Therefore in the entire and perfect nature of very man was born very God, whole in what was his, whole in what was ours. By "ours" we mean what the Creator formed in us at the beginning and what he assumed in order to restore; for of that which the deceiver brought in, and man, thus deceived, admitted, there was not a trace in the Saviour; and the fact that he took on himself a share in our infirmities did not make him a partaker in our transgressions. He assumed "the form of a servant" without the defilement of sin, enriching what was human, not impairing what was divine: because that "emptying of himself," whereby the Invisible made himself visible, and the Creator and Lord of all things willed to be one among mortals, was a stooping down in compassion, not a failure of power. Accordingly, the same who, remaining in the form of God, made man, was made man in the form of a servant. For each of the natures retains its proper character without defect; and as the form of God does not take away the form of a servant, so the form of a servant does not impair the form of God. For since the devil was glorying in the fact that man, deceived by his craft, was bereft of divine gifts and, being stripped of his endowment of immortality, had come under the grievous sentence of death, and that he himself, amid his miseries, had found a sort of consolation in having a transgressor as his companion, and that God, according to the requirements of the principle of justice, had changed his own resolution in regard to man, whom he had created in so high a position of honour; there was need of a dispensation of secret counsel, in order that the unchangeable God, whose will could not be deprived of its own benignity, should fulfil by a more secret mystery his original plan of loving kindness toward us, and that man, who had been led into fault by the wicked subtlety of the devil, should not perish contrary to God's purpose. Accordingly, the Son of God, descending from his seat in heaven, and not departing from the glory of the Father, enters this lower world, born after a new order, by a new mode of birth. After a new order; because he who in his own sphere is invisible, became visible in ours; He who could not be enclosed in space, willed to be enclosed; continuing to be before times, he began to exist in time; the Lord of the universe allowed his infinite majesty to be overshadowed, and took upon him the form of a servant; the impassible God did not disdain to be passible Man and the immortal One to be subjected to the laws of death. And born by a new mode of birth; because inviolate virginity, while ignorant of concupiscence, supplied the matter of his flesh. What was assumed from the Lord's mother was nature, not fault; nor does the wondrousness of the nativity of our Lord Jesus Christ, as born of a Virgin's womb, imply that his nature is unlike ours. For the selfsame who is very God, is also very man; and there is no illusion in this union, while the lowliness of man and the loftiness of Godhead meet together. For as "God" is not changed by the compassion [exhibited], so "Man" is not consumed by the dignity [bestowed]. For each "form" does the acts which belong to it, in communion with the other; the Word, that is, performing what belongs to the Word, and the flesh carrying out what belongs to the flesh; the one of these shines out in miracles, the other succumbs to injuries. And as the Word does not withdraw from equality with the Father in glory, so the flesh does not abandon the nature of our kind. For, as we must often be saying, he is one and the same, truly Son of God, and truly Son of Man. God, inasmuch as "in the beginning was the Word, and the Word was with God, and the Word was God." Man, inasmuch as "the Word was made flesh, and dwelt among us." God, inasmuch as "all things were made by him, and without him nothing was made." Man, inasmuch as he was "made of a woman, made under the law." The nativity of the flesh is a manifestation of human nature; the Virgin's child-bearing is an indication of Divine power. The infancy of the Babe is exhibited by the humiliation of swaddling clothes: the greatness of the Highest is declared by the voices of angels. He whom Herod impiously designs to slay is like humanity in its beginnings; but he whom the Magi rejoice to adore on their knees is Lord of all. Now when he came to the baptism of John his forerunner, lest the fact that the Godhead was covered with a veil of flesh should be concealed, the voice of the Father spoke in thunder from heaven, "This is my beloved Son, in whom I am well pleased." Accordingly, he who, as man, is tempted by the devil's subtlety, is the same to whom, as God, angels pay duteous service. To hunger, to thirst, to be weary, and to sleep, is evidently human. But to satisfy five thousand men with five loaves, and give to the Samaritan woman that living water, to draw which can secure him that drinks of it from ever thirsting again; to walk on the surface of the sea with feet that sink not, and by rebuking the storm to bring down the "uplifted waves," is unquestionably Divine. As then— to pass by many points — it does not belong to the same nature to weep with feelings of pity over a dead friend and, after the mass of stone had been removed from the grave where he had lain four days, by a voice of command to raise him up to life again; or to hang on the wood, and to make all the elements tremble after daylight had been turned into night; or to be transfixed with nails, and to open the gates of paradise to the faith of the robber; so it does not belong to the same nature to say, "I and the Father are one," and to say, "the Father is greater than I." For although in the Lord Jesus Christ there is one Person of God and man, yet that whereby contumely attaches to both is one thing, and that whereby glory attaches to both is another; for from what belongs to us he has that manhood which is inferior to the Father; while from the Father he has equal Godhead with the Father. Accordingly, on account of this unity of Person which is to be understood as existing in both the natures, we read, on the one hand, that "the Son of Man came down from heaven," inasmuch as the Son of God took flesh from that Virgin of whom he was born; and on the other hand, the Son of God is said to have been crucified and buried, inasmuch as he underwent this, not in his actual Godhead; wherein the Only-begotten is coeternal and consubstantial with the Father, but in the weakness of human nature. Wherefore we all, in the very Creed, confess that "the only-begotten Son of God was crucified and buried," according to that saying of the Apostle, "for if they had known it, they would not have crucified the Lord of Majesty."

But when our Lord and Saviour himself was by his questions instructing the faith of the disciples, he said, "Whom do men say that I the Son of Man am?" And when they had mentioned various opinions held by others, he said, "But whom do you say that I am?" that is, "I who am Son of Man, and whom you see in the form of a servant, and in reality of flesh, whom do you say that I am?" Whereupon the blessed Peter, as inspired by God, and about to benefit all nations by his confession, said, "You are the Christ, the Son of the living God." Not undeservedly, therefore, was he pronounced blessed by the Lord, and derived from the original Rock that solidity which belonged both to his virtue and to his name, who through revelation from the Father confessed the selfsame to be both the Son of God and the Christ; because one of these truths, accepted without the other, would not profit unto salvation, and it was equally dangerous to believe the Lord Jesus Christ to be merely God and not man, or merely man and not God. But after the resurrection of the Lord— which was in truth the resurrection of a real body, for no other person was raised again than he who had been crucified and had died— what else was accomplished during that interval of forty days than to make our faith entire and clear of all darkness? For while he conversed with his disciples, and dwelt with them, and ate with them, and allowed himself to be handled with careful and inquisitive touch by those who were under the influence of doubt, for this end he came in to the disciples when the doors were shut, and by his breath gave them the Holy Ghost, and opened the secrets of Holy Scripture after bestowing on them the light of intelligence, and again in his selfsame person showed to them the wound in the side, the prints of the nails, and all the flesh tokens of the Passion, saying, "Behold my hands and my feet, that it is I myself; handle me and see, for a spirit has not flesh and bones, as you see me have:" that the properties of the Divine and the human nature might be acknowledged to remain in him without causing a division, and that we might in such sort know that the Word is not what the flesh is, as to confess that the one Son of God is both Word and flesh. On which mystery of the faith this Eutyches must be regarded as unhappily having no hold, who does not recognise our nature to exist in the Only-begotten Son of God, either by way of the lowliness of mortality, or of the glory of resurrection. Nor has he been overawed by the declaration of the blessed Apostle and Evangelist John, saying, "Every spirit that confesses that Jesus Christ has come in the flesh is of God; and every spirit which dissolves Jesus is not of God, and this is Antichrist." Now what is to dissolve Jesus, but to separate the human nature from him, and to make void by shameless inventions that mystery by which alone we have been saved? Moreover, being in the dark as to the nature of Christ's body, he must needs be involved in the like senseless blindness with regard to his Passion also. For if he does not think the Lord's crucifixion to be unreal, and does not doubt that he really accepted suffering, even unto death, for the sake of the world's salvation; as he believes in his death, let him acknowledge his flesh also, and not doubt that he whom he recognises as having been capable of suffering is also Man with a body like ours; since to deny his true flesh is also to deny his bodily sufferings. If then he accepts the Christian faith, and does not turn away his ear from the preaching of the Gospel, let him see what nature it was that was transfixed with nails and hung on the wood of the cross; and let him understand whence it was that, after the side of the Crucified had been pierced by the soldier's spear, blood and water flowed out, that the Church of God might be refreshed both with a Laver and with a Cup. Let him listen also to the blessed Apostle Peter when he declares, that "sanctification by the Spirit" takes place through the "sprinkling of the blood of Christ," and let him not give a mere cursory reading to the words of the same Apostle, "Knowing that you were not redeemed with corruptible things, as silver and gold, from your vain way of life received by tradition from your fathers, but with the precious blood of Jesus Christ as of a Lamb without blemish and without spot." Let him also not resist the testimony of Blessed John the Apostle, "And the blood of Jesus the Son of God cleanses us from all sin." And again, "This is the victory which overcomes the world, even our faith;" and, "who is he that overcomes the world, but he that believes that Jesus is the Son of God? This is he that came by water and blood, even Jesus Christ; not in water only, but in water and blood; and it is the Spirit that bears witness, because the Spirit is truth. For there are three that bear witness— the Spirit, the water, and the blood; and the three are one." That is, the Spirit of sanctification, and the blood of redemption, and the water of baptism; which three things are one, and remain undivided, and not one of them is disjoined from connection with the others; because the Catholic Church lives and advances by this faith, that Christ Jesus we should believe neither manhood to exist without true Godhead, nor Godhead without true manhood. But when Eutyches, on being questioned in your examination of him, answered, "I confess that our Lord was of two natures before the union, but after the union I confess one nature;" I am astonished that so absurd and perverse a profession as this of his was not rebuked by a censure on the part of any of his judges, and that an utterance extremely foolish and extremely blasphemous was passed over, just as if nothing had been heard which could give offense: seeing that it is as impious to say that the Only-begotten Son of God was of two natures before the Incarnation as it is shocking to affirm that, since the Word became flesh, there has been in him one nature only. But lest Eutyches should think that what he said was correct, or was tolerable, because it was not confuted by any assertion of yours, we exhort your earnest solicitude, dearly beloved brother, to see that, if by God's merciful inspiration the case is brought to a satisfactory issue, the inconsiderate and inexperienced man be cleansed also from this pestilent notion of his; seeing that, as the record of the proceedings has clearly shown, he had fairly begun to abandon his own opinion when on being driven into a corner by authoritative words of yours, he professed himself ready to say what he had not said before, and to give his adhesion to that faith from which he had previously stood aloof. But when he would not consent to anathematize the impious dogma you understood, brother, that he continued in his own misbelief, and deserved to receive sentence of condemnation. For which if he grieves sincerely and to good purpose, and understands, even though too late, how properly the Episcopal authority has been put in motion, or if, in order to make full satisfaction, he shall condemn viva voce, and under his own hand, all that he has held amiss, no compassion, to whatever extent, which can be shown him when he has been set right, will be worthy of blame, for our Lord, the true and good Shepherd, who laid down his life for his sheep, and who came to save men's souls and not to destroy them, wills us to imitate his own loving kindness; so that justice should indeed constrain those who sin, but mercy should not reject those who are converted. For then indeed is the true faith defended with the best results, when a false opinion is condemned even by those who have followed it. But in order that the whole matter may be piously and faithfully carried out, we have appointed our brethren, Julius, Bishop, and Reatus, Presbyter (of the title of St. Clement) and also my son Hilarus, Deacon, to represent us; and with them we have associated Dulcitius, our Notary, of whose fidelity we have had good proof: trusting that the Divine assistance will be with you, so that he who has gone astray may be saved by condemning his own unsound opinion. May God keep you in good health, dearly beloved brother. Given on the Ides of June, in the Consulate of the illustrious men, Asterius and Protogenes.

Session II (Continued)

After the reading of the foregoing epistle, the most reverend bishops cried out: This is the faith of the fathers, this is the faith of the Apostles. So we all believe, thus the orthodox believe. Anathema to him who does not thus believe. Peter has spoken thus through Leo. So taught the Apostles. Piously and truly did Leo teach, so taught Cyril. Everlasting be the memory of Cyril. Leo and Cyril taught the same thing, anathema to him who does not so believe. This is the true faith. Those of us who are orthodox thus believe. This is the faith of the fathers. Why were not these things read at Ephesus [i.e. at the heretical synod held there]? These are the things Dioscorus hid away.

[Some explanations were asked by the Illyrian bishops and the answers were found satisfactory, but yet a delay of a few days was asked for, and some bishops petitioned for a general pardon of all who had been kept out. This proposition made great confusion, in the midst of which the session was dissolved by the judges. (Col. 371.)]

Session III

[The imperial representatives do not seem to have been present, and after Aëtius the Archdeacon of Constantinople had opened the Session,]

Paschasinus the bishop of Lilybæum, in the province of Silicia, and holding the place of the most holy Leo, archbishop of the Apostolic see of old Rome, said in Latin what being interpreted is as follows: It is well known to this beloved of God synod, that divine letters were sent to the blessed and apostolic pope Leo, inviting him to deign to be present at the holy synod. But since ancient custom did not sanction this, nor the general necessity of the time seemed to permit it, our littleness in the place of himself he τὰ τῆς ἁγίας συνόδου επέτρεψε, and therefore it is necessary that whatever things are brought into discussion should be examined by our interference (διαλαλιᾶς). [The Latin reads where I have placed the Greek of the ordinary text, thus, "commanded our littleness to preside in his place over this holy council."] Therefore let the book presented by our most beloved-of-God brother, and fellow bishop Eusebius be received, and read by the beloved of God archdeacon and primicerius of the notaries, Aëtius.

And Aëtius, the archdeacon and primicerius of the notaries, took the book and read as follows.

[Next follows the petition of Eusebius et post nonnulla four petitions each addressed to "The most holy and beloved-of-God ecumenical archbishop and patriarch of great Rome Leo, and to the holy and ecumenical Synod assembled at Chalcedon, etc., etc.;" The first two by deacons of Alexandria, the third by a quondam presbyter of the diocese, and the fourth by a layman also of Alexandria. After this Dioscorus was again summoned and, as he did not come, sentence was given against him, which was communicated to him in a letter contained in the acts. (L. and C., Conc., Tom. IV., col. 418.) The Bishops expressed their opinions for the most part one by one, but the Roman Legates spoke together, and in their speech occurs the following (Col. 426:)]

Wherefore the most holy and blessed Leo, archbishop of the great and elder Rome, through us, and through this present most holy synod together with the thrice blessed and all-glorious Peter the Apostle, who is the rock and foundation of the Catholic Church, and the foundation of the orthodox faith, has stripped him of the episcopate, and has alienated from him all hieratic worthiness. Therefore let this most holy and great synod sentence the before mentioned Dioscorus to the canonical penalties.

[The bishops then, one by one, spoke in favour of the deposition of Dioscorus, but usually on the ground of his refusal to appear when thrice summoned.]

And when all the most holy bishops had spoken on the subject, they signed this which follows.

The Condemnation Sent by the Holy and Ecumenical Synod to Dioscorus.

The holy and great and ecumenical Synod, which by the grace of God according to the constitution of our most pious and beloved of God emperors assembled together at Chalcedon the city of Bithynia, in the martyry of the most holy and victorious Martyr Euphemia to Dioscorus.

We do you to wit that on the thirteenth day of the month of October you were deposed from the episcopate and made a stranger to all ecclesiastical order (θεσμοῦ) by the holy and ecumenical synod, on account of your disregard of the divine canons, and of your disobedience to this holy and ecumenical synod and on account of the other crimes of which you have been found guilty, for even when called to answer your accusers three times by this holy and great synod according to the divine canons you did not come.

Session IV

The most magnificent and glorious judges and the great Senate said:

SEVEN ECUMENICAL COUNCILS OF THE CHURCH

Let the reverend council now declare what seems good concerning the faith, since those things which have already been disposed of have been made manifest. Paschasinus and Lucentius, the most reverend bishops, and Boniface the most reverend presbyter, legates of the Apostolic See through that most reverend man, bishop Paschasinus said: As the holy and blessed and Ecumenical Synod holds fast and follows the rule of faith (fidei regulam in the Latin Acts) which was set forth by the fathers at Nice, it also confirms the faith set forth by the Synod of 150 fathers gathered at Constantinople at the bidding of the great Theodosius of blessed memory. Moreover the exposition of their faith, of the illustrious Cyril of blessed memory set forth at the Council of Ephesus (in which Nestorius was condemned) is received. And in the third place the writings of that blessed man, Leo, Archbishop of all the churches, who condemned the heresy of Nestorius and Eutyches, show what the true faith is. Likewise the holy Synod holds this faith, this it follows— nothing further can it add nor can it take anything away.

When this had been translated into Greek by Beronician, the devout secretary of the divine consistory, the most reverend bishops cried out: So we all believe, so we were baptized, so we baptize, so we have believed, so we now believe.

The most glorious judges and the great senate said: Since we see that the Holy Gospels have been placed alongside of your holiness, let each one of the bishops here assembled declare whether the epistle of most blessed archbishop Leo is in accordance with the exposition of the 318 fathers assembled at Nice and with the decrees of the 150 fathers afterwards assembled in the royal city.

[To this question the bishops answered one by one, until 161 separate opinions had been given, when the rest of the bishops were asked by the imperial judges to give their votes in a body (col. 508).]

All the most reverend bishops cried out: We all acquiesce, we all believe thus; we are all of the same mind. So are we minded, so we believe, etc., etc.

Session V

Paschasinus and Lucentius the most reverend bishops and Boniface a presbyter, vicars of the Apostolic See of Rome, said: If they do not agree to the letter of that apostolic and blessed man, Pope Leo, give directions that we be given our letters of dismission, and let a synod be held there [i.e. in the

SEVEN ECUMENICAL COUNCILS OF THE CHURCH

West].

[A long debate then followed as to whether the decree drawn up and presented should be accepted. This seems to have been the mind of most of the bishops. At last the commissioners proposed a committee of twenty-two to meet with them and report to the council, and the Emperor imposed this with the threat that otherwise they all should be sent home and a new council called in the West. Even this did not make them yield (col. 560.)]

The most reverend bishops cried out: Many years to the Emperor! Either let the definition [i.e. the one presented at this session] stand or we go. Many years to the Emperor!

Cecropius, the most reverend bishop of Sebastopol, said: We ask that the definition be read again and that those who dissent from it, and will not sign, may go about their business; for we give our consent to these things which have been so beautifully drafted, and make no criticisms.

The most blessed bishops of Illyria said: Let those who contradict be made manifest. Those who contradict are Nestorians. Those who contradict, let them go to Rome.

The most magnificent and most glorious judges said: Dioscorus acknowledged that he accepted the expression "of two natures," but not that there were two natures. But the most holy archbishop Leo says that there are two natures in Christ unchangeably, inseparably, unconfusedly united in the one only-begotten Son our Saviour. Which would you follow, the most holy Leo or Dioscorus?

The most reverend bishops cried out: We believe as Leo. Those who contradict are Eutychians. Leo has rightly expounded the faith.

The most magnificent and glorious judges said: Add then to the definition, according to the judgment of our most holy father Leo, that there are two natures in Christ united unchangeably, inseparably, unconfusedly.

[The Committee then sat in the oratory of the most holy martyr Euphemis and afterwards reported a definition of faith which while teaching the same doctrine was not the Tome of Leo (col. 562).]

SEVEN ECUMENICAL COUNCILS OF THE CHURCH

The Definition of Faith of the Council of Chalcedon.

The holy, great, and ecumenical synod, assembled by the grace of God and the command of our most religious and Christian Emperors, Marcian and Valentinian, Augusti, at Chalcedon, the metropolis of the Bithynian Province, in the martyry of the holy and victorious martyr Euphemia, has decreed as follows:

Our Lord and Saviour Jesus Christ, when strengthening the knowledge of the Faith in his disciples, to the end that no one might disagree with his neighbour concerning the doctrines of religion, and that the proclamation of the truth might be set forth equally to all men, said, "My peace I leave with you, my peace I give unto you." But, since the evil one does not desist from sowing tares among the seeds of godliness, but ever invents some new device against the truth; therefore the Lord, providing, as he ever does, for the human race, has raised up this pious, faithful, and zealous Sovereign, and has called together unto him from all parts the chief rulers of the priesthood; so that, the grace of Christ our common Lord inspiring us, we may cast off every plague of falsehood from the sheep of Christ, and feed them with the tender leaves of truth. And this have we done with one unanimous consent, driving away erroneous doctrines and renewing the unerring faith of the Fathers, publishing to all men the Creed of the Three Hundred and Eighteen, and to their number adding, as their peers, the Fathers who have received the same summary of religion. Such are the One Hundred and Fifty holy Fathers who afterwards assembled in the great Constantinople and ratified the same faith. Moreover, observing the order and every form relating to the faith, which was observed by the holy synod formerly held in Ephesus, of which Celestine of Rome and Cyril of Alexandria, of holy memory, were the leaders, we do declare that the exposition of the right and blameless faith made by the Three Hundred and Eighteen holy and blessed Fathers, assembled at Nice in the reign of Constantine of pious memory, shall be pre-eminent: and that those things shall be of force also, which were decreed by the One Hundred and Fifty holy Fathers at Constantinople, for the uprooting of the heresies which had then sprung up, and for the confirmation of the same Catholic and Apostolic Faith of ours.

The Creed of the three hundred and eighteen Fathers at Nice.

We believe in one God, etc.

Item, the Creed of the one hundred and fifty holy Fathers who were

SEVEN ECUMENICAL COUNCILS OF THE CHURCH

assembled at Constantinople.

We believe in one God, etc.

This wise and salutary formula of divine grace sufficed for the perfect knowledge and confirmation of religion; for it teaches the perfect [doctrine] concerning Father, Son, and Holy Ghost, and sets forth the Incarnation of the Lord to them that faithfully receive it. But, forasmuch as persons undertaking to make void the preaching of the truth have through their individual heresies given rise to empty babblings; some of them daring to corrupt the mystery of the Lord's incarnation for us and refusing [to use] the name Mother of God (Θεοτόκος) in reference to the Virgin, while others, bringing in a confusion and mixture, and idly conceiving that the nature of the flesh and of the Godhead is all one, maintaining that the divine Nature of the Only Begotten is, by mixture, capable of suffering; therefore this present holy, great, and ecumenical synod, desiring to exclude every device against the Truth, and teaching that which is unchanged from the beginning, has at the very outset decreed that the faith of the Three Hundred and Eighteen Fathers shall be preserved inviolate. And on account of them that contend against the Holy Ghost, it confirms the doctrine afterwards delivered concerning the substance of the Spirit by the One Hundred and Fifty holy Fathers who assembled in the imperial City; which doctrine they declared unto all men, not as though they were introducing anything that had been lacking in their predecessors, but in order to explain through written documents their faith concerning the Holy Ghost against those who were seeking to destroy his sovereignty. And, on account of those who have taken in hand to corrupt the mystery of the dispensation [i.e. the Incarnation] and who shamelessly pretend that he who was born of the holy Virgin Mary was a mere man, it receives the synodical letters of the Blessed Cyril, Pastor of the Church of Alexandria, addressed to Nestorius and the Easterns, judging them suitable, for the refutation of the frenzied folly of Nestorius, and for the instruction of those who long with holy ardour for a knowledge of the saving symbol. And, for the confirmation of the orthodox doctrines, it has rightly added to these the letter of the President of the great and old Rome, the most blessed and holy Archbishop Leo, which was addressed to Archbishop Flavian of blessed memory, for the removal of the false doctrines of Eutyches, judging them to be agreeable to the confession of the great Peter, and as it were a common pillar against misbelievers. For it opposes those who would rend the mystery of the dispensation into a Duad of Sons; it repels from the sacred assembly those who dare to say that the Godhead of the Only Begotten is capable of suffering; it resists those who imagine a mixture or confusion of the two natures of Christ; it drives away those who fancy his form of a servant is of an heavenly or some substance other than that which was taken of us, and it anathematizes those who foolishly talk of two natures of our Lord before the union, conceiving that after the union there was only one.

Following the holy Fathers we teach with one voice that the Son [of God] and our Lord Jesus Christ is to be confessed as one and the same [Person], that he is perfect in Godhead and perfect in manhood, very God and very man, of a reasonable soul and [human] body consisting, consubstantial with the Father as touching his Godhead, and consubstantial with us as touching his manhood; made in all things like us, sin only excepted; begotten of his Father before the worlds according to his Godhead; but in these last days for us men and for our salvation born [into the world] of the Virgin Mary, the Mother of God according to his manhood. This one and the same Jesus Christ, the only-begotten Son [of God] must be confessed to be in two natures, unconfusedly, immutably, indivisibly, inseparably [united], and that without the distinction of natures being taken away by such union, but rather the peculiar property of each nature being preserved and being united in one Person and subsistence, not separated or divided into two persons, but one and the same Son and only-begotten, God the Word, our Lord Jesus Christ, as the Prophets of old time have spoken concerning him, and as the Lord Jesus Christ has taught us, and as the Creed of the Fathers has delivered to us.

These things, therefore, having been expressed by us with the greatest accuracy and attention, the holy Ecumenical Synod defines that no one shall be suffered to bring forward a different faith (ἑτέραν πίστιν), nor to write, nor to put together, nor to excogitate, nor to teach it to others. But such as dare either to put together another faith, or to bring forward or to teach or to deliver a different Creed (ἕτερον σύμβολον) to as wish to be converted to the knowledge of the truth, from the Gentiles, or Jews or any heresy whatever, if they be Bishops or clerics let them be deposed, the Bishops from the Episcopate, and the clerics from the clergy; but if they be monks or laics: let them be anathematized.

After the reading of the definition, all the most religious Bishops cried out: This is the faith of the fathers: let the metropolitans immediately subscribe it: let them immediately, in the presence of the judges, subscribe it: let that which has been well defined have no delay: this is the faith of the Apostles: by this we all stand: thus we all believe.

Session VI

[The Emperor was present in person and addressed the Council and afterwards suggested legislation under three heads, the drafts for which

were read.]

After this reading, the capitulas were handed by our most sacred and pious prince to the most beloved of God Anatolius, archbishop of royal Constantinople, which is New Rome, and all the most God-beloved bishops cried out: Many years to our Emperor and Empress, the pious, the Christian. May Christ whom you serve keep you. These things are worthy of the faith. To the Priest, the Emperor. You have straightened out the churches, victor of your enemies, teacher of the faith. Many years to the pious Empress, the lover of Christ. Many years to her that is orthodox. May God save your kingdom. You have put down the heretics, you have kept the faith. May hatred be far removed from your empire, and may your kingdom endure for ever!

Our most sacred and pious prince said to the holy synod: To the honour of the holy martyr Euphemia, and of your holiness, we decree that the city of Chalcedon, in which the synod of the holy faith has been held, shall have the honours of a metropolis, in name only giving it this honour, the proper dignity of the city of Nicomedia being preserved.

All cried out, etc., etc.

Decree on the Jurisdiction of Jerusalem and Antioch

Session VII

The most magnificent and glorious judges said:...The arrangement arrived at through the agreement of the most holy Maximus, the bishop of the city of Antioch, and of the most holy Juvenal, the bishop of Jerusalem, as the attestation of each of them declares, shall remain firm for ever, through our decree and the sentence of the holy synod; to wit, that the most holy bishop Maximus, or rather the most holy church of Antioch, shall have under its own jurisdiction the two Phœnicias and Arabia; but the most holy Juvenal, bishop of Jerusalem, or rather the most holy Church which is under him, shall have under his own power the three Palestines, all imperial pragmatics and letters and penalties being done away according to the bidding of our most sacred and pious prince.

The Ballerini, in their notes to the Works of St. Leo (Migne, Pat. Lat., LV., col. 733 et seqq.), cite fragments of the Acts of this council, which if they can be trusted, show that this matter of the rights of Antioch and Jerusalem was treated of again at a subsequent session (on Oct. 31) and determined in the same fashion. These fragments have generally been received as genuine, and have been inserted by Mansi (Tom. vii., 722 C.) in his Concilia.

The Decree with Regard to the Bishop of Ephesus.

Session XII

The most glorious judges said: Since the proposition of the God-beloved archbishop of royal Constantinople, Anatolius, and of the most reverend bishop Paschasinus, holding the place of Leo, the most God-beloved archbishop of old Rome, which orders that because both of them [i.e., Bassianus and Stephen] acted uncanonically, neither of them should rule, nor be called bishop of the most holy church of Ephesus, and since the whole holy synod taught that uncanonically they had performed these ordinations, and had agreed with the speeches of the most reverend bishops; the most reverend Bassianus and the most reverend Stephen will be removed from the holy church of Ephesus; but they shall enjoy the episcopal dignity, and from the revenues of the before-mentioned most holy church, for their nourishment and consolation, they shall receive each year two hundred gold pieces; and another bishop shall be ordained according to the canons for the most holy church.

And the whole holy synod cried out: This is a just sentence. This is a pious scheme. These things are fair to look upon.

The most reverend bishop Bassianus said: Pray give order that what was stolen from me be restored.

The most glorious judges said: If anything belonging to the most reverend bishop Bassianus personally has been taken from him, either by the most reverend bishop Stephen, or by any other persons whatsoever, this shall be restored, after judicial proof, by them who took it away or caused it to be taken.

Decree with Regard to Nicomedia

Session XIII

The most glorious judges said [after the reading of the imperial letters was finished]: These divine letters say nothing whatever with regard to the episcopate, but both refer to honour belonging to metropolitan cities. But the sacred letters of Valentinian and Valens of divine memory, which then bestowed metropolitan rights upon the city of Nice, carefully provided that nothing should be taken away from other cities. And the canon of the holy fathers decreed that there should be one metropolis in each province. What therefore is the pleasure of the holy synod in this matter?

The holy synod cried out: Let the canons be kept. Let the canons be sufficient.

Atticus the most reverend bishop of old Nicopolis in Epirus said: The canon thus defines, that a metropolitan should have jurisdiction in each province, and he should constitute all the bishops who are in that province. And this is the meaning of the canon. Now the bishop of Nicomedia, since from the beginning this was a metropolis, ought to ordain all the bishops who are in that province.

The holy synod said: This is what we all wish, this we all pray for, let this everywhere be observed, this is pleasing to all of us.

John, Constantine, Patrick [Peter] and the rest of the most reverend bishops of the Pontic diocese [through John who was one of them] said: The canons recognize the one more ancient as the metropolitan. And it is manifest that the most religious bishop of Nicomedia has the right of the ordination, and since the laws (as your magnificence has seen) have honoured Nice with the name only of metropolis, and so made its bishop superior to the rest of the bishops of the province in honour only.

The holy synod said: They have taught in accordance with the canons, beautifully have they taught. We all say the same things.

[Aëtius, Archdeacon of Constantinople, then put in a plea to save the rights of the throne of the royal city.]

The most glorious judges said: The most reverend the bishop of Nicomedia shall have the authority of metropolitan over the churches of the province of Bithynia, and Nice shall have the honour only of Metropolitical rank, submitting itself according to the example of the other bishops of the province of Nicomedia. For such is the pleasure of the Holy Synod.

Session XV

The 30 Canons of the Holy and Fourth Synods, of Chalcedon.

Canon 1

We have judged it right that the canons of the Holy Fathers made in every synod even until now, should remain in force.

Before the holding of the Council of Chalcedon, in the Greek Church, the canons of several synods, which were held previously, were gathered into one collection and provided with continuous numbers, and such a collection of canons, as we have seen, lay before the Synod of Chalcedon. As, however, most of the synods whose canons were received into the collection, e.g. those of Neocæsarea, Ancyra, Gangra, Antioch, were certainly not Ecumenical Councils, and were even to some extent of doubtful authority, such as the Antiochene Synod of 341, the confirmation of the Ecumenical Synod was now given to them, in order to raise them to the position of universally and unconditionally valid ecclesiastical rules. It is admirably remarked by the Emperor Justinian, in his 131st Novel, cap. j.; "We honour the doctrinal decrees of the first four Councils as we do Holy Scripture, but the canons given or approved by them as we do the laws."

It seems quite impossible to determine just what councils are included in this list, the Council in Trullo has entirely removed this ambiguity in its second canon.

Canon 2

If any Bishop should ordain for money, and put to sale a grace which cannot be sold, and for money ordain a bishop, or chorepiscopus, or presbyters, or deacons, or any other of those who are counted among the clergy; or if through lust of gain he should nominate for money a steward, or advocate, or prosmonarius, or any one whatever who is on the roll of the Church, let him who is convicted of this forfeit his own rank; and let him who is ordained be nothing profited by the purchased ordination or promotion; but let him be removed from the dignity or charge he has obtained for money. And if any one should be found negotiating such shameful and unlawful transactions, let him also, if he is a clergyman, be deposed from his rank, and if he is a layman or monk, let him be anathematized.

SEVEN ECUMENICAL COUNCILS OF THE CHURCH

According to Van Espen, however, who here supports himself upon Du Cange, by "prosmonarios" or "mansionarius," in the same way as by "oiconomos," a steward of church property was to be understood.

Canon 3

It has come to [the knowledge of] the holy Synod that certain of those who are enrolled among the clergy have, through lust of gain, become hirers of other men's possessions, and make contracts pertaining to secular affairs, lightly esteeming the service of God, and slip into the houses of secular persons, whose property they undertake through covetousness to manage. Wherefore the great and holy Synod decrees that henceforth no bishop, clergyman, nor monk shall hire possessions, or engage in business, or occupy himself in worldly engagements, unless he shall be called by the law to the guardianship of minors, from which there is no escape; or unless the bishop of the city shall commit to him the care of ecclesiastical business, or of unprovided orphans or widows and of persons who stand especially in need of the Church's help, through the fear of God. And if any one shall hereafter transgress these decrees, he shall be subjected to ecclesiastical penalties.

Canon 4

Let those who truly and sincerely lead the monastic life be counted worthy of becoming honour; but, forasmuch as certain persons using the pretext of monasticism bring confusion both upon the churches and into political affairs by going about promiscuously in the cities, and at the same time seeking to establish Monasteries for themselves; it is decreed that no one anywhere build or found a monastery or oratory contrary to the will of the bishop of the city; and that the monks in every city and district shall be subject to the bishop, and embrace a quiet course of life, and give themselves only to fasting and prayer, remaining permanently in the places in which they were set apart; and they shall meddle neither in ecclesiastical nor in secular affairs, nor leave their own monasteries to take part in such; unless, indeed, they should at any time through urgent necessity be appointed thereto by the bishop of the city. And no slave shall be received into any monastery to become a monk against the will of his master. And if any one shall transgress this our judgment, we have decreed that he shall be excommunicated, that the name of God be not blasphemed. But the bishop of the city must make the needful provision for the monasteries.

Hefele: Like the previous canon, this one was brought forward by the Emperor Marcian in the sixth session, and then as number one, and the synod accepted the Emperor's proposed canon almost verbally. Occasion for this canon seems to have been given by monks of Eutychian tendencies, and especially by the Syrian Barsumas, as appears from the fourth session. He and his monks had, as Eutychians, withdrawn themselves from the jurisdiction of their bishops, whom they suspected of Nestorianism.

Canon 5

Concerning bishops or clergymen who go about from city to city, it is decreed that the canons enacted by the Holy Fathers shall still retain their force.

It is supposed by Hefele that the bishops were thinking of the case of Bassian, who, in the eleventh session (Oct. 29), pleaded that he had been violently ejected from the see of Ephesus. Stephen the actual bishop, answered that Bassian had not been "ordained" for that see, but had invaded it and been justly expelled. Bassian rejoined that his original consecration for the see of Evasa had been forcible even to brutality; that he had never even visited Evasa, that therefore his appointment to Ephesus was not a translation. Ultimately, the Council cut the knot by ordering that a new bishop should be elected, Basalan and Stephen retaining the episcopal title and receiving allowances from the revenues of the see (Mansi, vii. 273 et seqq.)

Canon 6

Neither presbyter, deacon, nor any of the ecclesiastical order shall be ordained at large, nor unless the person ordained is particularly appointed to a church in a city or village, or to a martyry, or to a monastery. And if any have been ordained without a charge, the holy Synod decrees, to the reproach of the ordainer, that such an ordination shall be inoperative, and that such shall nowhere be suffered to officiate.

Hefele.

It is clear that our canon forbids the so-called absolute ordinations, and requires that every cleric must at the time of his ordination be designated to a definite church. The only titulus which is here recognized is that which was later known as titulus beneficii. As various kinds of this title we find here (a) the appointment to a church in the city; (b) to a village church; (c) that to the chapel of a martyr; (d) the appointment as chaplain of a monastery. For the right understanding of the last point, it must be remembered that the earliest monks were in no wise clerics, but that soon the custom was introduced in every larger convent, of having at least one monk ordained presbyter, that he might provide for divine service in the monastery.

SEVEN ECUMENICAL COUNCILS OF THE CHURCH

Bright.

By the word μαρτυρίῳ ("martyry") is meant a church or chapel raised over a martyr's grave. So the Laodicene Council forbids Churchmen to visit the "martyries of heretics" (can. ix.). So Gregory of Nyssa speaks of "the martyry" of the Holy Martyrs (Op. ii., 212); Chrysostom of a "martyry," and Palladius of "martyries" near Antioch (In Act. Apost. Hom., xxxviii. 5; Dial., p. 17), and Palladius of "the martyry of St. John" at Constantinople (Dial., p. 25). See Socrates, iv. 18, 23, on the "martyry" of St. Thomas at Edessa, and that of SS. Peter and Paul at Rome; and vi. 6, on the "martyry" of St. Euphenia at Chalcedon in which the Council actually met. In the distinct sense of a visible testimony, the word was applied to the church of the Resurrection at Jerusalem (Eusebius, Vit. Con., iii. 40, iv. 40; Mansi, vi. 564; Cyril, Catech., xiv. 3), and to the Holy Sepulchre itself (Vit. Con., iii. 28). Churches raised over martyrs' tombs were called in the West " memoriæ martyrum," see Cod. Afric., lxxxiii. (compare Augustine, De Cura pro Mortuis, VI.).

Canon 7

We have decreed that those who have once been enrolled among the clergy, or have been made monks, shall accept neither a military charge nor any secular dignity; and if they shall presume to do so and not repent in such wise as to turn again to that which they had first chosen for the love of God, they shall be anathematized.

Canon 8

Let the clergy of the poor-houses, monasteries, and martyries remain under the authority of the bishops in every city according to the tradition of the holy Fathers; and let no one arrogantly cast off the rule of his own bishop; and if any shall contravene this canon in any way whatever, and will not be subject to their own bishop, if they be clergy, let them be subjected to canonical censure, and if they be monks or laymen, let them be excommunicated.

Canon 9

If any Clergyman have a matter against another clergyman, he shall not forsake his bishop and run to secular courts; but let him first lay open the matter before his own Bishop, or let the matter be submitted to any person whom each of the parties may, with the Bishop's consent, select. And if any one shall contravene these decrees, let him be subjected to canonical penalties. And if a clergyman have a complaint against his own or any other bishop, let it be decided by the synod of the province. And if a bishop or clergyman should have a difference with the metropolitan of the province, let him have recourse to the Exarch of the Diocese, or to the throne of the Imperial City of Constantinople, and there let it be tried.

Canon 10

It shall not be lawful for a clergyman to be at the same time enrolled in the churches of two cities, that is, in the church in which he was at first ordained, and in another to which, because it is greater, he has removed from lust of empty honour. And those who do so shall be returned to their own church in which they were originally ordained, and there only shall they minister. But if any one has heretofore been removed from one church to another, he shall not intermeddle with the affairs of his former church, nor with the martyries, almshouses, and hostels belonging to it. And if, after the decree of this great and ecumenical Synod, any shall dare to do any of these things now forbidden, the synod decrees that he shall be degraded from his rank.

Here a new institution comes into view, of which there were many instances. Julian had directed Pagan hospices (ξενοδοχεῖα) to be established on the Christian model (Epist. xlix.). The Basiliad at Cæsarea was a ξενοδοχεῖον as well as a πτωχεῖον; it contained καταγώγια τοῖς ξένοις, as well as for wayfayers, and those who needed assistance on account of illness, and Basil distinguished various classes of persons engaged in charitable ministrations, including those who escorted the traveller on his way (τοὺς παραπέμποντας, Epist. xciv.). Jerome writes to Pammachius: "I hear that you have made a 'xenodochion' in the port of Rome," and adds that he himself had built a "diversorium" for pilgrims to Bethlehem (Epist. xvi., 11, 14). Chrysostom reminds his auditors at Constantinople that "there is a common dwelling set apart by the Church," and "called a xenon" (in Act. Hom., xlv. 4). His friend Olympias was munificent to "xenotrophia" (Hist. Lausiac, 144). There was a xenodochion near the church of the monastic settlement at Nitria (ib., 7). Ischyrion, in his memorial read in the 3d session of Chalcedon, complains of his patriarch Dioscorus for having misapplied funds bequeathed by a charitable lady τοῖς ξενεῶσι καὶ πτωχείοις in Egypt, and says that he himself had been confined by Dioscorus in a "xenon" for lepers (Mansi, vi. 1013, 1017). Justinian mentions xenodochia in Cod., i. 3, 49, and their wardens in Novell., 134, 16. Gregory the Great orders that the accounts of xenodochia should be audited by the bishop (Epist. iv., 27). Charles the Great provides for the restoration of decayed "senodochia" (Capitul. of 803; Pertz, Leg., i. 110); and Alcuin exhorts his pupil, archbishop Eanbald, to think where in the diocese of York he could establish "xenodochia, id est, hospitalia" (Epist. L.).

SEVEN ECUMENICAL COUNCILS OF THE CHURCH

Canon 11

We have decreed that the poor and those needing assistance shall travel, after examination, with letters merely pacifical from the church, and not with letters commendatory, inasmuch as letters commendatory ought to be given only to persons who are open to suspicion.

Canon 12

It has come to our knowledge that certain persons, contrary to the laws of the Church, having had recourse to secular powers, have by means of imperial rescripts divided one Province into two, so that there are consequently two metropolitans in one province; therefore the holy Synod has decreed that for the future no such thing shall be attempted by a bishop, since he who shall undertake it shall be degraded from his rank. But the cities which have already been honoured by means of imperial letters with the name of metropolis, and the bishops in charge of them, shall take the bare title, all metropolitan rights being preserved to the true Metropolis.

Canon 13

Strange and unknown clergymen without letters commendatory from their own Bishop, are absolutely prohibited from officiating in another city.

Canon 14

Since in certain provinces it is permitted to the readers and singers to marry, the holy Synod has decreed that it shall not be lawful for any of them to take a wife that is heterodox. But those who have already begotten children of such a marriage, if they have already had their children baptized among the heretics, must bring them into the communion of the Catholic Church; but if they have not had them baptized, they may not hereafter baptize them among heretics, nor give them in marriage to a heretic, or a Jew, or a heathen, unless the person marrying the orthodox child shall promise to come over to the orthodox faith. And if any one shall transgress this decree of the holy synod, let him be subjected to canonical censure.

Canon 15

A woman shall not receive the laying on of hands as a deaconess under forty years of age, and then only after searching examination. And if, after she has had hands laid on her and has continued for a time to minister, she shall despise the grace of God and give herself in marriage, she shall be

anathematized and the man united to her.
Canon 16

It is not lawful for a virgin who has dedicated herself to the Lord God, nor for monks, to marry; and if they are found to have done this, let them be excommunicated. But we decree that in every place the bishop shall have the power of indulgence towards them.

Canon 17

Outlying or rural parishes shall in every province remain subject to the bishops who now have jurisdiction over them, particularly if the bishops have peaceably and continuously governed them for the space of thirty years. But if within thirty years there has been, or is, any dispute concerning them, it is lawful for those who hold themselves aggrieved to bring their cause before the synod of the province. And if any one be wronged by his metropolitan, let the matter be decided by the exarch of the diocese or by the throne of Constantinople, as aforesaid. And if any city has been, or shall hereafter be newly erected by imperial authority, let the order of the ecclesiastical parishes follow the political and municipal example.

Canon 18

The crime of conspiracy or banding together is utterly prohibited even by the secular law, and much more ought it to be forbidden in the Church of God. Therefore, if any, whether clergymen or monks, should be detected in conspiring or banding together, or hatching plots against their bishops or fellow clergy, they shall by all means be deposed from their own rank.

Canon 19

Whereas it has come to our ears that in the provinces the Canonical Synods of Bishops are not held, and that on this account many ecclesiastical matters which need reformation are neglected; therefore, according to the canons of the holy Fathers, the holy Synod decrees that the bishops of every province shall twice in the year assemble together where the bishop of the Metropolis shall approve, and shall then settle whatever matters may have arisen. And bishops, who do not attend, but remain in their own cities, though they are in good health and free from any unavoidable and necessary business, shall receive a brotherly admonition.

Canon 20

It shall not be lawful, as we have already decreed, for clergymen officiating in one church to be appointed to the church of another city, but they shall cleave to that in which they were first thought worthy to minister; those, however, being excepted, who have been driven by necessity from their own country, and have therefore removed to another church. And if, after this decree, any bishop shall receive a clergyman belonging to another bishop, it is decreed that both the received and the receiver shall be excommunicated until such time as the clergyman who has removed shall have returned to his own church.

Canon 21

Clergymen and laymen bringing charges against bishops or clergymen are not to be received loosely and without examination, as accusers, but their own character shall first be investigated.

Canon 22

It is not lawful for clergymen, after the death of their bishop, to seize what belongs to him, as has been forbidden also by the ancient canons; and those who do so shall be in danger of degradation from their own rank.

Canon 23

It has come to the hearing of the holy Synod that certain clergymen and monks, having no authority from their own bishop, and sometimes, indeed, while under sentence of excommunication by him, betake themselves to the imperial Constantinople, and remain there for a long time, raising disturbances and troubling the ecclesiastical state, and turning men's houses upside down. Therefore the holy Synod has determined that such persons be first notified by the Advocate of the most holy Church of Constantinople to depart from the imperial city; and if they shall shamelessly continue in the same practices, that they shall be expelled by the same Advocate even against their will, and return to their own places.

Canon 24

Monasteries, which have once been consecrated with the consent of the bishop, shall remain monasteries for ever, and the property belonging to them shall be preserved, and they shall never again become secular dwellings. And they who shall permit this to be done shall be liable to ecclesiastical penalties.

SEVEN ECUMENICAL COUNCILS OF THE CHURCH

Canon 25

Forasmuch as certain of the metropolitans, as we have heard, neglect the flocks committed to them, and delay the ordinations of bishops the holy Synod has decided that the ordinations of bishops shall take place within three months, unless an inevitable necessity should some time require the term of delay to be prolonged. And if he shall not do this, he shall be liable to ecclesiastical penalties, and the income of the widowed church shall be kept safe by the steward of the same Church.

Canon 26

Forasmuch as we have heard that in certain churches the bishops managed the church-business without stewards, it has seemed good that every church having a bishop shall have also a steward from among its own clergy, who shall manage the church business under the sanction of his own bishop; that so the administration of the church may not be without a witness; and that thus the goods of the church may not be squandered, nor reproach be brought upon the priesthood; and if he [i.e., the Bishop] will not do this, he shall be subjected to the divine canons.

Canon 27

The holy Synod has decreed that those who forcibly carry off women under pretence of marriage, and the aiders or abettors of such ravishers, shall be degraded if clergymen, and if laymen be anathematized.

Canon 28

Following in all things the decisions of the holy Fathers, and acknowledging the canon, which has been just read, of the One Hundred and Fifty Bishops beloved-of-God (who assembled in the imperial city of Constantinople, which is New Rome, in the time of the Emperor Theodosius of happy memory), we also do enact and decree the same things concerning the privileges of the most holy Church of Constantinople, which is New Rome. For the Fathers rightly granted privileges to the throne of old Rome, because it was the royal city. And the One Hundred and Fifty most religious Bishops, actuated by the same consideration, gave equal privileges (ἴσα πρεσβεῖα) to the most holy throne of New Rome, justly judging that the city which is honoured with the Sovereignty and the Senate, and enjoys equal privileges with the old imperial Rome, should in ecclesiastical matters also be magnified as she is, and rank next after her; so that, in the Pontic, the Asian, and the Thracian dioceses, the metropolitans only and such bishops also of the

Dioceses aforesaid as are among the barbarians, should be ordained by the aforesaid most holy throne of the most holy Church of Constantinople; every metropolitan of the aforesaid dioceses, together with the bishops of his province, ordaining his own provincial bishops, as has been declared by the divine canons; but that, as has been above said, the metropolitans of the aforesaid Dioceses should be ordained by the archbishop of Constantinople, after the proper elections have been held according to custom and have been reported to him.

Canon 29

It is sacrilege to degrade a bishop to the rank of a presbyter; but, if they are for just cause removed from episcopal functions, neither ought they to have the position of a Presbyter; and if they have been displaced without any charge, they shall be restored to their episcopal dignity.

And Anatolius, the most reverend Archbishop of Constantinople, said: If those who are alleged to have been removed from the episcopal dignity to the order of presbyter, have indeed been condemned for any sufficient causes, clearly they are not worthy of the honour of a presbyter. But if they have been forced down into the lower rank without just cause, they are worthy, if they appear guiltless, to receive again both the dignity and priesthood of the Episcopate.

And all the most reverend Bishops cried out:

The judgment of the Fathers is right. We all say the same. The Fathers have righteously decided. Let the sentence of the Archbishops prevail.

And the most magnificent and glorious judges said:

Let the pleasure of the Holy Synod be established for all time.

From the Fourth Session of the same Holy Synod, having reference to the matter of the Egyptian Bishops.

The most magnificent and glorious judges, and the whole Senate, said:

Canon 30

Since the most religious bishops of Egypt have postponed for the present their subscription to the letter of the most holy Archbishop Leo, not because they oppose the Catholic Faith, but because they declare that it is the custom in the Egyptian diocese to do no such thing without the consent and order of their Archbishop, and ask to be excused until the ordination of the new bishop of the metropolis of Alexandria, it has seemed to us reasonable and kind that this concession should be made to them, they remaining in their official habit in the imperial city until the Archbishop of the Metropolis of Alexandria shall have been ordained.

And the most religious Bishop Paschasinus, representative of the Apostolic throne for Rome], said:

If your authority suggests and commands that any indulgence be shown to them, let them give securities that they will not depart from this city until the city of Alexandria receives a Bishop.

And the most magnificent and glorious judges, and the whole Senate, said:

Let the sentence of the most holy Paschasinus be confirmed.

And therefore let them [i.e., the most religious Bishops of the Egyptians] remain in their official habit, either giving securities, if they can, or being bound by the obligation of an oath.

Hefele.

This paragraph, like the previous one, is not a proper canon, but a verbal repetition of a proposal made in the fourth session by the imperial commissioners, improved by the legate Paschasinus, and approved by the Synod. Moreover, this so-called canon is not found in the ancient collections, and was probably added to the twenty-eight canons in the same manner and for the same reasons as the preceding.

Bright.

The council could insist with all plainness on the duty of hearing before condemning (see on Canon XXIX.); yet on this occasion bishop after bishop gave vent to harsh unfeeling absolutism, the only excuse for which consists in the fact that the outrages of the Latrocinium were fresh in their minds, and that three of the Egyptian supplicants, whom they were so eager to terrify or crush, had actually supported Dioscorus on the tragical August 8, 449. It was not in human nature to forget this; but the result is a blot on the history of the Council of Chalcedon.

SEVEN ECUMENICAL COUNCILS OF THE CHURCH

Session XVI

Paschasinus and Lucentius, the most reverend bishops, holding the place of the Apostolic See, said: If your magnificence so orders, we have something to lay before you.

The most glorious judges, said: Say what you wish. The most holy Paschasinus the bishop, holding the place of Rome, said: The rulers of the world, taking care of the holy Catholic faith, by which their kingdom and glory is increased, have deigned to define this, in order that unity through a holy peace may be preserved through all the churches. But with still greater care their clemency has vouchsafed to provide for the future, so that no contention may spring up again between God's bishops, nor any schisms, nor any scandal. But yesterday after your excellencies and our humility had left, it is said that certain decrees were made, which we esteem to have been done contrary to the canons, and contrary to ecclesiastical discipline. We request that your magnificence order these things to be read, that all the brethren may know whether the things done are just or unjust.

The most glorious judges said: If anything was done after our leaving let it be read.

And before the reading, Aëtius, the Archdeacon of the Church of Constantinople said: It is certain that the matters touching the faith received a suitable form. But it is customary at synods, after those things which are chiefest of all shall have been defined, that other things also which are necessary should be examined and put into shape. We have, I mean the most holy Church of Constantinople has, manifestly things to be attended to. We asked the lord bishops (κυρίοις τοις ἐπισκοποις) from Rome, to join with us in these matters, but they declined, saying they had received no instructions on the subject. We referred the matter to your magnificence and you bid the holy Synod to consider this very point. And when your magnificence had gone forth, as the affair was one of common interest, the most holy bishops, standing up, prayed that this thing might be done. And they were present here, and this was done in no hidden nor secret fashion, but in due course and in accordance with the canons.

The most glorious judges said: Let the acts be read.

[The canon (number XXVIII.), was then read, and the signatures, in all 192, including the bishops of Antioch, Jerusalem, and Heraclea, but not Thalassius of Cæsarea who afterwards assented. Only a week before 350 had signed the Definition of faith. When the last name was read a debate arose as follows.

SEVEN ECUMENICAL COUNCILS OF THE CHURCH

(Col. 810.).]

Lucentius, the most reverend bishop and legate of the Apostolic See, said: In the first place let your excellency notice that it was brought to pass by circumventing the holy bishops so that they were forced to sign the as yet unwritten canons, of which they made mention. [The Greek reads a little differently (I have followed the Latin as it is supposed by the critics to be more pure than the Greek we now have): Your excellency has perceived how many things were done in the presence of the bishops, in order that no one might be forced to sign the aforementioned canons; defining by necessity.]

The most reverend bishops cried out: No one was forced.

Lucentius the most reverend bishop and legate of the Apostolic See, said: It is manifest that the decrees of the 318 have been put aside, and that mention only has been made of those of the 150, which are not found to have any place in the synodical canons, and which were made as they acknowledge eighty years ago. If therefore they enjoyed this privilege during these years, what do they seek for now? If they never used it, why seek it? [The Greek reads: It is manifest that the present decrees have been added to the decrees of the 318 and to those of the 150 after them, decrees not received into the synodical canons, these things they pretend to be defined. If therefore in these times they used this benefit what now do they seek which according to the canons they had not used?]

Aëtius, the archdeacon of the most holy Church of Constantinople, said: If on this subject they had received any commands, let them be brought forward.

Bonifacius, a presbyter and vicar of the Apostolic See, said: The most blessed and Apostolic Pope, among other things, gave us this commandment. And he read from the chart, "The rulings of the holy fathers shall with no rashness be violated or diminished. Let the dignity of our person in all ways be guarded by you. And if any, influenced by the power of his own city, should undertake to make usurpations, withstand this with suitable firmness."

The most glorious judges said: Let each party quote the canons.

Paschasinus, the most reverend bishop and representative, read: Canon Six of the 318 holy fathers, "The Roman Church has always had the primacy. Let Egypt therefore so hold itself that the bishop of Alexandria have the authority over all, for this is also the custom as regards the bishop of Rome. So too at Antioch and in the other provinces let the churches of the larger cities have the primacy. [In the Greek 'let the primacy be kept to the churches.' a sentence which I do not understand, unless it means that for the advantage of the churches the primatial rights of Antioch must be upheld. But such a sentiment one would expect to find rather in the Latin than in the Greek.] And one thing is abundantly clear, that if any one shall have been ordained bishop contrary to the will of the metropolitan, this great synod has decreed that such an one ought not to be bishop. If however the judgment of all his own [fellows] is reasonable and according to the canons, and if two or three dissent through their own obstinacy, then let the vote of the majority prevail. For a custom has prevailed, and it is an ancient tradition, that the bishop of Jerusalem be honoured, let him have his consequent honour, but the rights of his own metropolis must be preserved."

Constantine, the secretary, read from a book handed him by Aëtius, the archdeacon; Canon Six of the 318 holy Fathers. "Let the ancient customs prevail, those of Egypt, so that the bishop of Alexandria shall have jurisdiction over all, since this also is the custom at Rome. Likewise at Antioch and in the rest of the provinces, let the rank (πρεσβεῖα) be preserved to the churches. For this is absolutely clear that if anyone contrary to the will of the metropolitan be ordained bishop, such an one the great synod decreed should not be a bishop. If however by the common vote of all, founded upon reason, and according to the canons, two or three moved by their own obstinacy, make opposition, let the vote of the majority stand."

The same secretary read from the same codex the determination of the Second Synod. "These things the bishops decreed who assembled by the grace of God in Constantinople from far separated provinces,...and bishops are not to go to churches which are outside the bounds of their dioceses, nor to confound the churches, but according to the canons the bishop of Alexandria shall take the charge of the affairs of Egypt only, and the bishops of Orient shall govern the Oriental diocese only, the honours due to the Church of Antioch being guarded according to the Nicene canons, and the Asiatic bishops shall care for the diocese of Asia only, and those of Pontus the affairs of Pontus only, and those of Thrace the affairs of Thrace only. But bishops shall not enter uncalled another diocese for ordination, or any other ecclesiastical function. And the aforesaid canon concerning dioceses being observed, it is evident that the synod of every province will administer the affairs of that particular province as was decreed at Nice. But the churches of God in heathen nations must be governed according to the custom which has prevailed from the times of the Fathers. The bishop of Constantinople however shall have the prerogative of honour next after the bishop of Rome,

SEVEN ECUMENICAL COUNCILS OF THE CHURCH

because Constantinople is new Rome."

The most glorious judges said: Let the most holy Asiatic and Pontic bishops who have signed the tome just read say whether they gave their signatures of their own judgment or compelled by any necessity. And when these had come into the midst, the most reverend Diogenes, the bishop of Cyzicum, said: I call God to witness that I signed of my own judgment. [And so on, one after the other.]

The rest cried out: We signed willingly.

The most glorious judges said: As it is manifest that the subscription of each one of the bishops was given without any necessity but of his own will, let the most holy bishops who have not signed say something.

Eusebius, the bishop of Ancyra, said: I am about to speak but for myself alone.

[His speech is a personal explanation of his own action with regard to consecrating a bishop for Gangra.]

The most glorious judges said: From what has been done and brought forward on each side, we perceive that the primacy of all (πρὸ πάντων τὰ πρωτεῖα) and the chief honour (τὴν ἐξαίρετον τιμὴν) according to the canons, is to be kept for the most God-beloved archbishop of Old Rome, but that the most reverend archbishop of the royal city Constantinople, which is new Rome, is to enjoy the honour of the same primacy, and to have the power to ordain the metropolitans in the Asiatic, Pontic, and Thracian dioceses, in this manner: that there be elected by the clergy, and substantial (κτητόρων) and most distinguished men of each metropolis and moreover by all the most reverend bishops of the province, or a majority of them, and that he be elected whom those afore mentioned shall deem worthy of the metropolitan episcopate and that he should be presented by all those who had elected him to the most holy archbishop of royal Constantinople, that he might be asked whether he [i.e., the Patriarch of Constantinople] willed that he should there be ordained, or by his commission in the province where he received the vote to the episcopate. The most reverend bishops of the ordinary towns should be ordained by all the most reverend bishops of the province or by a majority of them, the metropolitan having his power according to the established canon of the fathers, and making with regard to such ordinations no communications to the most holy archbishop of royal Constantinople. Thus the matter appears to us to stand. Let the holy Synod vouchsafe to teach its view of the case.

The most reverend bishops cried out: This is a just sentence. So we all say. These things please us all. This is a just determination. Establish the proposed form of decree. This is a just vote. All has been decreed as should be. We beg you to let us go. By the safety of the Emperor let us go. We all will remain in this opinion, we all say the same things.

Lucentius, the bishop, said: The Apostolic See gave orders that all things should be done in our presence [This sentence reads in the Latin: The Apostolic See ought not to be humiliated in our presence. I do not know why Canon Bright in his notes on Canon XXVIII. has followed this reading]; and therefore whatever yesterday was done to the prejudice of the canons during our absence, we beseech your highness to command to be rescinded. But if not, let our opposition be placed in the minutes, and pray let us know clearly [Lat. that we may know] what we are to report to that most apostolic bishop who is the ruler of the whole church, so that he may be able to take action with regard to the indignity done to his See and to the setting at naught of the canons.

[John, the most reverend bishop of Sebaste, said: We all will remain of the opinion expressed by your magnificence.]

The most glorious judges said: The whole synod has approved what we proposed.

SEVEN ECUMENICAL COUNCILS OF THE CHURCH

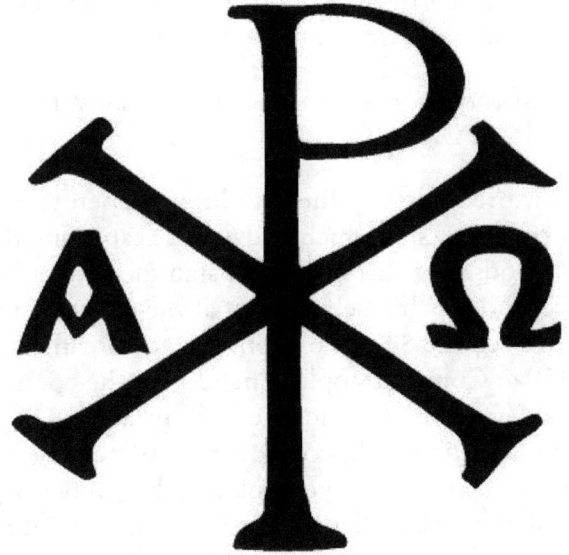

COUNCIL OF SECOND CONSTANTINOPLE

SEVEN ECUMENICAL COUNCILS OF THE CHURCH

Session I - Extracts from the Acts

[*The Emperor's Letter which was read to the Fathers.*]

In the Name of our Lord God Jesus Christ. The Emperor Flavius Justinian, German, Gothic, etc., and always Augustus, to the most blessed bishops and patriarchs, Eutychius of Constantinople, Apollinarius of Alexandria, Domninus of Theopolis, Stephen, George, and Damian, the most religious bishops taking the place of that man of singular blessedness, Eustochius, the Archbishop and Patriarch of Jerusalem, and the other most religious bishops stopping in this royal city from the different provinces.

[*The following is the letter condensed, including Hefele's digest.* History of the Councils, *Vol. IV., p. 298.*]

The effort of my predecessors, the orthodox Emperors, ever aimed at the settling of controversies which had arisen respecting the faith by the calling of Synods. For this cause Constantine assembled 318 Fathers at Nice, and was himself present at the Council, and assisted those who confessed the Son to be consubstantial with the Father. Theodosius, 150 at Constantinople, Theodosius the younger, the Synod of Ephesus, the Emperor Marcian, the bishops at Chalcedon. As, however, after Marcian's death, controversies respecting the Synod of Chalcedon had broken out in several places, the Emperor Leo wrote to all bishops of all places, in order that everyone might declare his opinion in writing with regard to this holy Council. Soon afterwards, however, had arisen again the adherents of Nestorius and Eutyches, and caused great divisions, so that many Churches had broken off communion with one another. When, now, the grace of God raised us to the throne, we regarded it as our chief business to unite the Churches again, and to bring the Synod of Chalcedon, together with the three earlier, to universal acceptance. We have won many who previously opposed that Synod; others, who persevered in their opposition, we banished, and so restored the unity of the Church again. But the Nestorians want to impose their heresy upon the Church; and, as they could not use Nestorius for that purpose, they made haste to introduce their errors through Theodore of Mopsuestia, the teacher of Nestorius, who taught still more grievous blasphemies than his. He maintained, *e.g.*, that God the Word was one, and Christ another. For the same purpose they made use of those impious writings of Theodoret which were directed against the first Synod of Ephesus, against Cyril and his Twelve Chapters, and also the shameful letter which Ibas is said to have written. They maintain that this letter was accepted by the Synod of Chalcedon, and so would free from condemnation Nestorius and Theodore who were commended in the letter. If they were to succeed, the Logos could no longer be said to be made man, nor Mary called the Mother (*genetrix*) of God. We, therefore, following the holy Fathers, have first asked you in writing to give your judgment on the three impious chapters named, and you have answered, and have joyfully confessed the true faith. Because, however, after the condemnation proceeding from you, there are still some who defend the Three Chapters, therefore we have summoned you to the capital, that you may here, in common assembly, place again your view in the light of day. When, for example, Vigilius, Pope of Old Rome, came hither, he, in answer to our questions, repeatedly anathematised in writing the Three Chapters, and confirmed his steadfastness in this view by much, even by the condemnation of his deacons, Rusticus and Sebastian. We possess still his declarations in his own hand. Then he issued his *Judicatum*, in which he anathematised the Three Chapters, with the words, *Et quoniam*, etc. You know that he not only deposed Rusticus and Sebastian because they defended the Three Chapters, but also wrote to Valentinian, bishop of Scythia, and Aurelian, bishop of Arles, that nothing might be undertaken against the *Judicatum*. When you afterwards came hither at my invitation, letters were exchanged between you and Vigilius in order to a common assembly. But now he had altered his view, would no longer have a synod, but required that only the three patriarchs and one other bishop (in communion with the Pope and the three bishops about him) should decide the matter. In vain we sent several commands to him to take part in the synod. He rejected also our two proposals, either to call a tribunal for decision, or to hold a smaller assembly, at which, besides him and his three bishops, every other patriarch should have place and voice, with from three to five bishops of his diocese.* We further declare that we hold fast to the decrees of the four Councils, and in every way follow the holy Fathers, Athanasius, Hilary, Basil, Gregory the Theologian, Gregory of Nyssa, Ambrose, Theophilus, John (Chrysostom) of Constantinople, Cyril, Augustine, Proclus, Leo and their writings on the true faith. As, however, the heretics are resolved to defend Theodore of Mopsuestia and Nestorius with their impieties, and maintain that that letter of Ibas was received by the Synod of Chalcedon, so do we exhort you to direct your attention to the impious writings of Theodore, and especially to his Jewish Creed which was brought forward at Ephesus and Chalcedon, and anathematized by each synod with those who had so held or did so hold; and we further exhort you to consider what the holy Fathers have written concerning him and his blasphemies, as well as what our predecessors have promulgated, as also what the Church historians have set forth concerning him. You will thence see that he and his heresies have since been condemned and that therefore his name has long since been struck from the diptychs of the Church of Mopsuestia. Consider the absurd assertion that heretics ought not to be anathematized after their deaths; and we exhort you further to follow in this matter the doctrine of the holy Fathers, who condemned not only living heretics but also anathematized after their death those who had died in their iniquity, just as those who had been unjustly condemned they restored after their death and wrote their names in the sacred diptychs; which took place in the case of John and of Flavian of pious memory, both of them bishops of Constantinople. Moreover we exhort you to examine the writing of Theodoret and the supposed letter of Ibas, in which the incarnation of the Word is denied, the expression Mother of God and the holy Synod of Ephesus rejected, Cyril called a heretic, and Theodore and Nestorius defended and praised. And as they say that the Council of Chalcedon has received this letter, you must compare the declarations of this Council relating to the faith with the contents of the impious letter. Finally, we entreat you to accelerate the matter. For he who when asked concerning the right faith, puts off his answer for a long while, does nothing else but deny the right faith. For in questioning and answering on things which are of faith, it is not he who is found first or second, but he who is the more ready with a right confession, that is acceptable to God. May God keep you, most holy and religious fathers, for many years. Given IV. Nones of May, at Constantinople, in the twenty-seventh year of the reign of the imperial lord Justinian, the perpetual Augustus, and in the twelfth year after the consulate of the most illustrious Basil.

Session VII - Extracts from the Acts

(*From the Paris manuscript found in* Hardouin *Concilia*, Tom. III., 171 et seqq.; Mansi, Tom. ix., 346 et seqq. *This speech is not found in full in any other ms. The Ballerini [Hefele notes] raise objections to the genuineness of the additions* [in Noris. *Opp.*, Tom. IV., 1037], *but Hefele does not consider the objections of serious moment.* [*Hist. of the Councils*, Vol. IV., p. 323, note 2.] *All the mss. agree that* The most glorious quæster of the sacred palace, Constantine, was sent by the most pious Emperor, and when he had entered the Council spoke as follows: Certum est vestræ beatitudini, quantum, etc. *The rest of the speech differs in the different manuscripts. I follow that of Paris.*)

You know how much care the most invincible Emperor has always had that the contention raised up by certain persons with regard to the Three Chapters should have a termination....For this intent he has required the most religious Vigilius to assemble with you and draw up a decree on this matter in accordance with the Orthodox faith. Although therefore, Vigilius has already frequently condemned the Three Chapters in writing, and has done this also by word of mouth in the presence of the Emperor, and of the most glorious judges and of many members of this synod, and has always been ready to smite with anathema the defenders of Theodore of Mopsuestia, and the letter which was attributed to Ibas, and the writings of Theodoret which he set forth against the orthodox faith and against the twelve capitula of the holy Cyril: yet he has refused to do this in communion with you and your synod.

Yesterday Vigilius sent Servus Dei, a most reverend Subdeacon of the Roman Church, and invited Belisarius, Cethegus, as also Justinus and Constantine the most glorious consuls, as well as bishops Theodore, Ascidas, Benignus, and Phocas, to come to him as he wished to give through them an answer to the Emperor. They came, but speedily returned and informed the most pious lord, that we had visited Vigilius, the most religious bishop, and that he had said to us: We have called you for this reason, that you may know what things have been done in the past days. To this end I have written a document about the disputed Three Chapters, addressed to the most pious Emperor, pray be good enough to read it, and to carry it to his Serenity. But when we had heard this and had seen the document written to your serenity, we said to him that we could not by any means receive any document written to the most pious Emperor without his bidding. But you have deacons for running with messages, by whom you can send it. He, however, said to us: You now know that I have made the document.

But we, bishops, answered him: If your blessedness is willing to meet together with us and the most holy Patriarchs, and the most religious bishops, and to treat of the Three Chapters and to give, in unison with us all, a suitable form of the orthodox faith, as the Holy Apostles and the holy Fathers and the four Councils have done, we will hold you as our head, as a father and primate. But if your holiness has drawn up a document for the Emperor, you have errand-runners, as we have said; send it by them. And when he had heard these things from us, he sent Servus Dei the Subdeacon, who now awaits the answer of your serenity. And when his Piety had heard this, he commanded through the aforesaid most religious and glorious men, the before-named subdeacon to carry back this message to the most religious Vigilius: We invited him (*you*) to meet together with the most blessed patriarchs and other religious bishops, and with them in common to examine and judge the Three Chapters. But since you have refused to do this, and you say that you alone have written by yourself somewhat on the Three Chapters; if you have condemned them, in accordance with those things which you did before, we have already many such statements and need no more; but if you have written now something contrary to these things which were done by you before, you have condemned yourself by your own writing, since you have departed from orthodox doctrine and have defended impiety. And how can you expect us to receive such a document from you?

And when this answer was given by the most pious Emperor, he did not send through the same deacon any document in writing from himself. And all this was done without writing as also to your blessedness.

[*He then, according to all the mss., presented certain documents to be read, in the ms. printed by Labbe and Cossart, Tom. V., col. 549 et seqq. These are fewer than in the Paris ms., which last also contains the following just after the reading of the documents and after the Council had declared that they proved the Emperor's zeal for the faith.*]

Constantine, the most glorious Quæstor, said: While I am still present at your holy council by reason of the reading of the documents which have been presented to you, I would say that the most pious Emperor has sent a minute (*formam*), to your Holy Synod, concerning the name of Vigilius, that it be no more inserted in the holy diptychs of the

Church, on account of the impiety which he defended. Neither let it be recited by you, nor retained, either in the church of the royal city, or in other churches which are entrusted to you and to the other bishops in the State committed by God to his rule. And when you hear this minute, again you will perceive by it how much the most serene Emperor cares for the unity of the holy churches and for the purity of the holy mysteries.

[The letter was then read.]

The holy Synod said: What has seemed good to the most pious Emperor is congruous to the labours which he bears for the unity of the churches. Let us preserve unity to (*ad*) the Apostolic See of the most holy Church of ancient Rome, carrying out all things according to the tenor of what has been read. De proposita vero quæstione quod jam promisimus procedat.

The Sentence of the Synod

Our Great God and Saviour Jesus Christ, as we learn from the parable in the Gospel, distributes talents to each man according to his ability, and at the fitting time demands an account of the work done by every man. And if he to whom but one talent has been committed is condemned because he has not worked with it but only kept it without loss, to how much greater and more horrible judgment must he be subject who not only is negligent concerning himself, but even places a stumbling-block and cause of offense in the way of others? Since it is manifest to all the faithful that whenever any question arises concerning the faith, not only the impious man himself is condemned, but also he who when he has the power to correct impiety in others, neglects to do so.

We therefore, to whom it has been committed to rule the church of the Lord, fearing the curse which hangs over those who negligently perform the Lord's work, hasten to preserve the good seed of faith pure from the tares of impiety which are being sown by the enemy.

When, therefore, we saw that the followers of Nestorius were attempting to introduce their impiety into the church of God through the impious Theodore, who was bishop of Mopsuestia, and through his impious writings; and moreover through those things which Theodoret impiously wrote, and through the wicked epistle which is said to have been written by Ibas to Maris the Persian, moved by all these sights we rose up for the correction of what was going on, and assembled in this royal city called there by the will of God and the bidding of the most religious Emperor.

And because it happened that the most religious Vigilius stopping in this royal city, was present at all the discussions with regard to the Three Chapters, and had often condemned them orally and in writing, nevertheless afterwards he gave his consent in writing to be present at the Council and examine together with us the Three Chapters, that a suitable definition of the right faith might be set forth by us all. Moreover the most pious Emperor, according to what had seemed good between us, exhorted both him and us to meet together, because it is comely that the priesthood should after common discussion impose a common faith. On this account we besought his reverence to fulfil his written promises; for it was not right that the scandal with regard to these Three Chapters should go any further, and the Church of God be disturbed thereby. And to this end we brought to his remembrance the great examples left us by the Apostles, and the traditions of the Fathers. For although the grace of the Holy Spirit abounded in each one of the Apostles, so that no one of them needed the counsel of another in the execution of his work, yet they were not willing to define on the question then raised touching the circumcision of the Gentiles, until being gathered together they had confirmed their own several sayings by the testimony of the divine Scriptures.

And thus they arrived unanimously at this sentence, which they wrote to the Gentiles: It has seemed good to the Holy Ghost and to us, to lay upon you no other burden than these necessary things, that you abstain from things offered to idols, and from blood, and from things strangled, and from fornication.

But also the Holy Fathers, who from time to time have met in the four holy councils, following the example of the ancients, have by a common discussion, disposed of by a fixed decree the heresies and questions which had sprung up, as it was certainly known, that by common discussion when the matter in dispute was presented by each side, the light of truth expels the darkness of falsehood.

SEVEN ECUMENICAL COUNCILS OF THE CHURCH

Nor is there any other way in which the truth can be made manifest when there are discussions concerning the faith, since each one needs the help of his neighbour, as we read in the Proverbs of Solomon: A brother helping his brother shall be exalted like a walled city; and he shall be strong as a well-founded kingdom; and again in Ecclesiastes he says: Two are better than one; because they have a good reward for their labour.

So also the Lord himself says: Verily I say unto you that if two of you shall agree upon earth as touching anything they shall seek for, they shall have it from my Father which is in heaven. For wheresoever two or three are gathered together in my name, there am I in the midst of them.

But when often he had been invited by us all, and when the most glorious judges had been sent to him by the most religious Emperor, he promised to give sentence himself on the Three Chapters (*sententiam proferre*): And when we heard this answer, having the Apostle's admonition in mind, that each one must give an account of himself to God and fearing the judgment that hangs over those who scandalize one, even of the least important, and knowing how much sorer it must be to give offense to so entirely Christian an Emperor, and to the people, and to all the Churches; and further recalling what was said by God to Paul: Fear not, but speak, and be not silent, for I am with you, and no one can harm you. Therefore, being gathered together, before all things we have briefly confessed that we hold that faith which our Lord Jesus Christ, the true God, delivered to his holy Apostles, and through them to the holy churches, and which they who after them were holy fathers and doctors, handed down to the people credited to them.

We confessed that we hold, preserve, and declare to the holy churches that confession of faith which the 318 holy Fathers more at length set forth, who were gathered together at Nice, who handed down the holy *mathema* or creed. Moreover, the 150 gathered together at Constantinople set forth our faith, who followed that same confession of faith and explained it. And the consent of the 200 holy fathers gathered for the same faith in the first Council of Ephesus. And what things were defined by the 630 gathered at Chalcedon for the one and the same faith, which they both followed and taught. And all those who from time to time have been condemned or anathematized by the Catholic Church, and by the aforesaid four Councils, we confessed that we hold them condemned and anathematized. And when we had thus made profession of our faith we began the examination of the Three Chapters, and first we brought into review the matter of Theodore of Mopsuestia; and when all the blasphemies contained in his writings were made manifest, we marvelled at the long-suffering of God, that the tongue and mind which had framed such blasphemies were not immediately consumed by the divine fire; and we never would have suffered the reader of the aforenamed blasphemies to proceed, fearing [as we did] the indignation of God for their record alone (as each blasphemy surpassed its predecessor in the magnitude of its impiety and moved from its foundation the mind of the hearer) had it not been that we saw they who gloried in such blasphemies stood in need of the confusion which would come upon them through their manifestation. So that all of us, moved with indignation by these blasphemies against God, both during and after the reading, broke forth into denunciations and anathematisms against Theodore, as if he had been living and present. O Lord be merciful, we cried, not even devils have dared to utter such things against you.

O intolerable tongue! O the depravity of the man! O that high hand he lifted up against his Creator! For the wretched man who had promised to know the Scriptures, had no recollection of the words of the Prophet Hosea, Woe unto them! For they have fled from me: they have become famous because they were impious as touching me; they spoke iniquities against me, and when they had thought them out, they spoke the violent things against me. Therefore shall they fall in the snare by reason of the wickedness of their own tongues. Their contempt shall turn into their own bosom: because they have transgressed my covenant and have acted impiously against my laws.

To these curses the impious Theodore is justly subject. For the prophecies concerning Christ he rejected and hastened to destroy, so far as he had the power, the great mystery of the dispensation for our salvation; attempting in many ways to show the divine words to be nothing but fables, for the mirth of the gentiles, and spurned the other prophetic announcements made against the impious, especially that which the divine Habacuc said of those who teach falsely, Woe to him that gives his neighbour drink, that puts your bottle to him and makes him drunken that you may look on their nakedness, that is, their doctrines full of darkness and altogether foreign to the light.

And why should we add anything further? For anyone can take in his hands the writings of the impious Theodore or the impious chapters which from his impious writings were inserted by us in our acts, and find the incredible foolishness and the detestable things which he said. For we are afraid to proceed further and again to remember these infamies.

There was also read to us what had been written by the holy Fathers against him, and his foolishness which exceeded that of all heretics, and moreover the histories and the imperial laws, setting forth his impiety from the beginning, and since after all these things the defenders of his impiety, glorying in the injuries uttered by him against his Creator, said that it was not right to anathematize him after death, although we knew the ecclesiastical tradition concerning the impious, that even after death, heretics are anathematized; nevertheless we thought it necessary concerning this also to make examination, and there were found in the acts how various heretics had been anathematized after death; and in many ways it was manifest to us that those who were saying this cared nothing for the judgment of God, nor for the Apostolic announcements, nor for the tradition of the Fathers. And we would like to ask them what they have to say to the Lord's having said of himself: Whosoever should have believed in him, is not judged: but who should not have believed in him is judged already, because he has not believed in the name of the only begotten Son of God, and of that exclamation of the Apostle: Although we or an angel from heaven were to preach to you another gospel than that we have preached unto you, let him be anathema: as we have said, so now I say again, If anyone preach to you another gospel than that you have received, let him be anathema.

For when the Lord says: he is judged already, and when the Apostle anathematizes even angels, if they teach anything different from what we have preached, how can even those who dare all things, presume to say that these words refer only to the living? Or are they ignorant, or is it not rather that they feign to be ignorant, that the judgment of anathema is nothing else than that of separation from God? For the impious person, although he may not have been verbally anathematized by anyone, nevertheless he really is anathematized, having separated himself from the true life by his impiety.

For what have they to answer to the Apostle again when he says, A man that is an heretic reject after the first and second corrections. Knowing that such a man is perverse, and sins, and is condemned by himself.

In accordance with which words Cyril of blessed memory, in the books which he wrote against Theodore, says as follows: They are to be avoided who are in the grasp of such awful crimes whether they be among the quick or not. For it is necessary always to flee from that which is hurtful, and not to have respect of persons, but to consider what is pleasing to God. And again the same Cyril of holy memory, writing to John, bishop of Antioch, and to the synod assembled in that city concerning Theodore who was anathematized together with Nestorius, says thus: It was therefore necessary to keep a brilliant festival, since every voice which agreed with the blasphemies of Nestorius had been cast out no matter whose. For it proceeded against all those who held these same opinions or had at one time held them, which is exactly what we and your holiness have said: We anathematize those who say that there are two Sons and two Christs. For one is he who is preached by us and you, as we have said, Christ, the Son and Lord, only begotten as man, according to the saying of the most learned Paul. And also in his letter to Alexander and Martinian and John and Paregorius and Maximus, presbyters and monastic fathers, and those who with them were leading the solitary life, he so says: The holy synod of Ephesus, gathered together according to the will of God against the Nestorian perfidy with a just and keen sentence condemned together with him the empty words of those who afterwards should embrace or who had in time past embraced the same opinions with him, and who presumed to say or write any such thing, laying upon them an equal condemnation. For it followed naturally that when one was condemned for such profane emptiness of speech, the sentence should not come against one only, but (so to speak) against every one of their heresies or calumnies, which they utter against the pious doctrines of the Christ, worshipping two Sons, and dividing the indivisible, and bringing in the crime of man-worship (*anthropolatry*), both into heaven and earth. For with us the holy multitude of the supernal spirits adore one Lord Jesus Christ. Moreover several letters of Augustine, of most religious memory, who shone forth resplendent among the African bishops, were read, showing that it was quite right that heretics should be anathematized after death. And this ecclesiastical tradition, the other most reverend bishops of Africa have preserved: and the holy Roman Church as well had anathematized certain bishops after their death, although they had not been accused of any falling from the faith during their lives: and of each we have the evidence in our hands.

But since the disciples of Theodore and of his impiety, who are so manifestly enemies of the truth, have attempted to bring forward certain passages of Cyril of holy memory and of Proclus, as though they had been written in favour of Theodore, it is opportune to fit to them the words of the prophet when he says: The ways of the Lord are right and the just walk therein; but the wicked shall be weak in them. For these, evilly receiving the things which have been well and opportunely written by the holy Fathers, and making excuses in their sins, quote these words. The fathers do not appear as delivering Theodore from anathema, but rather as economically using certain expressions on account of those who defended Nestorius and his impiety, in order to draw them away from this error, and to lead them to perfection and to teach them to condemn not only Nestorius, the disciple of the impiety, but also his teacher Theodore. So in these very words of economy the Fathers show their intention on this point, that Theodore should be anathematized, as has been abundantly demonstrated by us in our acts from the writings of Cyril and Proclus of holy memory with regard to the condemnation of Theodore and his impiety. And such economy is found in divine Scripture: and it is evident that Paul the Apostle made use of this in the beginning of his ministry, in relation to those who had been brought up as Jews, and circumcised Timothy, that by this economy and condescension he might lead them on to perfection. But afterwards he forbade circumcision, writing thus to the Galatians: Behold, I Paul say to you, that if you be circumcised Christ profits you nothing. But we found that that which heretics were wont to do, the defenders of Theodore had done also. For cutting out certain of the things which the holy Fathers had written, and placing with them and mixing up certain false things of their own, they have tried by a letter of Cyril of holy memory as though from a testimony of the Fathers, to free from anathema the aforesaid impious Theodore: in which very passages the truth was demonstrated, when the parts which had been cut off were read in their proper order, and the falsehood was thoroughly evinced by the collation of the true. But in all these things, they who spoke such vanities, trusted in falsehood, as it is written, they trust in falsehood, and speak vanity; they conceive grief and bring forth iniquity, weaving the spider's web. When we had thus considered Theodore and his impiety, we took care to have recited and inserted in our acts a few of these things which had been impiously written by Theodoret against the right faith and against the Twelve Chapters of St. Cyril and against the First Council of Ephesus, also certain things written by him in defense of those impious ones Theodore and Nestorius, for the satisfaction of the reader; that all might know that these had been justly cast out and anathematized. In the third place the letter which is said to have been written by Ibas to Maris the Persian, was brought forward for examination, and we found that it, too, should be read. When it was read immediately its impiety was manifest to all. And it was right to make the condemnation and anathematism of the aforesaid Three Chapters, as even to this time there had been some question on the subject. But because the defenders of these impious ones, Theodore and Nestorius, were scheming in some way or other to confirm these persons and their impiety, and were saying that this impious letter, which praised and defended Theodore and Nestorius and their impiety, had been received by the holy Council of Chalcedon we thought it necessary to show that the holy synod was free of the impiety which was contained in that letter, that it might be clear that they who say such things do not do so with the favour of this holy council, but that through its name they may confirm their own impiety. And it was shown in the acts that in former times Ibas had been accused because of the very impiety which is contained in this letter; at first by Proclus, of holy memory, the bishop of Constantinople, and afterwards by Theodosius, of pious memory, and by Flavian, who was ordained bishop in succession to Proclus, who delegated the examination of the matter to Photius, bishop of Tyre, and to Eustathius, bishop of the city of Beyroot. Afterwards the same Ibas, being found guilty, was cast out of his bishopric. Such was the state of the case, how could anyone presume to say that that impious letter was received by the holy council of Chalcedon and that the holy council of Chalcedon agreed with it throughout? Nevertheless in order that they who thus calumniate the holy council of Chalcedon may have no further opportunity of doing so, we ordered to be recited the decisions of the holy Synods, to wit, of first Ephesus, and of Chalcedon, with regard to the Epistles of Cyril of blessed memory and of Leo, of pious memory, sometime Pope of Old Rome. And since we had learned from these that nothing written by anyone else ought to be received unless it had been proved to agree with the orthodox faith of the holy Fathers, we interrupted our proceedings so as to recite also the definition of the faith which was set forth by the holy council of Chalcedon, so that we might compare the things in the epistle with this decree. And when this was done it was perfectly clear that the contents of the epistle were wholly opposite to those of the definition.

For the definition agreed with the one and unchanging faith set forth as well by the 318 holy Fathers as by the 150 and by those who assembled at the first synod at Ephesus. But that impious letter, on the other hand, contained the blasphemies of the heretics Theodore and Nestorius, and defended them, and calls them doctors, while it calls the holy Fathers heretics.

And this we made manifest to all, that we did not have any intention of omitting the Fathers of the first and second interlocutions, which the followers of Theodore and Nestorius cited on their side, but these and all the others having been read and their contents examined, we found that the aforesaid Ibas was not allowed to be received without being compelled to anathematize Nestorius and his impious teachings, which were defended in that epistle. And this the rest of the religious bishops of the aforesaid holy Council did as well as those two whose interlocutions certain tried to use.

For this they observed in the case of Theodoret, and required him to anathematize those things of which he was accused. If therefore they were willing to allow the reception of Ibas in no other manner unless he condemned the impiety which was contained in his letters, and subscribed the definition of faith adopted by the Council, how can they attempt to make out that this impious letter was received by the same holy council? For we are taught, What fellowship has righteousness with unrighteousness? And what communion has light with darkness? And what concord has Christ with Belial? Or what part has he that believes with an infidel? And what agreement has the temple of God with idols.

SEVEN ECUMENICAL COUNCILS OF THE CHURCH

Having thus detailed all that has been done by us, we again confess that we receive the four holy Synods, that is, the Nicene, the Constantinopolitan, the first of Ephesus, and that of Chalcedon, and we have taught, and do teach all that they defined respecting the one faith. And we account those who do not receive these things aliens from the Catholic Church. Moreover we condemn and anathematize, together with all the other heretics who have been condemned and anathematized by the before-mentioned four holy Synods, and by the holy Catholic and Apostolic Church, Theodore who was Bishop of Mopsuestia, and his impious writings, and also those things which Theodoret impiously wrote against the right faith, and against the Twelve Chapters of the holy Cyril, and against the first Synod of Ephesus, and also those which he wrote in defense of Theodore and Nestorius. In addition to these we also anathematize the impious Epistle which Ibas is said to have written to Maris, the Persian, which denies that God the Word was incarnate of the holy Mother of God, and ever Virgin Mary, and accuses Cyril of holy memory, who taught the truth, as an heretic, and of the same sentiments with Apollinaris, and blames the first Synod of Ephesus as deposing Nestorius without examination and inquiry, and calls the Twelve Chapters of the holy Cyril impious, and contrary to the right faith, and defends Theodorus and Nestorius, and their impious dogmas and writings. We therefore anathematize the Three Chapters before-mentioned, that is, the impious Theodore of Mopsuestia, with his execrable writings, and those things which Theodoret impiously wrote, and the impious letter which is said to be of Ibas, and their defenders, and those who have written or do write in defense of them, or who dare to say that they are correct, and who have defended or attempt to defend their impiety with the names of the holy Fathers, or of the holy Council of Chalcedon. These things therefore being settled with all accuracy, we, bearing in remembrance the promises made respecting the holy Church, and who it was that said that the gates of hell should not prevail against her, that is, the deadly tongues of heretics; remembering also what was prophesied respecting it by Hosea, saying, I will betroth you unto me in faithfulness, and you shall know the Lord, and numbering together with the devil, the father of lies, the unbridled tongues of heretics who persevered in their impiety unto death, and their most impious writings, will say to them, Behold, as you kindle a fire, and cause the flame of the fire to grow strong, you shall walk in the light of your fire, and the flame which you kindle. But we, having a commandment to exhort the people with right doctrine, and to speak to the heart of Jerusalem, that is, the Church of God, do rightly make haste to sow in righteousness, and to reap the fruit of life; and kindling for ourselves the light of knowledge from the holy Scriptures, and the doctrine of the Fathers, we have considered it necessary to comprehend in certain Capitula, both the declaration of the truth, and the condemnation of heretics, and of their wickedness.

The Capitula of the Council

1

If anyone shall not confess that the nature or essence of the Father, of the Son, and of the Holy Ghost is one, as also the force and the power; [if anyone does not confess] a consubstantial Trinity, one Godhead to be worshipped in three subsistences or Persons: let him be anathema. For there is but one God even the Father of whom are all things, and one Lord Jesus Christ through whom are all things, and one Holy Spirit in whom are all things.

2

If anyone shall not confess that the Word of God has two nativities, the one from all eternity of the Father, without time and without body; the other in these last days, coming down from heaven and being made flesh of the holy and glorious Mary, Mother of God and always a virgin, and born of her: let him be anathema.

3

If anyone shall say that the wonder-working Word of God is one [Person] and the Christ that suffered another; or shall say that God the Word was with the woman-born Christ, or was in him as one person in another, but that he was not one and the same our Lord Jesus Christ, the Word of God, incarnate and made man, and that his miracles and the sufferings which of his own will he endured in the flesh were not of the same [Person]: let him be anathema.

4

If anyone shall say that the union of the Word of God to man was only according to grace or energy, or dignity, or equality of honour, or authority, or relation, or effect, or power, or according to good pleasure in this sense that God the Word was pleased with a man, that is to say, that he loved him for his own sake, as says the senseless Theodorus, or [if anyone pretends that this union exists only] so far as likeness of name is concerned, as the Nestorians understand, who call also the Word of God Jesus and Christ, and even accord to the man the names of Christ and of Son, speaking thus clearly of two persons, and only designating disingenuously one Person and one Christ when the reference is to his honour, or his dignity, or his worship; if anyone shall not acknowledge as the Holy Fathers teach, that the union of God the Word is made with the flesh animated by a reasonable and living soul, and that such union is made synthetically and hypostatically, and that therefore there is only one Person, to wit: our Lord Jesus Christ, one of the Holy Trinity: let him be anathema. As a matter of fact the word union (τῆς ἑνώςεως) has many meanings, and the partisans of Apollinaris and Eutyches have affirmed that these natures are confounded *inter se*, and have asserted a union produced by the mixture of both. On the other hand the followers of Theodorus and of Nestorius rejoicing in the division of the natures, have taught only a relative union. Meanwhile the Holy Church of God, condemning equally the impiety of both sorts of heresies, recognises the union of God the Word with the flesh synthetically, that is to say, hypostatically. For in the mystery of Christ the synthetical union not only preserves unconfusedly the natures which are united, but also allows no separation.

5

If anyone understands the expression one only Person of our Lord Jesus Christ in this sense, that it is the union of many hypostases, and if he attempts thus to introduce into the mystery of Christ two hypostases, or two Persons, and, after having introduced two persons, speaks of one Person only out of dignity, honour or worship, as both Theodorus and Nestorius insanely have written; if anyone shall calumniate the holy Council of Chalcedon, pretending that it made use of this expression [one hypostasis] in this impious sense, and if he will not recognize rather that the Word of God is united with the flesh hypostatically, and that therefore there is but one hypostasis or one only Person, and that the holy Council of Chalcedon has professed in this sense the one Person of our Lord Jesus Christ: let him be anathema. For since one of the Holy Trinity has been made man, viz.: God the Word, the Holy Trinity has not been increased by the addition of another person or hypostasis.

6

If anyone shall not call in a true acceptation, but only in a false acceptation, the holy, glorious, and ever-virgin Mary, the Mother of God, or shall call her so only in a relative sense, believing that she bare only a simple man and that God the word was not incarnate of her, but that the incarnation of God the Word resulted only from the fact that he united himself to that man who was born [of her]; if he shall calumniate the Holy Synod of Chalcedon as though it had asserted the Virgin to be Mother of God according to the impious sense of Theodore; or if anyone shall call her the mother of a man (ἀνθρωποτόκον) or the Mother of Christ (Χριστοτόκον), as if Christ were not God, and shall not confess that she is exactly and truly the Mother of God, because that God the Word who before all ages was begotten of the Father was in these last days made flesh and born of her, and if anyone shall not confess that in this sense the holy Synod of Chalcedon acknowledged her to be the Mother of God: let him be anathema.

7

If anyone using the expression, in two natures, does not confess that our one Lord Jesus Christ has been revealed in the divinity and in the humanity, so as to designate by that expression a difference of the natures of which an ineffable union is unconfusedly made, [a union] in which neither the nature of the Word was changed into that of the flesh, nor that of the flesh into that of the Word, for each remained that it was by nature, the union being hypostatic; but shall take the expression with regard to the mystery of Christ in a sense so as to divide the parties, or recognising the two natures in the only Lord Jesus, God the Word made man, does not content himself with taking in a theoretical manner the difference of the natures which compose him, which difference is not destroyed by the union between them, for one is composed of the two and the two are in one, but shall make use of the number [two] to divide the natures or to make of them Persons properly so called: let him be anathema.

8

If anyone uses the expression of two natures, confessing that a union was made of the Godhead and of the humanity, or the expression the one nature made flesh of God the Word, and shall not so understand those expressions as the holy Fathers have taught, to wit: that of the divine and human nature there was made an hypostatic union, whereof is one Christ; but from these expressions shall try to introduce one nature or substance [made by a mixture] of the Godhead and manhood of Christ; let him be anathema. For in teaching that the only-begotten Word was united hypostatically [to humanity] we do not mean to say that there was made a mutual confusion of natures, but rather each [nature] remaining what it was, we understand that the Word was united to the flesh. Wherefore there is one Christ, both God and man, consubstantial with the Father as touching his Godhead, and consubstantial with us as touching his manhood. Therefore they are equally condemned and anathematized by the Church of God, who divide or part the mystery of the divine dispensation of Christ, or who introduce confusion into that mystery.

9

If anyone shall take the expression, Christ ought to be worshipped in his two natures, in the sense that he wishes to introduce thus two adorations, the one in special relation to God the Word and the other as pertaining to the man; or if anyone to get rid of the flesh, [that is of the humanity of Christ,] or to mix together the divinity and the humanity, shall speak monstrously of one only nature or essence (φύσιν ἤγουν οὐσίαν) of the united (natures), and so worship Christ, and does not venerate, by one adoration, God the Word made man, together with his flesh, as the Holy Church has taught from the beginning: let him be anathema.

10

If anyone does not confess that our Lord Jesus Christ who was crucified in the flesh is true God and the Lord of Glory and one of the Holy Trinity: let him be anathema.

11

If anyone does not anathematize Arius, Eunomius, Macedonius, Apollinaris, Nestorius, Eutyches and Origen, as well as their impious writings, as also all other heretics already condemned and anathematized by the Holy Catholic and Apostolic Church, and by the aforesaid four Holy Synods and [if anyone does not equally anathematize] all those who have held and hold or who in their impiety persist in holding to the end the same opinion as those heretics just mentioned: let him be anathema.

12

If anyone defends the impious Theodore of Mopsuestia, who has said that the Word of God is one person, but that another person is Christ, vexed by the sufferings of the soul and the desires of the flesh, and separated little by little above that which is inferior, and become better by the progress in good works and irreproachable in his manner of life, as a mere man was baptized in the name of the Father, and of the Son, and of the Holy Ghost, and obtained by this baptism the grace of the Holy Spirit, and became worthy of Sonship, and to be worshipped out of regard to the Person of God the Word (just as one worships the image of an emperor) and that he has become, after the resurrection, unchangeable in his thoughts and altogether without sin. And, again, this same impious Theodore has also said that the union of God the Word with Christ is like to that which, according to the doctrine of the Apostle, exists between a man and his wife, They two shall be in one flesh. The same [Theodore] has dared, among numerous other blasphemies, to say that when after the resurrection the Lord breathed upon his disciples, saying, Receive the Holy Ghost, he did not really give them the Holy Spirit, but that he breathed upon them only as a sign. He likewise has said that the profession of faith made by Thomas when he had, after the resurrection, touched the hands and the side of the Lord, viz.: My Lord and my God, was not said in reference to Christ, but that Thomas, filled with wonder at the miracle of the resurrection, thus thanked God who had raised up Christ. And moreover (which is still more scandalous) this same Theodore in his Commentary on the Acts of the Apostles compares Christ to Plato, Manichæus, Epicurus and Marcion, and says that as each of these men having discovered his own doctrine, had given his name to his disciples, who were called Platonists, Manicheans, Epicureans and Marcionites, just so Christ, having discovered his doctrine, had given the name Christians to his disciples. If, then, anyone shall defend this most impious Theodore and his impious writings, in which he vomits the blasphemies mentioned above, and countless others besides against our Great God and Saviour Jesus Christ, and if anyone does not anathematize him or his impious writings, as well as all those who protect or defend him, or who assert that his exegesis is orthodox, or who write in favour of him and of his impious works, or those who share the same opinions, or those who have shared them and still continue unto the end in this heresy: let him be anathema.

13

If anyone shall defend the impious writings of Theodoret, directed against the true faith and against the first holy Synod of Ephesus and against St. Cyril and his XII. Anathemas, and [defends] that which he has written in defense of the impious Theodore and Nestorius, and of others having the same opinions as the aforesaid Theodore and Nestorius, if anyone admits them or their impiety, or shall give the name of impious to the doctors of the Church who profess the hypostatic union of God the Word; and if anyone does not anathematize these impious writings and those who have held or who hold these sentiments, and all those who have written contrary to the true faith or against St. Cyril and his XII. Chapters, and who die in their impiety: let him be anathema.

14

If anyone shall defend that letter which Ibas is said to have written to Maris the Persian, in which he denies that the Word of God incarnate of Mary, the Holy Mother of God and ever-virgin, was made man, but says that a mere man was born of her, whom he styles a Temple, as though the Word of God was one Person and the man another person; in which letter also he reprehends St. Cyril as a heretic, when he teaches the right faith of Christians, and charges him with writing things like to the wicked Apollinaris. In addition to this he vituperates the First Holy Council of Ephesus, affirming that it deposed Nestorius without discrimination and without examination. The aforesaid impious epistle styles the XII. Chapters of Cyril of blessed memory, impious and contrary to the right faith and defends Theodore and Nestorius and their impious teachings and writings. If anyone therefore shall defend the aforementioned epistle and shall not anathematize it and those who defend it and say that it is right or that a part of it is right, or if anyone shall defend those who have written or shall write in its favour, or in defense of the impieties which are contained in it, as well as those who shall presume to defend it or the impieties which it contains in the name of the Holy Fathers or of the Holy Synod of Chalcedon, and shall remain in these offenses unto the end: let him be anathema.

The Anathemas Against Origen

1

If anyone asserts the fabulous pre-existence of souls, and shall assert the monstrous restoration which follows from it: let him be anathema.

2

If anyone shall say that the creation (τὴυ παραγωγὴν) of all reasonable things includes only intelligences (νόας) without bodies and altogether immaterial, having neither number nor name, so that there is unity between them all by identity of substance, force and energy, and by their union with and knowledge of God the Word; but that no longer desiring the sight of God, they gave themselves over to worse things, each one following his own inclinations, and that they have taken bodies more or less subtle, and have received names, for among the heavenly Powers there is a difference of names as there is also a difference of bodies; and thence some became and are called Cherubims, others Seraphims, and Principalities, and Powers, and Dominations, and Thrones, and Angels, and as many other heavenly orders as there may be: let him be anathema.

3

If anyone shall say that the sun, the moon and the stars are also reasonable beings, and that they have only become what they are because they turned towards evil: let him be anathema.

4

If anyone shall say that the reasonable creatures in whom the divine love had grown cold have been hidden in gross bodies such as ours, and have been called men, while those who have attained the lowest degree of wickedness have shared cold and obscure bodies and have become and called demons and evil spirits: let him be anathema,.

5

If anyone shall say that a psychic (ψυχικὴν) condition has come from an angelic or archangelic state, and moreover that a demoniac and a human condition has come from a psychic condition, and that from a human state they may become again angels and demons, and that each order of heavenly virtues is either all from those below or from those above, or from those above and below: let him be anathema.

6

If anyone shall say that there is a twofold race of demons, of which the one includes the souls of men and the other the superior spirits who fell to this, and that of all the number of reasonable beings there is but one which has remained unshaken in the love and contemplation of God, and that that spirit has become Christ and the king of all reasonable beings, and that he has created all the bodies which exist in heaven, on earth, and between heaven and earth; and that the world which has in itself elements more ancient than itself, and which exists by themselves, viz.: dryness, damp, heat and cold, and the image (ιδέαν) to which it was formed, was so formed, and that the most holy and consubstantial Trinity did not create the world, but that it was created by the working intelligence (Ν οὖς δημιουργός) which is more ancient than the world, and which communicates to it its being: let him be anathema.

7

If anyone shall say that Christ, of whom it is said that he appeared in the form of God, and that he was united before all time with God the Word, and humbled himself in these last days even to humanity, had (according to their expression) pity upon the various falls which had appeared in the spirits united in the same unity (of which he himself is part), and that to restore them he passed through various classes, had different bodies and different names, became all to all, an Angel among Angels, a Power among Powers, has clothed himself in the different classes of reasonable beings with a form corresponding to that class, and finally has taken flesh and blood like ours and has become man for men; [if anyone says all this] and does not profess that God the Word humbled himself and became man: let him be anathema.

8

If anyone shall not acknowledge that God the Word, of the same substance with the Father and the Holy Ghost, and who was made flesh and became man, one of the Trinity, is Christ in every sense of the word, but [shall affirm] that he is so only in an inaccurate manner, and because of the abasement (κενώσαντα), as they call it, of the intelligence (νοῦς); if anyone shall affirm that this intelligence united (συνημμένον) to God the Word, is the Christ in the true sense of the word, while the Logos is only called Christ because of this union with the intelligence, and *e converso* that the intelligence is only called God because of the Logos: let him be anathema.

9

If anyone shall say that it was not the Divine Logos made man by taking an animated body with a ψυχὴ˙ λογικὴ and νοερὰ, that he descended into hell and ascended into heaven, but shall pretend that it is the Ν οῦς which has done this, that Ν οῦς of which they say (in an impious fashion) he is Christ properly so called, and that he has become so by the knowledge of the Monad: let him be anathema.

10

If anyone shall say that after the resurrection the body of the Lord was ethereal, having the form of a sphere, and that such shall be the bodies of all after the resurrection; and that after the Lord himself shall have rejected his true body and after the others who rise shall have rejected theirs, the nature of their bodies shall be annihilated: let him be anathema.

11

If anyone shall say that the future judgment signifies the destruction of the body and that the end of the story will be an immaterial ψύσις, and that thereafter there will no longer be any matter, but only spirit νοῦς): let him be anathema.

12

If anyone shall say that the heavenly Powers and all men and the Devil and evil spirits are united with the Word of God in all respects, as the Νοῦς which is by them called Christ and which is in the form of God, and which humbled itself as they say; and [if anyone shall say] that the Kingdom of Christ shall have an end: let him be anathema.

13

If anyone shall say that Christ [i.e., the Νοῦς] is in no wise different from other reasonable beings, neither substantially nor by wisdom nor by his power and might over all things but that all will be placed at the right hand of God, as well as he that is called by them Christ [the Νοῦς], as also they were in the feigned pre-existence of all things: let him be anathema.

14

If anyone shall say that all reasonable beings will one day be united in one, when the hypostases as well as the numbers and the bodies shall have disappeared, and that the knowledge of the world to come will carry with it the ruin of the worlds, and the rejection of bodies as also the abolition of [all] names, and that there shall be finally an identity of the γνῶσις and of the hypostasis; moreover, that in this pretended apocatastasis, spirits only will continue to exist, as it was in the feigned pre-existence: let him be anathema.

15

If anyone shall say that the life of the spirits (νοῶν) shall be like to the life which was in the beginning while as yet the spirits had not come down or fallen, so that the end and the beginning shall be alike, and that the end shall be the true measure of the beginning: let him be anathema.

The Anathemas of the Emperor Justinian Against Origen

1

Whoever says or thinks that human souls pre-existed, i.e., that they had previously been spirits and holy powers, but that, satiated with the vision of God, they had turned to evil, and in this way the divine love in them had died out (ἀπψυγείσας) and they had therefore become souls (ψυχάς) and had been condemned to punishment in bodies, shall be anathema.

2

If anyone says or thinks that the soul of the Lord pre-existed and was united with God the Word before the Incarnation and Conception of the Virgin, let him be anathema.

3

If anyone says or thinks that the body of our Lord Jesus Christ was first formed in the womb of the holy Virgin and that afterwards there was united with it God the Word and the pre-existing soul, let him be anathema.

4

If anyone says or thinks that the Word of God has become like to all heavenly orders, so that for the cherubim he was a cherub, for the seraphim a seraph: in short, like all the superior powers, let him be anathema.

5

If anyone says or thinks that, at the resurrection, human bodies will rise spherical in form and unlike our present form, let him be anathema.

6

If anyone says that the heaven, the sun, the moon, the stars, and the waters that are above heavens, have souls, and are reasonable beings, let him be anathema.

7

If anyone says or thinks that Christ the Lord in a future time will be crucified for demons as he was for men, let him be anathema.

8

If anyone says or thinks that the power of God is limited, and that he created as much as he was able to compass, let him be anathema.

9

If anyone says or thinks that the punishment of demons and of impious men is only temporary, and will one day have an end, and that a restoration (ἀποκατάστασις) will take place of demons and of impious men, let him be anathema.

Anathema to Origen and to that Adamantius, who set forth these opinions together with his nefarious and execrable and wicked doctrine and to whomsoever there is who thinks thus, or defends these opinions, or in any way hereafter at any time shall presume to protect them.

The Decretal Epistle of Pope Vigilius in Confirmation of the Fifth Ecumenical Synod

At last the Pope Vigilius resigned himself to the advice of the Council, and six months afterwards wrote a letter to the Patriarch Eutychius, wherein he confesses that he has been wanting in charity in dividing from his brethren. He adds, that one ought not to be ashamed to retract, when one recognises the truth, and brings forward the example of Augustine. He says, that, after having better examined the matter of the Three Chapters, he finds them worthy of condemnation. We recognize for our brethren and colleagues all those who have condemned them, and annul by this writing all that has been done by us or by others for the defense of the three chapters.

The manuscript from which this letter was printed was found in the Royal Library of Paris by Peter de Marca and by him first published, with a Latin translation and with a dissertation. Both of these with the Greek text are found in Labbe and Cossart's *Concilia*, Tom. V., col. 596 *et seqq.*; also in Migne's *Patr. Lat.*, Tom. LXIX., col. 121 *et seqq*. Some doubts have been expressed about its genuineness and Hardouin is of opinion that the learned Jesuit, Garnerius, in his notes on the Deacon Leberatus's *Breviary*, has proved its supposititious character. But the learned have not generally been of this mind but have accepted the letter as genuine.

Vigilius to his beloved brother Eutychius.

No one is ignorant of the scandals which the enemy of the human race has stirred up in all the world: so that he made each one with a wicked object in view, striving in some way to fulfil his wish to destroy the Church of God spread over the whole world, not only in his own name but even in ours and in those of others to compose diverse things as well in words as in writing; in so much that he attempted to divide us who, together with our brethren and fellow bishops, are stopping in this royal city, and who defend with equal reverence the four synods, and sincerely persist in the one and the same faith of those four synods, by his sophistries and machinations he tried to part from them; so that we ourselves who were and are of the same opinion as they touching the faith, went apart into discord, brotherly love being despised.

But since Christ our God, who is the true light, whom the darkness comprehends not, has removed all confusion from our minds, and has so recalled peace to the whole world and to the Church, so that what things should be defined by us have been healthfully fulfilled through the revelation of the Lord and through the investigation of the truth.

Therefore, my dear brothers, I do you to wit, that in common with all of you, our brethren, we receive in all respects the four synods, that is to say the Nicene, the Constantinopolitan, the first Ephesian, and the Chalcedonian; and we venerate them with devout mind, and watch over them with all our mind. And should there be any who do not follow these holy synods in all things which they have defined concerning the faith, we judge them to be aliens to the communion of the holy and Catholic Church.

Wherefore on account of our desire that you, my brothers, should know what we have done in this matter, we make it known to you by this letter. For no one can doubt how many were the discussions raised on account of the Three Chapters, that is, concerning Theodore, sometime bishop of Mopsuestia, and his writings, as well as concerning the writings of Theodoret, and concerning that letter which is said to have been written by Ibas to Maris the Persian: and how diverse were the things spoken and written concerning these Three Chapters. Now if in every business sound wisdom demands that there should be a retractation of what was propounded after examination, there ought to be no shame when what was at first omitted is made public after it is discovered by a further study of the truth. [And if this is the case in ordinary affairs] how much more in ecclesiastical strifes should the same dictate of sound reason be observed? Especially since it is manifest that our Fathers, and especially the blessed Augustine, who was in very truth illustrious in the Divine Scriptures, and a master in Roman eloquence, retracted some of his own writings, and corrected some of his own sayings, and added what he had omitted and afterward found out. We, led by their example never gave over the study of the questions raised by the controversy with regard to the before-mentioned Three Chapters, nor our search for passages in the writings of our Fathers which were applicable to the matter.

As a result of this investigation it became evident that in the sayings of Theodore of Mopsuestia (which are spoken against on all hands) there are contained very many things contrary to the right faith and to the teachings of the holy Fathers; and for this very reason these same holy Fathers have left for the instruction of the Church treatises which they had written against him.

For among other blasphemies of his we find that he openly said that God the Word was one [Person] and Christ another [Person], vexed with the passions of the soul and with the desires of the flesh, and that he little by little advanced from a lower to a higher stage of excellence by the improvement (προκοπῇ, *per profectum operum*) of his works, and became irreprehensible in his manner of life. And further he taught that it was a mere man who was baptized in the Name of the Father and of the Son and of the Holy Ghost, and that he received through his baptism the grace of the Holy Spirit, and merited his adoption; and therefore that Christ could be venerated in the same way that the image of the Emperor is venerated as being the persona (εἰς πρόσωπον) of God the Word. And he also taught that [only] after his resurrection he became immutable in his thoughts and altogether impeccable.

Moreover he said that the union of the Word of God was made with Christ as the Apostle says the union is made between a man and his wife: They two shall be one flesh; and that after his resurrection, when the Lord breathed upon his disciples and said, Receive the Holy Ghost, he did not give to them the Holy Spirit. In like strain of profanity he dared to say that the confession which Thomas made, when he touched the hands and side of the Lord after his resurrection, saying, My Lord and my God, did not apply to Christ (for Theodore did not acknowledge Christ to be God); but that Thomas gave glory to God being filled with wonder at the miracle of the resurrection, and so said these words.

But what is still worse is this, that in interpreting the Acts of the Apostles, Theodore makes Christ like to Plato, and Manichæus, and Epicurus, and Marcian, saying: Just as each of these were the authors of their own peculiar teachings, and called their disciples after their own names, Platonists, and Manichæans, and Epicureans, and Marcionites, just so Christ invented dogmas and called his followers Christians after himself.

Let therefore the whole Catholic Church know that justly and irreproachably we have arrived at the conclusions contained in this our constitution. Wherefore we condemn and anathematize Theodore, formerly bishop of Mopsuestia, and his impious writings, together with all other heretics, who (as is manifest) have been condemned and anathematized by the four holy Synods aforesaid, and by the Catholic Church: also the writings of Theodoret which are opposed to the right faith, and are against the Twelve Chapters of St. Cyril, and against the first Council of Ephesus, which were written by him in defense of Theodore and Nestorius.

Moreover we anathematize and condemn the letter to the Persian heretic Maris, which is said to have been written by Ibas, which denies that Christ the Word was incarnate of the holy Mother of God and ever-virgin Mary, and was made man, but declares that a mere man was born of her, and this man it styles a temple, so from this we are given to understand that God the Word is one [Person] and Christ another [Person]. Moreover it calumniates Saint Cyril, the master and herald of the orthodox faith, calling him a heretic, and charging him with writing things similar to Apollinaris; and it reviles the first Synod of Ephesus, as having condemned Nestorius without deliberation or investigation; it likewise declares the twelve chapters of St. Cyril to be impious and contrary to the right faith; and further still it defends Theodore and Nestorius, and their impious teachings and writings.

Therefore we anathematize and condemn the aforesaid impious Three Chapters, to-wit, the impious Theodore of Mopsuestia and his impious writings; And all that Theodoret impiously wrote, as well as the letter said to have been written by Ibas, in which are contained the above mentioned profane blasphemies. We likewise subject to anathema whoever shall at any time believe that these chapters should be received or defended; or shall attempt to subvert this present condemnation.

And further we define that they are our brethren and fellow priests who ever keep the right faith set forth by those afore-mentioned synods, and shall have condemned the above-named Three Chapters, or even do now condemn them.

And further we annul and evacuate by this present written definition of ours whatever has been said by me (*a me*) or by others in defense of the aforesaid Three Chapters.

Far be it from the Catholic Church that anyone should say that all the blasphemies above related or they who held and followed such things, were received by the before-mentioned four synods or by any one of them. For it is most clear, that no one was admitted by the before-mentioned holy Fathers and especially by the Council of Chalcedon, about whom there was any suspicion, unless he had first repelled the above-named blasphemies and all like to them, or else had denied and condemned the heresy or blasphemies of which he was suspected.

Subscription

May God preserve you in health, most honourable brother. Dated VI. Id. Dec. in the twenty-second year of our lord the Emperor Justinian, eternal Augustus, the twelfth year after the consulate of the illustrious Basil.

SEVEN ECUMENICAL COUNCILS OF THE CHURCH

COUNCIL OF THIRD CONSTANTINOPLE

SEVEN ECUMENICAL COUNCILS OF THE CHURCH

Session I
Extracts from the Acts

After a history of the assembly of the Council, the Acts begin with the Speech of the Papal Legates, as follows:

Most benign lord, in accordance with the Sacra to our most holy Pope from your God-instructed majesty, we have been sent by him to the most holy footsteps of your God-confirmed serenity, bearing with us his suggestion (ἀναφορᾶς, suggestione) as well as the other suggestion of his Synod equally addressed to your divinely preserved Piety by the venerable bishops subject to it, which also we offered to your God-crowned Fortitude. Since, then, during the past forty-six years, more or less, certain novelties in expression, contrary to the Orthodox faith, have been introduced by those who were at several times bishops of this, your royal and God-preserved city, to wit: Sergius, Paul, Pyrrhus, and Peter, as also by Cyrus, at one time archbishop of the city of Alexandria, as well also as by Theodore, who was bishop of a city called Pharan, and by certain others their followers, and since these things have in no small degree brought confusion into the Church throughout the whole world, for they taught dogmatically that there was but one will in the dispensation of the Incarnation of our Lord Jesus Christ, one of the Holy Trinity, and one operation; and since many times your servant, our apostolic see, has fought against this, and then prayed against it, and by no means been able, even up to now, to draw away from such a depraved opinion its advocates, we beseech your God-crowned fortitude, that such as share these views of the most holy church of Constantinople may tell us, what is the source of this new-fangled language.

Answer of the Monothelites made at the Emperor's bidding:

We have brought out no new method of speech, but have taught whatever we have received from the holy Ecumenical Synods, and from the holy approved Fathers, as well as from the archbishops of this imperial city, to wit: Sergius, Paul, Pyrrhus, and Peter, as also from Honorius who was Pope of Old Rome, and from Cyrus who was Pope of Alexandria, that is to say with reference to will and operation, and so we have believed, and so we believe, so we preach; and further we are ready to stand by, and defend this faith.
The Letter of Agatho, Pope of Old Rome, to the Emperor, and the Letter of Agatho and of 125 Bishops of the Roman Synod, Addressed to the Sixth Council

Read at the Fourth Session, November 15, at the request of George, Patriarch of Constantinople and his Suffragans.

SEVEN ECUMENICAL COUNCILS OF THE CHURCH

Introductory Note

All the fathers spoke one by one, and only after examination were the letters of St. Agatho and the whole Western Council approved. Agatho, indeed, and the Western Bishops put forth their decrees thus ['We have directed persons from our humility to your valour protected of God, which shall offer to you the report of us all, that is, of all the Bishops in the Northern or Western Regions, in which too we have summed up the confession of our Apostolic Faith, yet] not as those who wished to contend about these things as being uncertain, but, being certain and unchangeable to see them forth in a brief definition, [suppliantly beseeching you that, by the favour of your sacred majesty, you would command these same things to be preached to all, and to have force with all.'] Undoubtedly, therefore, so far as in them lay, they defined the matter. The question was, whether the other Churches throughout the world would agree, and a matter so great was only made clear after Episcopal examination. But the high, magnificent, yet true expressions, which St. Agatho had used of his See, namely, that resting on the promise of the Lord it had never turned aside from the path of truth, and that its Pontiffs, the predecessors of Agatho, who were charged in the person of Peter to strengthen their brethren, had ever discharged that office, this the Fathers of the Council hear and receive. But not the less they examine the matter, they inquire into the decrees of Roman Pontiffs, and, after inquiry held, approve Agatho's decrees, condemn those of Honorius: a certain proof that they did not understand Agatho's expressions as if it were necessary to receive without discussion every decree of Roman Pontiffs even de fide, inasmuch as they are subjected to the supreme and final examination of a General Council: but as if these expressions taken as a whole, in their total, hold good in the full and complete succession of Peter, as we have often said, and in its proper place shall say at greater length.

SEVEN ECUMENICAL COUNCILS OF THE CHURCH

The Letter of Pope Agatho

Agatho a bishop and servant of the servants of God to the most devout and serene victors and conquerors, our most beloved sons and lovers of God and of our Lord Jesus Christ, the Emperor Constantine the Great, and to Heraclius and Tiberius, Augustuses.

While contemplating the various anxieties of human life, and while groaning with vehement weeping before the one true God, in prayer that he might impart to my wavering soul the comfort of his divine mercy, and might lift me by his right hand out of the depths of grief and anxiety, I most gratefully recognize, my most illustrious lords and sons, that your purpose [i.e. of holding a Council] afforded me deep and wonderful consolation. For it was most pious and emanated from your most meek tranquillity, taught by the divine benignity for the benefit of the Christian commonwealth divinely entrusted to your keeping, that your imperial power and clemency might have a care to enquire diligently concerning the things of God (through whom Kings do reign, who is himself King of Kings and Lord of Lords) and might seek after the truth of his spotless faith as it has been handed down by the Apostles and by the Apostolic Fathers, and be zealously affected to command that in all the churches the pure tradition be held. And that no one may be ignorant of this pious intention of yours, or suspect that we have been compelled by force, and have not freely consented to the carrying into effect of the imperial decrees touching the preaching of our evangelical faith which was addressed to our predecessor Donus, a pontiff of Apostolic memory, they have through our ministry been sent to and entirely approved by all nations and peoples; for these decrees the Holy Spirit by his grace dictated to the tongue of the imperial pen, out of the treasure of a pure heart, as the words of an adviser not of an oppressor, defending himself, not looking with contempt upon others; not afflicting, but exhorting; and inviting to those things which are of God in godly wise, because he, the Maker and Redeemer of all men, who had he come in the majesty of his Godhead into the world, might have terrified mortals, preferred to descend through his inestimable clemency and humility to the estate of us whom he had created and thus to redeem us, who also expects from us a willing confession of the true faith.

And this it is that the blessed Peter, the prince of the Apostles, teaches: "Feed the flock of Christ which is among you, not by constraint, but willingly, exhorting it according to God." Therefore, encouraged by these imperial decrees, O most meek lords of all things, and relieved from the depths of affliction and raised to the hope of consolation, I have begun, refreshed somewhat by a better confidence, to comply with promptness with the things which were sometime ago bidden by the Sacra of your gentlest fortitude, and am endeavouring in obedience therewith to find persons, such as our deficient times and the quality of this obedient province permit, and taking advice with my fellow-servant bishops, as well concerning the approaching synod of this Apostolic See, as concerning our own clergy, the lovers of the Christian Empire, and, afterwards concerning the religious servants of God, that I might exhort them to follow in haste the footsteps of your most pious Tranquillity. And, were it not that the great compass of the provinces, in which our humility's council is situated had caused so great a loss of time, our servitude a while ago could have fulfilled with studious obedience what even now has scarcely been done. For while from the various provinces a council has been gathering about us, and while we have been able to select some persons of those from this very Roman city immediately subject to your most serene power, or from those near by, others again we have been obliged to wait for from far distant provinces, in which the word of Christian faith was preached by those sent by the predecessors of my littleness; and thus quite a space of time has elapsed: and I pass over my bodily pains in consequence of which life to a perpetually suffering person is neither possible nor pleasant. Therefore, most Christian lords and sons, in accordance with the most pious jussio of your God-protected clemency, we have had a care to send, with the devotion of a prayerful heart (from the obedience we owe you, not because we relied on the [superabundant] knowledge of those whom we send to you), our fellow-servants here present, Abundantius, John, and John, our most reverend brother bishops, Theodore and George our most beloved sons and presbyters, with our most beloved son John, a deacon, and with Constantine, a subdeacon of this holy spiritual mother, the Apostolic See, as well as Theodore, the presbyter legate of the holy Church of Ravenna and the religious servants of God the monks. For, among men placed amid the Gentiles, and earning their daily bread by bodily labour with considerable distraction, how could a knowledge of the Scriptures, in its fullness, be found unless what has been canonically defined by our holy and apostolic predecessors, and by the venerable five councils, we preserve in simplicity of heart, and without any distorting keep the faith come to us from the Fathers, always desirous and endeavouring to possess that one and chiefest good, viz.: that nothing be diminished from the things canonically defined, and that nothing be changed nor added thereto, but that those same things, both in words and sense, be guarded untouched? To these same commissioners we also have given the witness of some of the holy Fathers, whom this Apostolic Church of Christ receives, together with their books, so that, having obtained from the power of your most benign Christianity the privilege of suggesting, they might out of these endeavour to give satisfaction, (when your imperial Meekness shall have so commanded) as to what this Apostolic Church of Christ, their spiritual mother and the mother of your God-sprung empire, believes and preaches, not in words of worldly eloquence, which are not at the command of ordinary men, but in the integrity of the apostolic faith, in which having been taught from the cradle, we pray that we may serve and obey the Lord of heaven, the Propagator of your Christian empire, even unto the end. Consequently, we have granted them faculty or authority with your most tranquil mightiness, to afford satisfaction with simplicity whenever your clemency shall command, it being enjoined on them as a limitation that they presume not to add to, take away, or to change anything; but that they set forth this tradition of the Apostolic See in all sincerity as it has been taught by the apostolic pontiffs, who were our predecessors. For these delegates we most humbly implore with bent knees of the mind your clemency ever full of condescension, that agreeably to the most benign and most august promise of the imperial Sacra, your Christlike Tranquillity may deem them worthy of acceptance and may deign to give a favourable hearing to their most humble suggestions. Thus may your meekest Piety find the ears of Almighty God open to your prayers, and may you order that they return to their own unharmed in their rectitude of our Apostolic faith, as well as in the integrity of their bodies. And thus may the supernal Majesty restore to the benign rule of your government through the most heroic and unconquerable labours of your God-strengthened clemency, the whole Christian commonwealth, and may he subdue hostile nations to your mighty sceptre, that there may be satisfaction from this time forth to every soul and to all nations, because what you deigned to promise solemnly by your most august letters about the immunity and safety of those who came to the Council, you have fulfilled in all respects. It is not their wisdom that gave us confidence to make bold to send them to your pious presence; but our littleness obediently complied with what your imperial benignity, with a gracious order, exhorted to. And briefly we shall intimate to your divinely instructed Piety, what the strength of our Apostolic faith contains, which we have received through Apostolic tradition and through the tradition of the Apostolical pontiffs, and that of the five holy general synods, through which the foundations of Christ's Catholic Church have been strengthened and established; this then is the status [and the regular tradition] of our Evangelical and Apostolic faith, to wit, that as we confess the holy and inseparable Trinity, that is, the Father, the Son and the Holy Ghost, to be of one deity, of one nature and substance or essence, so we will profess also that it has one natural will, power, operation, domination, majesty, potency, and glory. And whatever is said of the same Holy Trinity essentially in singular number we understand to refer to the one nature of the three consubstantial Persons, having been so taught by canonical logic. But when we make a confession concerning one of the same three Persons of that Holy Trinity, of the Son of God, or God the Word, and of the mystery of his adorable dispensation according to the flesh, we assert that all things are double in the one and the same our Lord and Saviour Jesus Christ according to the Evangelical tradition, that is to say, we confess his two natures, to wit the divine and the human, of which and in which he, even after the wonderful and inseparable union, subsists. And we confess that each of his natures has its own natural propriety, and that the divine, has all things that are divine, without any sin. And we recognize that each one (of the two natures) of the one and the same incarnated, that is, humanated (humanati) Word of God is in him unconfusedly, inseparably and unchangeably, intelligence alone discerning a unity, to avoid the error of confusion. For we equally detest the blasphemy of division and of commixture. For when we confess two natures and two natural wills, and two natural operations in our one Lord Jesus Christ, we do not assert that they are contrary or opposed one to the other (as those who err from the path of truth and accuse the apostolic tradition of doing. Far be this impiety from the hearts of the faithful!), nor as though separated (per se separated) in two persons or subsistences, but we say that as the same our Lord Jesus Christ has two natures so also he has two natural wills and operations, to wit, the divine and the human: the divine will and operation he has in common with the coessential Father from all eternity: the human, he has received from us, taken with our nature in time. This is the apostolic and evangelic tradition, which the spiritual mother of your most felicitous empire, the Apostolic Church of Christ, holds.

This is the pure expression of piety. This is the true and immaculate profession of the Christian religion, not invented by human cunning, but which was taught by the Holy Ghost through the princes of the Apostles. This is the firm and irreprehensible doctrine of the holy Apostles, the integrity of the sincere piety of which, so long as it is preached freely, defends the empire of your Tranquillity in the Christian

SEVEN ECUMENICAL COUNCILS OF THE CHURCH

commonwealth, and exults [will defend it, will render it stable; and exulting], and (as we firmly trust) will demonstrate it full of happiness. Believe your most humble [servant], my most Christian lords and sons, that I am pouring forth these prayers with my tears, or its stability and exultation [in Greek exaltation]. And these things I (although unworthy and insignificant) dare advise through my sincere love, because your God-granted victory is our salvation, the happiness of your Tranquillity is our joy, the harmlessness of your kindness is the security of our littleness. And therefore I beseech you with a contrite heart and rivers of tears, with prostrated mind, deign to stretch forth your most clement right hand to the Apostolic doctrine which the co-worker of your pious labours, the blessed apostle Peter, has delivered, that it be not hidden under a bushel, but that it be preached in the whole earth more shrilly than a bugle: because the true confession thereof for which Peter was pronounced blessed by the Lord of all things, was revealed by the Father of heaven, for he received from the Redeemer of all himself, by three commendations, the duty of feeding the spiritual sheep of the Church; under whose protecting shield, this Apostolic Church of his has never turned away from the path of truth in any direction of error, whose authority, as that of the Prince of all the Apostles, the whole Catholic Church, and the Ecumenical Synods have faithfully embraced, and followed in all things; and all the venerable Fathers have embraced its Apostolic doctrine, through which they as the most approved luminaries of the Church of Christ have shone; and the holy orthodox doctors have venerated and followed it, while the heretics have pursued it with false criminations and with derogatory hatred. This is the living tradition of the Apostles of Christ, which his Church holds everywhere, which is chiefly to be loved and fostered, and is to be preached with confidence, which conciliates with God through its truthful confession, which also renders one commendable to Christ the Lord, which keeps the Christian empire of your Clemency, which gives far-reaching victories to your most pious Fortitude from the Lord of heaven, which accompanies you in battle, and defeats your foes; which protects on every side as an impregnable wall your God-sprung empire, which throws terror into opposing nations, and smites them with the divine wrath, which also in wars celestially gives triumphal palms over the downfall and subjection of the enemy, and ever guards your most faithful sovereignty secure and joyful in peace. For this is the rule of the true faith, which this spiritual mother of your most tranquil empire, the Apostolic Church of Christ, has both in prosperity and in adversity always held and defended with energy; which, it will be proved, by the grace of Almighty God, has never erred from the path of the apostolic tradition, nor has she been depraved by yielding to heretical innovations, but from the beginning she has received the Christian faith from her founders, the princes of the Apostles of Christ, and remains undefiled unto the end, according to the divine promise of the Lord and Saviour himself, which he uttered in the holy Gospels to the prince of his disciples: saying, "Peter, Peter, behold, Satan has desired to have you, that he might sift you as wheat; but I have prayed for you, that (your) faith fail not. And when you are converted, strengthen your brethren." Let your tranquil Clemency therefore consider, since it is the Lord and Saviour of all, whose faith it is, that promised that Peter's faith should not fail and exhorted him to strengthen his brethren, how it is known to all that the Apostolic pontiffs, the predecessors of my littleness, have always confidently done this very thing: of whom also our littleness, since I have received this ministry by divine designation, wishes to be the follower, although unequal to them and the least of all. For woe is me, if I neglect to preach the truth of my Lord, which they have sincerely preached. Woe is me, if I cover over with silence the truth which I am bidden to give to the exchangers, i.e., to teach to the Christian people and imbue it therewith. What shall I say in the future examination by Christ himself, if I blush (which God forbid!) to preach here the truth of his words? What satisfaction shall I be able to give for myself, what for the souls committed to me, when he demands a strict account of the office I have received? Who, then, my most clement and most pious lords and sons, (I speak trembling and prostrate in spirit) would not be stirred by that admirable promise, which is made to the faithful: "Whoever shall confess me before men, him also will I confess before my Father, who is in heaven"? And which one even of the infidels shall not be terrified by that most severe threat, in which he protests that he will be full of wrath, and declares that "Whoever shall deny me before men, him also will I deny before my Father, who is in heaven"? Whence also blessed Paul, the apostle of the Gentiles, gives warning and says: "But though we, or an angel from the heaven should preach to you any other Gospel from what we have evangelized to you, let him be anathema." Since, therefore, such an extremity of punishment overhangs the corruptors, or suppressors of truth by silence, would not any one flee from an attempt at curtailing the truth of the Lord's faith? Wherefore the predecessors of Apostolic memory of my littleness, learned in the doctrine of the Lord, ever since the prelates of the Church of Constantinople have been trying to introduce into the immaculate Church of Christ an heretical innovation, have never ceased to exhort and warn them with many prayers, that they should, at least by silence, desist from the heretical error of the depraved dogma, lest from this they make the beginning of a split in the unity of the Church, by asserting one will, and one operation of the two natures in the one Jesus Christ our Lord: a thing which the Arians and the Apollinarists, the Eutychians, the Timotheans, the Acephali, the Theodosians and the Gaianitæ taught, and every heretical madness, whether of those who confound, or of those who divide the mystery of the Incarnation of Christ. Those that confound the mystery of the holy Incarnation, inasmuch as they say that there is one nature of the deity and humanity of Christ, contend that he has one will, as of one, and (one) personal operation. But they who divide, on the other hand, the inseparable union, unite the two natures which they acknowledge that the Saviour possesses, not however in an union which is recognized to be hypostatic; but blasphemously join them by concord, through the affection of the will, like two subsistences, i.e., two somebodies. Moreover, the Apostolic Church of Christ, the spiritual mother of your God-founded empire, confesses one Jesus Christ our Lord existing of and in two natures, and she maintains that his two natures, to wit, the divine and the human, exist in him unconfused even after their inseparable union, and she acknowledges that each of these natures of Christ is perfect in the proprieties of its nature, and she confesses that all things belonging to the proprieties of the natures are double, because the same our Lord Jesus Christ himself is both perfect God and perfect man, of two and in two natures: and after his wonderful Incarnation, his deity cannot be thought of without his humanity, nor his humanity without his deity. Consequently, therefore, according to the rule of the holy Catholic and Apostolic Church of Christ, she also confesses and preaches that there are in him two natural wills and two natural operations. For if anybody should mean a personal will, when in the holy Trinity there are said to be three Persons, it would be necessary that there should be asserted three personal wills, and three personal operations (which is absurd and truly profane). Since, as the truth of the Christian faith holds, the will is natural, where the one nature of the holy and inseparable Trinity is spoken of, it must be consistently understood that there is one natural will, and one natural operation. But when in truth we confess that in the one person of our Lord Jesus Christ the mediator between God and men, there are two natures (that is to say the divine and the human), even after his admirable union, just as we canonically confess the two natures of one and the same person, so too we confess his two natural wills and two natural operations. But that the understanding of this truthful confession may become clear to your Piety's mind from the God-inspired doctrine of the Old and the New Testament, (for your Clemency is incomparably more able to penetrate the meaning of the sacred Scriptures, than our littleness to set it forth in flowing words), our Lord Jesus Christ himself, who is true and perfect God, and true and perfect man, in his holy Gospels shows forth in some instances human things, in others, divine, and still in others both together, making a manifestation concerning himself in order that he might instruct his faithful to believe and preach that he is both true God and true man. Thus as man he prays to the Father to take away the cup of suffering, because in him our human nature was complete, sin only excepted, "Father, if it be possible, let this cup pass from me; nevertheless not as I will, but as you will." And in another passage: "Not my will, but yours be done." If we wish to know the meaning of which testimony as explained by the holy and approved Fathers, and truly to understand what "my will" and "yours" signify, the blessed Ambrose in his second book to the Emperor Gratian, of blessed memory, teaches us the meaning of this passage in these words, saying: "He then, receives my will, he takes my sorrow, I confidently call it sorrow as I am speaking of the cross, mine is the will, which he calls his, because he bears my sorrow as man, he spoke as a man, and therefore he says: 'Not as I will but as you will.'" Mine is the sadness which he has received according to my affection. See, most pious of princes, how clearly here this holy Father sets forth that the words our Lord used in his prayer, "Not my will," pertain to his humanity; through which also he is said, according to the teaching of Blessed Paul the Apostle of the Gentiles, to have "become obedient unto death, even the death of the Cross." Wherefore also it is taught us that he was obedient to his parents, which must piously be understood to refer to his voluntary obedience, not according to his divinity (by which he governs all things), but according to his humanity, by which he spontaneously submitted himself to his parents. St. Luke the Evangelist likewise bears witness to the same thing, telling how the same our Lord Jesus Christ prayed according to his humanity to his Father, and said, "Father, if it be possible let the cup pass from me; nevertheless not my will but yours be done,"— which passage Athanasius, the Confessor of Christ, and Archbishop of the Church of Alexandria, in his book against Apollinaris the heretic, concerning the Trinity and the Incarnation, also understanding the wills to be two, thus explains: And when he says, "Father, if it be possible, let this cup pass from me, nevertheless not my will but yours be done," and again, "The spirit is willing, but the flesh is weak;" he shows that there are two wills, the one human which is the will of the flesh, but the other divine. For his human will, out of the weakness of the flesh was fleeing away from the passion, but his divine will was ready for it. What truer explanation could be found? For how is it possible not to acknowledge in him two wills, to wit, a human and a divine, when in him, even after the inseparable union, there are two natures according to the definitions of the synods? For John also, who leaned upon the Lord's breast, his beloved disciple, shows forth the same self-restraint in these words: "I came down from heaven not to do my own will but the will of the Father that sent me." And again: "This is the will of him that sent me, that of all that he gave me I should lose nothing, but should raise it up again at the last day." Again he introduces the Lord as disputing with the Jews, and saying among other things: "I seek not my own will, but the will of him that sent me." On the meaning of which divine words blessed Augustine, a most illustrious doctor, thus writes in his book against Maximinus the Arian. He says, "When the Son says to the Father 'Not what I will, but what you will,' what does it profit you, that you brought your words into subjection and sayest, It shows truly that his will was subject to his Father, as though we would deny that the will of man should be subject to the will of God? For that the Lord said this in his human nature, anyone will quickly see who studies attentively this place of the Gospel. For therein he says, 'My soul is exceeding sorrowful even unto death.' Can this possibly be said of the nature of the One Word? But, O man, who thinkest to make the nature of the Holy Ghost to groan, why do you say that the nature of the Only-begotten Word of God cannot be sad? But to prevent anyone arguing in this way, he does not say 'I am sad;' (and even if he had so said, it could properly only have been understood of his human nature) but he says 'My soul is sad,' which soul he has as man; however in this also which he said, 'Not what I will' he showed that he willed something different from what the Father did, which he could not have done except in his human nature, since he did not introduce our infirmity into his divine nature, but would transfigure human affection. For had he not been made man, the Only Word could in no way have said to the Father, 'Not what I will.' For it could never be possible for that immutable nature to will anything different from what the Father willed. If you would but make this distinction, O you Arians, you would not be heretics."

In this disputation this venerable Father shows that when the Lord says "his own" he means the will of his humanity, and when he says not to do "his own will," he teaches us not chiefly to seek our own wills but that through obedience we should submit our wills to the Divine Will. From all which it is evident that he had a human will by which he obeyed his Father, and that he had in himself this same human will immaculate from all sin, as true God and man. Which thing St. Ambrose also thus treats of in his explanation of St. Luke the Evangelist.

After this follows a catena of Patristic quotations which I have not thought worth while to produce in full. After St. Ambrose he cites St. Leo, then St. Gregory Nazianzen, then St. Augustine.

From which testimonies it is clear that each of those natures which the spiritual Doctor has here enumerated has its own natural property, and that to each one a will ought to be assigned. For an angelic nature cannot have a divine or a human will, neither can a human nature have a divine or an angelic will. For no nature can have anything or any motion which pertains to another nature but only that which is naturally given by creation. And as this is the truth of the matter it is most certainly clear that we must needs confess that in our Lord Jesus Christ there are two natures and substances, to wit, the Divine and human, united in his one subsistence or person, and that we further confess that there are in him two natural wills, viz.: the divine and the human, for his divinity so far as its nature is concerned could not be said to possess a human will, nor should his humanity be believed to have naturally a divine will: And again, neither of these two substances of Christ must be confessed as being without a natural will; but his human will was lifted up by the omnipotency of his divinity, and his divine will was revealed to men through his humanity. Therefore it is necessary to refer to him as God such things as are divine, and as man such things as are human; and each must be truly recognized through the hypostatic union of the one and the same our Lord Jesus Christ, which the most true decree of the Council of Chalcedon sets forth— [Here follows citation.] This same thing also the holy synod which was gathered together in Constantinople in the time of the Emperor Justinian of august memory, teaches in the seventh chapter of its definitions. [Here follows the citation.] Moreover it is necessary that we should faithfully keep what those Venerable Synods taught, so that we never take away the difference of natures as a result of the union, but confess one Christ, true and perfect God and also true and perfect man, the propriety of each nature being kept intact. Wherefore, if in no respect the difference of the natures of our Lord Jesus Christ has been taken away, it is necessary that we preserve this same difference in all its proprieties. For whoso teaches that the difference is in no respect to be taken away, declares that it must be preserved in all things. But when the heretics and the followers of heretics say that there is but one will and one operation, how is this difference recognized? Or where is the difference which has been defined by this holy Synod preserved? While if it is asserted that there is but one will in him (which is absurd), those who make this assertion must needs say that that will is either human or divine, or else composite from both, mixed and confused, or (according to the teaching of all heretics) that Christ has one will and one operation, proceeding from his one composite nature (as they hold). And thus, without any doubt, the difference of nature is destroyed, which the holy synods declared to be preserved in all respects even after the admirable union. Because, though they taught that Christ was one, his person and substance one, yet on account of the union of the natures which was made hypostatically, they likewise decreed that we should clearly acknowledge and teach the difference of those natures which were united in him, after the admirable union. Therefore if the proprieties of the natures in the same our one Lord Jesus Christ were preserved on account of the difference [of the natures], it is congruous that we should with full faith confess also the difference of his natural wills and operations, in order that we may be shown to have followed in all respects their doctrine, and may admit into the Church of Christ no heretical novelty.

And although there exist numerous works of the other holy Fathers, nevertheless we subjoin to this our humble exposition a few testimonies out of the books which are in Greek, for the sake of fastidiousness.

Here follows a catena of passages from the Greek fathers, viz.: St. Gregory Theologus, St. Gregory Nyssen, St. John bishop of Constantinople, St. Cyril, bishop of Alexandria.

From these truthful testimonies it is also demonstrated that these venerable fathers predicated in the one and the same Lord Jesus Christ two natural wills, viz.: a divine and a human, for when St. Gregory Nazianzen says, "The willing of that man who is understood to be the Saviour," he shows that the human will of the Saviour was deified through its union with the Word, and therefore it is not contrary to God. So likewise he proves that he had a human, although deified will, and this same he had (as he teaches in what follows) as well as his divine will, which was one and the same with that of the Father. If therefore he had a divine and a deified will, he had also two wills. For what is divine by nature has no need of being deified; and what is deified is not truly divine by nature. And when St. Gregory Nyssen, a great bishop, says that the true confession of the mystery is, that there should be understood one human will and another a divine will in Christ, what does he bid us understand when he says one and another will, except that there are manifestly two wills?

He next proceeds to comment upon the passage cited from St. John, then upon that from St. Cyril of Alexandria. After this follow quotations from St. Hilary, St. Athanasius, St. Denys the Areopagite, St. Ambrose, St. Leo, St. Gregory Nyssen, St. Cyril of Alexandria, which are next commented on in their order. He then proceeds:

There are not lacking most telling passages in other of the venerable fathers, who speak clearly of the two natural operations in Christ, not to mention St. Cyril of Jerusalem, St. John of Constantinople, or those who afterwards conducted the laborious conflicts in defence of the venerable council of Chalcedon and of the Tome of St. Leo against the heretics from whose error the assertion of this new dogma has arisen: that is to say, John, bishop of Scythopolis, Eulogius, bishop of Alexandria, Euphræmius and Anastasius the elder, most worthy rulers of the church of Theopolis, and above all that emulator of the true and apostolic faith, the Emperor Justinian of pious memory, whose uprightness of faith exalted the Christian State as much as his sincere confession pleased God. And his pious memory is esteemed worthy of veneration by all nations, whose uprightness of faith was disseminated with praise throughout the whole world by his most august edicts: one of these, to wit, that addressed to Zoilus, the patriarch of Alexandria, against the heresy of the Acephali to satisfy them of the rectitude of the apostolic faith, we offer to your most tranquil Christianity, sending it together with this paper of our lowliness through the same carriers. But lest this declaration should be thought burdensome on account of its length, we have inserted in this declaration of our humility only a few of the testimonies of the Holy Fathers, especially [when writing to those] on whom the care and arrangement of the whole world as on a firm foundation are recognized to rest; since this is altogether incomparable and great, that the care of the whole Christian State being laid aside for a little out of love and zeal for true religion, your august and most religious clemency should desire to understand more clearly the doctrine of preaching. For from the different approved fathers the truth of the Orthodox faith has become clear although the treatment is short. For the approved fathers thought it to be superfluous to discourse at length upon what was evident and clear to all; for who, even if he be dull of wit, does not perceive what is evident to all? For it is impossible and contrary to the order of nature that there should be a nature without a natural operation: and even the heretics did not dare to say this, although they were, all of them, hunting for human craftiness and cunning questions against the orthodoxy of the faith, and arguments agreeable to their depravities.

SEVEN ECUMENICAL COUNCILS OF THE CHURCH

How then can that now be asserted which never was said by the holy orthodox fathers, nor even was presumptuously invented by the profane heretics, viz.: that of the two natures of Christ, the divine and the human, the proprieties of each of which are recognized as being preserved in Christ, that anyone in sound mind should declare there was but one operation? Since if there is one, let them say whether it be temporal or eternal, divine or human, uncreated or created: the same as that of the Father or different from that of the Father. If therefore it is one, that one and the same must be common to the divinity and to the humanity (which is absurd), therefore while the Son of God, who is both God and man, wrought human things on earth, likewise also the Father worked with him according to his nature (naturaliter, φυσικῶς); for what things the Father does these the Son also does likewise. But if (as is the truth) the human acts which Christ did are to be referred to his person alone as the Son, which is not the same as that of the Father; in one nature Christ worked one set of works, and in the other another, so that according to his divinity the Son does the same things that the Father does; and likewise according to his humanity, what things are proper to the manhood, those same, he as man, did because he is truly both God and man. For which reason we rightly believe that that same person, since he is one, has two natural operations, to wit, the divine and the human, one uncreated, and the other created, as true and perfect God and as true and perfect man, the one and the same, the mediator between God and men, the Lord Jesus Christ. Wherefore from the quality of the operations there is recognized a difference void of offense (ἀπρόσκοπος) of the natures which are joined in Christ through the hypostatic union. We now proceed to cite some passages from the execrable writings of the heretics hated of God, whose words and sayings we equally abominate, for the demonstration of those things which our inventors of new dogma have followed teaching that in Christ there is but one will and one operation.

Then follow quotations from Apollinaris, Severus, Theodosius of Alexandria.

Behold, most pious lords and sons, by the testimonies of the holy Fathers, as by spiritual rays, the doctrine of the Catholic and Apostolic Church has been illustrated and the darkness of heretical blindness, which is offering error to men for imitation, has been revealed. Now it is necessary that the new doctrine should follow somebody, and by whose authority it is supported, we shall note.

Here follow quotations from Cyrus of Alexandria, Theodore of Pharon, Sergius of Constantinople, Pyrrhus, Paulus his successor, Peter his successor.

Let then your God-founded clemency with the internal eye of discrimination, which for the guidance of the Christian people you have been deemed worthy to receive by the Grace of God, take heed which one of such doctors you think the Christian people should follow, the doctrine of which one of these they should embrace so as to be saved; for they condemn all, and each one of them the other, according as the various and unstable definitions in their writings assert sometimes that there is one will and one operation, sometimes that there is neither one nor two operations, sometimes one will and operation, and again two wills and two operations, likewise one will and one operation, and again neither one, nor two, and somebody else one

SEVEN ECUMENICAL COUNCILS OF THE CHURCH

and two.

Who does not hate, and rage against, and avoid such blind errors, if he have any desire to be saved and seek to offer to the Lord at his coming a right faith? Therefore the Holy Church of God, the mother of your most Christian power, should be delivered and liberated with all your might (through the help of God) from the errors of such teachers, and the evangelical and apostolic uprightness of the orthodox faith, which has been established upon the firm rock of this Church of blessed Peter, the Prince of the Apostles, which by his grace and guardianship remains free from all error, [that faith I say] the whole number of rulers and priests, of the clergy and of the people, unanimously should confess and preach with us as the true declaration of the Apostolic tradition, in order to please God and to save their own souls.

And these things we have taken pains to insert in the tractate of our humility, for we have been afflicted and have groaned without ceasing that such grievous errors should be entertained by bishops of the Church, who are zealous to establish their own peculiar views rather than the truth of the faith, and think that our sincere fraternal admonition has its spring in a contempt for them. And indeed the apostolic predecessors of my humility admonished, begged, upbraided, besought, reproved, and exercised every kind of exhortation that the recent wound might receive a remedy, moved thereto not by a mind filled with hatred (God is my witness) nor through the elation of boasting, nor through the opposition of contention, nor through an inane desire to find some fault with their teachings, nor through anything akin to the love of arrogance, but out of zeal for the uprightness of the truth, and for the rule of the confession of the pure Gospel, and for the salvation of souls, and for the stability of the Christian state, and for the safety of those who rule the Roman Empire. Nor did they cease from their admonitions after the long duration of this domesticated error, but always exhorted and bore record, and that with fraternal charity, not through malice or pertinacious hatred (far be it from the Christian heart to rejoice at another's fall, when the Lord of all teaches, "I desire not the death of a sinner, but that he be converted and live;" and who rejoices over one sinner that repents more than over ninety-and-nine just persons: who came down from heaven to earth to deliver the lost sheep, inclining the power of his majesty), but desiring them with outstretched spiritual arms, and exhorting to embrace them returning to the unity of the orthodox faith, and awaiting their conversion to the full rectitude of the orthodox faith: that they might not make themselves aliens from our communion, that is from the communion of blessed Peter the Apostle, whose ministry, we (though unworthy) exercise, and preach the faith he has handed down, but that they should together with us pray Christ the Lord, the spotless sacrifice, for the stability of your most strong and serene Empire.

We believe, most pious lords [singular in the Latin] of all things, that there has been left no possible ambiguity which can prevent the recognizing of those who have followed the inventors of new dogma. For the sweetness of spiritual understanding with which the sayings of the Fathers are full has become evident to the eyes of all; and the stench of the heretics, to be avoided by all the faithful, has been made notorious. Nor has it remained unknown that the inventors of new dogma have been shown to be the followers of heretics, and not the walkers in the footsteps of the holy

SEVEN ECUMENICAL COUNCILS OF THE CHURCH

Fathers: therefore whoever wishes to colour any error of his whatever, is condemned by the light of truth, as the Apostle of the Gentiles says, "For everything that does make manifest is light," for the truth ever remains constant and the same, but falsehood is ever varying, and in its wanderings adopting things mutually contradictory. On this account the inventors of the new dogma have been shown to have taught things mutually contradictory, because they were not willing to be followers of the Evangelical and Apostolic faith. Wherefore since the truth has shone forth by the observations of your God-inspired piety, and falsity which has been exposed has attained the contempt which it deserved, it remains that the crowned truth may shine forth victoriously through the pious favours of your God-crowned clemency; and that the error of novelty with its inventors and with those who follow their doctrine, may receive the punishment due their presumption, and be cast forth from the midst of the orthodox prelates for the heretical pravity of their innovation, which into the holy, Catholic and Apostolic Church of Christ they have endeavoured to introduce, and to stain with the contagion of heretical pravity the indivisible and unspotted body of the Church [of Christ]. For it is not just that the injurious should injure the innocent, nor that the offenses of some should be visited upon the inoffensive, for even if in this world to the condemned mercy is extended, yet they who are thus spared reap for that sparing no benefit in the judgment of God, and by those thus sparing them there is incurred no little danger for their unlawful compassion.

But we believe that Almighty God has reserved for the happy days of your gentleness the amending of these things, that filling on earth the place and zeal of our Lord Jesus Christ himself, who has vouchsafed to crown your rule, you may judge just judgment for his Evangelical and Apostolical truth: for although he be the Redeemer and Saviour of the human race yet he suffered injury, and bore it even until now, and inspired the empire of your fortitude, so that you should be worthy to follow the cause of his faith (as equity demanded, and as the determination of the Holy Fathers and of the Five General Synods decreed), and that you should avenge, through his guardianship, on the spurners of his faith, the injury done your Redeemer and Colleague in reigning, thus fulfilling magnanimously with imperial clemency that prophetic utterance with which David the King and Prophet, spoke to God, saying, "The zeal of your house has eaten me up." Wherefore having been extolled for so God-pleasing a zeal, he was deemed fit to hear that blessed word spoken by the Creator of all men, "I have found David, a man after my heart, who will do all my will." And to him also it was promised in the Psalms, "I have found David, my servant, with my holy oil have I anointed him: My hand shall aid him and my arm shall comfort him," so that the most pious majesty of your Christian clemency may work to further the cause of Christ with burning zeal for the sake of remuneration, and may he make all the acts of your most powerful empire both happy and prosperous, who has stored up his promise in the Holy Gospels, saying, "Seek first the kingdom of God and all these things shall be added unto you." For all, to whom has come the knowledge of the sacred heads, have been offering innumerable thanksgivings and unceasing praises to the defender of your most powerful dominion, being filled with admiration for the greatness of your clemency, in that you have so benignly set forth the kind intention of your august magnanimity; for in truth, as most pious and most just princes, you have deigned to treat divine things with the fear of God, having promised every immunity to those persons sent to you from our littleness.

And we are confident that what your pious clemency has promised, you are powerful to carry out, in order that what has been vowed and promised to God by the religious philanthropy beyond your Christian power, may nevertheless be fulfilled by the aid of his omnipotency.

Wherefore let praise by all Christian nations, and eternal memory, and frequent prayer be poured forth before the Lord Christ, whose is the cause, for your safety, and your triumphs, and your complete victory, that the nations of the Gentiles, being impressed by the terror of the supernal majesty, may lay down most humbly their necks beneath the sceptre of your most powerful rule, that the power of your most pious kingdom may continue until the ceaseless joy of the eternal kingdom succeeds to this temporal reign. Nor could anything be found more likely to commend the clemency of your unconquerable fortitude to the divine majesty, than that those who err from the rule of truth should be repelled and the integrity of our Evangelical and Apostolic faith should be everywhere set forth and preached.

Moreover, most pious and God-instructed sons and lords, if the Archbishop of the Church of Constantinople shall choose to hold and to preach with us this most unblameable rule of Apostolic doctrine of the Sacred Scriptures, of the venerable synods, of the spiritual Fathers, according to their evangelical understanding, through which the form of the truth has been set forth by us through the assistance of the Spirit, there will ensue great peace to them that love the name of God, and there will remain no scandal of dissension, and that will come to pass which is recorded in the Acts of the Apostles, when through the grace of the Holy Spirit the people had come to the acknowledging of Christianity, all of us will be of one heart and of one mind. But if (which God forbid!) he shall prefer to embrace the novelty but lately introduced by others; and shall ensnare himself with doctrines which are alien to the rule of orthodox truth and of our Apostolic faith, to decline which as injurious to souls these have put off, despite the exhortation and admonitions of our predecessors in the Apostolic See, down to this day, he himself should know what kind of an answer he will have to give for such contempt in the divine examination of Christ before the judge of all, who is in heaven, to whom when he comes to judgment also we ourselves are about to give an account of the ministry of preaching the truth which has been committed to us, or for the toleration of things contrary to the Christian religion: and may we (as I humbly pray) preserve unconfusedly and freely, with simplicity and purity, whole and undefiled, the Apostolic and Evangelical rule of the right faith as we have received it from the beginning. And may your most august serenity, for the affection and reverence which you bear to the Catholic and Apostolic right faith, receive the perfect reward of your pious labours from our Lord Jesus Christ himself, the ruler with you of your Christian empire, whose true confession you desire to preserve undefiled, because nothing in any respect has been neglected or omitted by your God-crowned clemency, which could minister to the peace of the churches, provided always that the integrity of the true faith was maintained: since God, the Judge of all, who disposes the ending of all matters as he deems most expedient, seeks out the intent of the heart, and will accept a zeal for piety. Therefore

SEVEN ECUMENICAL COUNCILS OF THE CHURCH

I exhort you, O most pious and clement Emperor, and together with my littleness every Christian man exhorts you on bended knee with all humility, that to all the God-pleasing goodnesses and admirable imperial benefits which the heavenly condescension has vouchsafed to grant to the human race through your God-accepted care, this also you would order, for the redintegration of perfect piety, to offer an acceptable sacrifice to Christ the Lord your fellow-ruler, granting entire impunity, and free faculty of speech to each one wishing to speak, and to urge a word in defence of the faith which he believes and holds, so that it may most manifestly be recognized by all that by no terror, by no force, by no threat or aversion any one wishing to speak for the truth of the Catholic and Apostolic faith, has been prohibited or repulsed, and that all unanimously may glorify your imperial (divinam) majesty, throughout the whole space of their lives for so great and so inestimable a good, and may pour forth unceasing prayers to Christ the Lord that your most strong empire may be preserved untouched and exalted. The Subscription. May the grace from above keep your empire, most pious lords, and place beneath its feet the neck of all the nations.

The Letter of Agatho and of the Roman Synod of 125 Bishops which was to Serve as an Instruction to the Legates Sent to Attend the Sixth Synod.

To the most pious Lords and most serene victors and conquerors, our own sons beloved of God and of our Lord Jesus Christ, Constantine, the great Emperor, and Heraclius and Tiberius, Augustuses, Agatho, the bishop and servant of the servants of God, together with all the synods subject to the council of the Apostolic See.

The Letter opens with a number of compliments to the Emperor, much in style and matter like the introduction of the preceding letter. I have not thought it worth while to translate this, but have begun at the doctrinal part, which is given to the reader in full.

We believe in God the Father Almighty, maker of heaven and earth, and of all things visible and invisible; and in his only-begotten Son, who was begotten of him before all worlds; very God of Very God, Light of Light, begotten not made, being of one substance with the Father, that is of the same substance as the Father; by him were all things made which are in heaven and which are in earth; and in the Holy Ghost, the Lord and giver of life, who proceeds from the Father, and with the Father and the Son together is worshipped and glorified; the Trinity in unity and Unity in trinity; a unity so far as essence is concerned, but a trinity of persons or subsistences; and so we confess God the Father, God the Son, and God the Holy Ghost; not three gods, but one God, the Father, the Son, and the Holy Ghost: not a subsistency of three names, but one substance of three subsistences; and of these persons one is the essence, or substance or nature, that is to say one is the godhead, one the eternity, one the power, one the kingdom, one the glory, one the adoration, one the essential will and operation of the same Holy and inseparable Trinity, which has created all things, has made disposition of them, and still contains them.

Moreover we confess that one of the same holy consubstantial Trinity, God the Word, who was begotten of the Father before the worlds, in the last days of the world for us and for our salvation came down from heaven, and was incarnate of the Holy Ghost, and of our Lady, the holy, immaculate, ever-virgin and glorious Mary, truly and properly the Mother of God, that is to say according to the flesh which was born of her; and was truly made man, the same being very God and very man. God of God his Father, but man of his Virgin Mother, incarnate of her flesh with a reasonable and intelligent soul: of one substance with God the Father, as touching his godhead, and consubstantial with us as touching his manhood, and in all points like us, but without sin. He was crucified for us under Pontius Pilate, he suffered, was buried and rose again; ascended into heaven, and sits at the right hand of the Father, and he shall come again to judge both the quick and the dead, and of his kingdom there shall be no end.

And this same one Lord of ours, Jesus Christ, the only-begotten Son of God, we acknowledge to subsist of and in two substances unconfusedly, unchangeably, indivisibly, inseparably, the difference of the natures being by no means taken away by the union, but rather the proprieties of each nature being preserved and concurring in one Person and one Subsistence, not scattered or divided into two Persons, nor confused into one composite nature; but we confess one and the same only-begotten Son, God the Word, our Lord Jesus Christ, not one in another, nor one added to another, but himself the same in two natures— that is to say in the Godhead and in the manhood even after the hypostatic union: for neither was the Word changed into the nature of flesh, nor was the flesh transformed into the nature of the Word, for each remained what it was by nature. We discern by contemplation alone the distinction between the natures united in him of which inconfusedly, inseparably and unchangeably he is composed; for one is of both, and through one both, because there are together both the height of the deity and the humility of the flesh, each nature preserving after the union its own proper character without any defect; and each form acting in communion with the other what is proper to itself. The Word working what is proper to the Word, and the flesh what is proper to the flesh; of which the one shines with miracles, the other bows down beneath injuries. Wherefore, as we confess that he truly has two natures or substances, viz.: the Godhead and the manhood, inconfusedly, indivisibly and unchangeably [united], so also the rule of piety instructs us that he has two natural wills and two natural operations, as perfect God and perfect man, one and the same our Lord Jesus Christ. And this the apostolic and evangelical tradition and the authority of the Holy Fathers (whom the Holy Apostolic and Catholic Church and the venerable Synods receive), has plainly taught us.

The letter goes on to say that this is the traditional faith, and is that which was set forth in a council over which Pope Martin presided, and that those opposed to this faith have erred from the truth, some in one way, and some in another. It next apologizes for the delay in sending the persons ordered by the imperial Sacra, and proceeds thus:

In the first place, a great number of us are spread over a vast extent of country even to the sea coast, and the length of their journey necessarily took much time. Moreover we were in hopes of being able to join to our humility our fellow-servant and brother bishop, Theodore, the archbishop and philosopher of the island of Great

SEVEN ECUMENICAL COUNCILS OF THE CHURCH

Britain, with others who have been kept there even till today; and to add to these various bishops of this council who have their sees in different parts, that our humble suggestion [i.e., the doctrinal definition contained in the letters] might proceed from a council of wide-spread influence, lest if only a part were cognizant of what was being done, it might escape the notice of a part; and especially because among the Gentiles, as the Longobards, and the Sclavi, as also the Franks, the French, the Goths, and the Britains, there are known to be very many of our fellow-servants who do not cease curiously to enquire on the subject, that they may know what is being done in the cause of the Apostolic faith: who as they can be of advantage so long as they hold the true faith with us, and think in unison with us, so are they found troublesome and contrary, if (which may God forbid!) they stumble at any article of the faith. But we, although most humble, yet strive with all our might that the commonwealth of your Christian empire may be shown to be more sublime than all the nations, for in it has been founded the See of Blessed Peter, the prince of the Apostles, by the authority of which, all Christian nations venerate and worship with us, through the reverence of the blessed Apostle Peter himself. (This is the Latin, which appears to me to be corrupt, the Greek reads as follows: "The authority of which for the truth, all the Christian nations together with us worship and revere, according to the honour of the blessed Peter the Apostle himself.")

The letter ends with prayers for constancy, and blessings on the State and Emperor, and hopes for the universal diffusion and acceptance of the truth.

Session VIII
Extracts from the Acts

The Emperor said:

Let George, the most holy archbishop of this our God-preserved city, and let Macarius, the venerable archbishop of Antioch, and let the synod subject to them [i.e., their suffragans] say, if they submit to the force (εἰ στοιχοῦσι τῇ δυνάμει) of the suggestions sent by the most holy Agatho Pope of Old Rome and by his Synod.

The answer of George, with which all his bishops, many of them, speaking one by one, agreed except Theodore of Metilene (who handed in his assent at the end of the Tenth Session).

I have diligently examined the whole force of the suggestions sent to your most pious Fortitude, as well by Agatho, the most holy Pope of Old Rome, as by his synod, and I have scrutinized the works of the holy and approved Fathers, which are laid up in my venerable patriarchate, and I have found that all the testimonies of the holy and accepted Fathers, which are contained in those suggestions agree with, and in no particular differ from, the holy and accepted Fathers. Therefore I give my submission to them and thus I profess and believe.

The answer of all the rest of the Bishops subject to the See of Constantinople.

And we, most pious Lord, accepting the teaching of the suggestion sent to your most gentle Fortitude by the most holy and blessed Agatho, Pope of Old Rome, and of that other suggestion which was adopted by the council subject to him, and following the sense therein contained, so we are minded, so we profess, and so we believe that in our one Lord Jesus Christ, our true God, there are two natures unconfusedly, unchangeably, undividedly, and two natural wills and two natural operations; and all who have taught, and who now say, that there is but one will and one operation in the two natures of our one Lord Jesus Christ our true God, we anathematize.

The Emperor's demand to Macarius.

Let Macarius, the Venerable Archbishop of Antioch, who has now heard what has been said by this holy and Ecumenical Synod [demanding the expression of his faith], answer what seems him good.

The answer of Macarius.

I do not say that there are two wills or two operations in the dispensation of the incarnation of our Lord Jesus Christ, but one will and one theandric operation.

Session XIII
The Sentence Against the Monothelites

The holy council said: After we had reconsidered, according to our promise which we had made to your highness, the doctrinal letters of Sergius, at one time patriarch of this royal god-protected city to Cyrus, who was then bishop of Phasis and to Honorius some time Pope of Old Rome, as well as the letter of the latter to the same Sergius, we find that these documents are quite foreign to the apostolic dogmas, to the declarations of the holy Councils, and to all the accepted Fathers, and that they follow the false teachings of the heretics; therefore we entirely reject them, and execrate them as hurtful to the soul. But the names of those men whose doctrines we execrate must also be thrust forth from the holy Church of God, namely, that of Sergius some time bishop of this God-preserved royal city who was the first to write on this impious doctrine; also that of Cyrus of Alexandria, of Pyrrhus, Paul, and Peter, who died bishops of this God-preserved city, and were like-minded with them; and that of Theodore sometime bishop of Pharan, all of whom the most holy and thrice blessed Agatho, Pope of Old Rome, in his suggestion to our most pious and God-preserved lord and mighty Emperor, rejected, because they were minded contrary to our orthodox faith, all of whom we define are to be subjected to anathema. And with these we define that there shall be expelled from the holy Church of God and anathematized Honorius who was some time Pope of Old Rome, because of what we found written by him to Sergius, that in all respects he followed his view and confirmed his impious doctrines. We have also examined the synodal letter of Sophronius of holy memory, some time Patriarch of the Holy City of Christ our God, Jerusalem, and have found it in accordance with the true faith and with the Apostolic teachings, and with those of the holy approved Fathers. Therefore we have received it as orthodox and as salutary to the holy Catholic and Apostolic Church, and have decreed that it is right that his name be inserted in the diptychs of the Holy Churches.

SEVEN ECUMENICAL COUNCILS OF THE CHURCH

Session XVI
Extracts from the Acts

The Acclamations of the Fathers.

Many years to the Emperor! Many years to Constantine, our great Emperor! Many years to the Orthodox King! Many years to our Emperor that makes peace! Many years to Constantine, a second Martian! Many years to Constantine, a new Theodosius! Many years to Constantine, a new Justinian! Many years to the keeper of the orthodox faith! O Lord preserve the foundation of the Churches! O Lord preserve the keeper of the faith!

Many years to Agatho, Pope of Rome! Many years to George, Patriarch of Constantinople! Many years to Theophanus, Patriarch of Antioch! Many years to the orthodox council! Many years to the orthodox Senate!

> To Theodore of Pharan, the heretic, anathema!
> To Sergius, the heretic, anathema!
> To Cyrus, the heretic, anathema!
> To Honorius, the heretic, anathema!
> To Pyrrhus, the heretic, anathema!
> To Paul the heretic, anathema!
> To Peter the heretic, anathema!
> To Macarius the heretic, anathema!
> To Stephen the heretic, anathema!
> To Polychronius the heretic, anathema!
> To Apergius of Perga the heretic, anathema!
> To all heretics, anathema! To all who side with heretics, anathema!

May the faith of the Christians increase, and long years to the orthodox and Ecumenical Council!

The Definition of Faith

The holy, great, and Ecumenical Synod which has been assembled by the grace of God, and the religious decree of the most religious and faithful and mighty Sovereign Constantine, in this God-protected and royal city of Constantinople, New Rome, in the Hall of the imperial Palace, called Trullus, has decreed as follows.

The only-begotten Son, and Word of God the Father, who was made man in all things like us without sin, Christ our true God, has declared expressly in the words of the Gospel, "I am the light of the world; he that follows me shall not walk in darkness, but shall have the light of life." And again, "My peace I leave with you, my peace I give unto you." Our most gentle Sovereign, the champion of orthodoxy, and opponent of evil doctrine, being reverentially led by this divinely uttered doctrine of peace, and having convened this our holy and Ecumenical assembly, has united the judgment of the whole Church. Wherefore this our holy and Ecumenical Synod having driven away the impious error which had prevailed for a certain time until now, and following closely the straight path of the holy and approved Fathers, has piously given its full assent to the five holy and Ecumenical Synods (that is to say, to that of the 318 holy Fathers who assembled in Nice against the raging Arius; and the next in Constantinople of the 150 God-inspired men against Macedonius the adversary of the Spirit, and the impious Apollinaris; and also the first in Ephesus of 200 venerable men convened against Nestorius the Judaizer; and that in Chalcedon of 630 God-inspired Fathers against Eutyches and Dioscorus hated of God; and in addition to these, to the last, that is the Fifth holy Synod assembled in this place, against Theodore of Mopsuestia, Origen, Didymus, and Evagrius, and the writings of Theodoret against the Twelve Chapters of the celebrated Cyril, and the Epistle which was said to be written by Ibas to Maris the Persian), renewing in all things the ancient decrees of religion, and chasing away the impious doctrines of irreligion. And this our holy and Ecumenical Synod inspired of God has set its seal to the Creed which was put forth by the 318 Fathers, and again religiously confirmed by the 150, which also the other holy synods cordially received and ratified for the taking away of every soul-destroying heresy.

The Nicene Creed of the 318 holy Fathers.

We believe, etc.

The Creed of the 150 holy Fathers assembled at Constantinople. We believe, etc.

The holy and Ecumenical Synod further says, this pious and orthodox Creed of the Divine grace would be sufficient for the full knowledge and confirmation of the orthodox faith. But as the author of evil, who, in the beginning, availed himself of the aid of the serpent, and by it brought the poison of death upon the human race, has not desisted, but in like manner now, having found suitable instruments for working out his will (we mean Theodorus, who was Bishop of Pharan, Sergius, Pyrrhus, Paul and Peter, who were Archbishops of this royal city, and moreover, Honorius who was Pope of the elder Rome, Cyrus Bishop of Alexandria, Macarius who was lately bishop of Antioch, and Stephen his disciple), has actively employed them in raising up for the whole Church the stumbling-blocks of one will and one operation in the two natures of Christ our true God, one of the Holy Trinity; thus disseminating, in novel terms, among the orthodox people, an heresy similar to the mad and wicked doctrine of the impious Apollinaris, Severus, and Themistius, and endeavouring craftily to destroy the perfection of the incarnation of the same our Lord Jesus Christ, our God, by blasphemously representing his flesh endowed with a rational soul as devoid of will or operation. Christ, therefore, our God, has raised up our faithful Sovereign, a new David, having found him a man after his own heart, who as it is written, "has not suffered his eyes to sleep nor his eyelids to slumber," until he has found a perfect declaration of orthodoxy by this our God-collected and holy Synod; for, according to the sentence spoken of God, "Where two or three are gathered together in my name, there am I in the midst of them," the present holy and Ecumenical Synod faithfully receiving and saluting with uplifted hands as well the suggestion which by the most holy and blessed Agatho, Pope of ancient Rome, was sent to our most pious and faithful Emperor Constantine, which rejected by name those who taught or preached one will and one operation in the dispensation of the incarnation of our Lord Jesus Christ who is our very God, has likewise adopted that other synodal suggestion which was sent by the Council holden under the same most holy Pope, composed of 125 Bishops, beloved of God, to his God-instructed tranquillity, as consonant to the holy Council of Chalcedon and to the Tome of the most holy and blessed Leo, Pope of the same old Rome, which was directed to St. Flavian, which also this Council called the Pillar of the right faith; and also agrees with the Synodal Epistles which were written by Blessed Cyril against the impious Nestorius and addressed to the Oriental Bishops. Following the five holy Ecumenical Councils and the holy and approved Fathers, with one voice defining that our Lord Jesus Christ must be confessed to be very God and very man, one of the holy and consubstantial and life-giving Trinity, perfect in Deity and perfect in humanity, very God and very man, of a reasonable soul and human body subsisting; consubstantial with the Father as touching his Godhead and consubstantial with us as touching his manhood; in all things like us, sin only excepted; begotten of his Father before all ages according to his Godhead, but in these last days for us men and for our salvation made man of the Holy Ghost and of the Virgin Mary, strictly and properly the Mother of God according to the flesh; one and the same Christ our Lord the only-begotten Son of two natures unconfusedly, unchangeably, inseparably indivisibly to be recognized, the peculiarities of neither nature being lost by the union but rather the proprieties of each nature being preserved, concurring in one Person and in one subsistence, not parted or divided into two persons but one and the same only-begotten Son of God, the Word, our Lord Jesus Christ, according as the Prophets of old have taught us and as our Lord Jesus Christ himself has instructed us, and the Creed of the holy Fathers has delivered to us; defining all this we likewise declare that in him are two natural wills and two natural operations indivisibly, inconvertibly, inseparably, inconfusedly, according to the teaching of the holy Fathers. And these two natural wills are not contrary the one to the other (God forbid!) as the impious heretics assert, but his human will follows and that not as resisting and reluctant, but rather as subject to his divine and omnipotent will. For it was right that the flesh should be moved but subject to the divine will, according to the most wise Athanasius. For as his flesh is called and is the flesh of God the Word, so also the natural will of his flesh is called and is the proper will of God the Word, as he himself says: "I came down from heaven, not that I might do my own will but the will of the Father which sent me!" where he calls his own will the will of his flesh, inasmuch as his flesh was also his own. For as his most holy and immaculate animated flesh was not destroyed because it was deified but continued in its own state and nature (ὅρῳ τε καὶ λόγῳ), so also his human will, although deified, was not suppressed, but was rather preserved according to the saying of Gregory Theologus: "His will [i.e., the Saviour's] is not contrary to God but altogether deified."

We glorify two natural operations indivisibly, immutably, inconfusedly, inseparably in the same our Lord Jesus Christ our true God, that is to say a divine operation and a human operation, according to the divine preacher Leo, who most distinctly asserts as follows: "For each form (μορφή) does in communion with the other what pertains properly to it, the Word, namely, doing that which pertains to the Word, and the flesh that which pertains to the flesh."

For we will not admit one natural operation in God and in the creature, as we will not exalt into the divine essence what is created, nor will we bring down the glory of the divine nature to the place suited to the creature.

We recognize the miracles and the sufferings as of one and the same [Person], but of one or of the other nature of which he is and in which he exists, as Cyril admirably says. Preserving therefore the inconfusedness and indivisibility, we make briefly this whole confession, believing our Lord Jesus Christ to be one of the Trinity and after the incarnation our true God, we say that his two natures shone forth in his one subsistence in which he both performed the miracles and endured the sufferings through the whole of his economic conversation (δι ὅλης αὐτοῦ τῆς οἰκονομικῆς ἀναστροφῆς), and that not in appearance only but in very deed, and this by reason of the difference of nature which must be recognized in the same Person, for although joined together yet each nature wills and does the things proper to it and that indivisibly and inconfusedly. Wherefore we confess two wills and two operations, concurring most fitly in him for the salvation of the human race.

These things, therefore, with all diligence and care having been formulated by us, we define that it be permitted to no one to bring forward, or to write, or to compose, or to think, or to teach a different faith. Whosoever shall presume to compose a different faith, or to propose, or teach, or hand to those wishing to be converted to the knowledge of the truth, from the Gentiles or Jews, or from any heresy, any different Creed; or to introduce a new voice or invention of speech to subvert these things which now have been determined by us, all these, if they be Bishops or clerics let them be deposed, the Bishops from the Episcopate, the clerics from the clergy; but if they be monks or laymen: let them be anathematized.

SEVEN ECUMENICAL COUNCILS OF THE CHURCH

The Prosphoneticus to the Emperor

This address begins with many compliments to the Emperor, especially for his zeal for the true faith.

But because the adversary Satan allows no rest, he has raised up the very ministers of Christ against him, as if armed and carrying weapons, etc.

The various heretics are then named and how they were condemned by the preceding five councils is set forth.

Things being so, it was necessary that your beloved of Christ majesty should gather together this all holy, and numerous assembly.

Thereafter being inspired by the Holy Ghost, and all agreeing and consenting together, and giving our approval to the doctrinal letter of our most blessed and exalted pope, Agatho, which he sent to your mightiness, as also agreeing to the suggestion of the holy synod of one hundred and twenty-five fathers held under him, we teach that one of the Holy Trinity, our Lord Jesus Christ, was incarnate, and must be celebrated in two perfect natures without division and without confusion. For as the Word, he is consubstantial and eternal with God his father; but as taking flesh of the immaculate Virgin Mary, the Mother of God, he is perfect man, consubstantial with us and made in time. We declare therefore that he is perfect in Godhead and that the same is perfect likewise in manhood, according to the pristine tradition of the fathers and the divine definition of Chalcedon.

And as we recognize two natures, so also we recognize two natural wills and two natural operations. For we dare not say that either of the natures which are in Christ in his incarnation is without a will and operation: lest in taking away the proprieties of those natures, we likewise take away the natures of which they are the proprieties. For we neither deny the natural will of his humanity, or its natural operation: lest we also deny what is the chief thing of the dispensation for our salvation, and lest we attribute passions to the Godhead. For this they were attempting who have recently introduced the detestable novelty that in him there is but one will and one operation, renewing the malignancy of Arius, Apollinaris, Eutyches and Severus. For should we say that the human nature of our Lord is without will and operation, how could we affirm in safety the perfect humanity? For nothing else constitutes the integrity of human nature except the essential will, through which the strength of free-will is marked in us; and this is also the case with the substantial operation. For how shall we call him perfect in humanity if he in no wise suffered and acted as a man? For like as the union of two natures preserves for us one subsistence without confusion and without division; so this one subsistence, showing itself in two natures, demonstrates as its own what things belong to each.

Therefore we declare that in him there are two natural wills and two natural operations, proceeding commonly and without division: but we cast out of the

SEVEN ECUMENICAL COUNCILS OF THE CHURCH

Church and rightly subject to anathema all superfluous novelties as well as their inventors: to wit, Theodore of Pharan, Sergius and Paul, Pyrrhus, and Peter (who were archbishops of Constantinople), moreover Cyrus, who bore the priesthood of Alexandria, and with them Honorius, who was the ruler (πρόεδρον) of Rome, as he followed them in these things. Besides these, with the best of cause we anathematize and depose Macarius, who was bishop of Antioch, and his disciple Stephen (or rather we should say master), who tried to defend the impiety of their predecessors, and in short stirred up the whole world, and by their pestilential letters and by their fraudulent institutions devastated multitudes in every direction. Likewise also that old man Polychronius, with an infantile intelligence, who promised he would raise the dead and who when they did not rise, was laughed at; and all who have taught, or do teach, or shall presume to teach one will and one operation in the incarnate Christ....But the highest prince of the Apostles fought with us: for we had on our side his imitator and the successor in his see, who also had set forth in his letter the mystery of the divine word (θεολογίας). For the ancient city of Rome handed you a confession of divine character, and a chart from the sunsetting raised up the day of dogmas, and made the darkness manifest, and Peter spoke through Agatho, and you, O autocratic King, according to the divine decree, with the Omnipotent Sharer of your throne, judged.

But, O benign and justice-loving Lord, do this favour in return to him who has bestowed your power upon you; and give, as a seal to what has been defined by us, your imperial ratification in writing, and so confirm them with the customary pious edicts and constitutions, that no one may contradict the things which have been done, nor raise any fresh question. For rest assured, O serene majesty, that we have not falsified anything defined by the Ecumenical Councils and by the approved fathers, but we have confirmed them. And now we all cry out with one mind and one voice, "O God, save the King! etc., etc."

Then follow numerous compliments to the Emperor and prayers for his preservation.

Letter of the Council to St. Agatho

A copy of the letter sent by the holy and Ecumenical Sixth Council to Agatho, the most blessed and most holy pope of Old Rome.

The holy and ecumenical council which by the grace of God and the pious sanction of the most pious and faithful Constantine, the great Emperor, has been gathered together in this God-preserved and royal city, Constantinople, the new Rome, in the Secretum of the imperial (θείου, sacri) palace called Trullus, to the most holy and most blessed pope of Old Rome, Agatho, health in the Lord.

Serious illnesses call for greater helps, as you know, most blessed [father]; and therefore Christ our true God, who is the creator and governing power of all things, gave a wise physician, namely your God-honoured sanctity, to drive away by force the contagion of heretical pestilence by the remedies of orthodoxy, and to give the strength of health to the members of the church. Therefore to you, as to the bishop of the first see of the Universal Church, we leave what must be done, since you willingly take for your standing ground the firm rock of the faith, as we know from having read your true confession in the letter sent by your fatherly beatitude to the most pious emperor: and we acknowledge that this letter was divinely written (perscriptas) as by the Chief of the Apostles, and through it we have cast out the heretical sect of many errors which had recently sprung up, having been urged to making a decree by Constantine who divinely reigns, and wields a most clement sceptre. And by his help we have overthrown the error of impiety, having as it were laid siege to the nefarious doctrine of the heretics. And then tearing to pieces the foundations of their execrable heresy, and attacking them with spiritual and paternal arms, and confounding their tongues that they might not speak consistently with each other, we overturned the tower built up by these followers of this most impious heresy; and we slew them with anathema, as lapsed concerning the faith and as sinners, in the morning outside the camp of the tabernacle of God, that we may express ourselves after the manner of David, in accordance with the sentence already given concerning them in your letter, and their names are these: Theodore, bishop of Pharan, Sergius, Honorius, Cyrus, Paul, Pyrrhus and Peter. Moreover, in addition to these, we justly subjected to the anathema of heretics those also who live in their impiety which they have received, or, to speak more accurately, in the impiety of these God-hated persons, Apollinaris, Severus and Themestius, to wit, Macarius, who was the bishop of the great city of Antioch (and him we also stripped deservedly of his pastor's robes on account of his impenitence concerning the orthodox faith and his obstinate stubbornness), and Stephen, his disciple in craziness and his teacher in impiety, also Polychronius, who was inveterate in his heretical doctrines, thus answering to his name; and finally all those who impenitently have taught or do teach, or now hold or have held similar doctrines.

Up to now grief, sorrow, and many tears have been our portion. For we cannot laugh at the fall of our neighbours, nor exult with joy at their unbridled madness, nor have we been elated that we might fall all the more grievously because of this thing; not thus, O venerable and sacred head, have we been taught, we who hold Christ, the Lord of the universe, to be both benign and man-loving in the highest degree; for he exhorts us to be imitators of him in his priesthood so far as is possible, as becomes the good, and to obtain the pattern of his pastoral and conciliatory government. But also to true repentance the most Serene Emperor and ourselves have exhorted them in various ways, and we have conducted the whole matter with great religiousness and care. Nor have we been moved to do so for the sake of gain, nor by hatred, as you can easily see from what things have been done in each session, and related in the minutes, which are herewith sent to your blessedness: and you will understand from your holiness's vicars, Theodore and George, presbyters beloved of God, and from John, the most religious deacon, and from Constantine, the most venerable subdeacon, all of them your spiritual children and our well-loved brethren. So too you will hear the same things from those sent by your holy synod, the holy bishops who rightly and uprightly, in accordance with your discipline, decreed with us in the first chapter of the faith.

Thus, illuminated by the Holy Spirit, and instructed by your doctrine, we have cast forth the vile doctrines of impiety, making smooth the right path of orthodoxy, being in every way encouraged and helped in so doing by the wisdom and power of our most pious and serene Emperor Constantine. And then one of our number, the most holy præsul of this reigning Constantinople, in the first place assenting to the orthodox compositions sent by you to the most pious emperor as in all respects agreeable to the teaching of the approved Fathers and of the God-instructed Fathers, and of the holy five universal councils, we all, by the help of Christ our God, easily accomplished what we were striving after. For as God was the mover, so God also he crowned our council.

Thereupon, therefore, the grace of the Holy Spirit shone upon us, displaying his power, through your assiduous prayers, for the uprooting of all weeds and every tree which brought not forth good fruit, and giving command that they should be consumed by fire. And we all agree both in heart and tongue, and hand, and have put forth, by the assistance of the life-giving Spirit, a definition, clean from all error, certain, and infallible; not 'removing the ancient landmarks,' as it is written (God forbid!), but remaining steadfast in the testimonies and authority of the holy and approved fathers, and defining that, as of two and in two natures (to wit, the divinity and the humanity) of which he is composed and in which he exists, Christ our true God is preached by us, and is glorified inseparably, unchangeably, unconfusedly, and undividedly; just so also we predicate of him two natural operations, undividedly, incontrovertibly, unconfusedly, inseparably, as has been declared in our synodal definition. These decrees the majesty of our God-copying Emperor assented to, and subscribed them with his own hand. And, as has been said, we rejected and condemned that most impious and unsubstantial heresy which affirmed but one will and one operation in the incarnate Christ our true God, and by so doing we have pressed sore upon the crowd who confound and who divide, and have extinguished the inflamed storm of other heresies, but we have set forth clearly with you the shining light of the orthodox faith, and we pray your paternal sanctity to confirm our decree by your honourable rescript; through which we confide in good hope in Christ that his merciful kindness will grant freely to the Roman State, committed to the care of our most clement Emperor, stability; and will adorn with daily yokes and victories his most serene clemency; and that in addition to the good things he has here bestowed upon us, he will set your God-honoured holiness before his tremendous tribunal as one who has sincerely confessed the true faith, preserving it unsullied and keeping good ward over the orthodox flocks committed to him by God.

We and all who are with us salute all the brethren in Christ who are with your blessedness.

The Imperial Edict Posted in the Third Atrium of the Great Church Near What is Called Dicymbala

In the name of our Lord and Master Jesus Christ, our God and Saviour, the most pious Emperor, the peaceful and Christ-loving Constantine, an Emperor faithful to God in Jesus Christ, to all our Christ-loving people living in this God-preserved and royal city.

The document is very long, Hefele gives the following epitome, which is all sufficient for the ordinary reader, who will remember that it is an Edict of the Emperor and not anything proceeding from the council.

"The heresy of Apollinaris, etc., has been renewed by Theodore of Pharan and confirmed by Honorius, sometime Pope of Old Rome, who also contradicted himself. Also Cyrus, Pyrrhus, Paul, Peter; more recently. Macarius, Stephen, and Polychronius had diffused Monothelitism. He, the Emperor, had therefore convoked this holy and Ecumenical Synod, and published the present edict with the confession of faith, in order to confirm and establish its decrees. (There follows here an extended confession of faith, with proofs for the doctrine of two wills and operations.) As he recognized the five earlier Ecumenical Synods, so he anathematized all heretics from Simon Magus, but especially the originator and patrons of the new heresy, Theodore and Sergius; also Pope Honorius, who was their adherent and patron in everything, and confirmed the heresy (τὸν κατὰ πάντα τούτοις συναιρέτην καὶ σύνδρομον καὶ βεβαιωτὴν τῆς αἱρέσεως, further, Cyrus, etc., and ordained that no one henceforth should hold a different faith, or venture to teach one will and one energy. In no other than the orthodox faith could men be saved. Whoever did not obey the imperial edict should, if he were a bishop or cleric be deposed; if an official, punished with confiscation of property and loss of the girdle (ζώνη); if a private person, banished from the residence and all other cities."

SEVEN ECUMENICAL COUNCILS OF THE CHURCH

Canons of the Synod of Trullo
Anno Domini 692

Canon 1

That order is best of all which makes every word and act begin and end in God. Wherefore that piety may be clearly set forth by us and that the Church of which Christ is the foundation may be continually increased and advanced, and that it may be exalted above the cedars of Lebanon; now therefore we, by divine grace at the beginning of our decrees, define that the faith set forth by the God-chosen Apostles who themselves had both seen and were ministers of the Word, shall be preserved without any innovation, unchanged and inviolate.

Moreover the faith of the three hundred and eighteen holy and blessed fathers who were assembled at Nice under Constantine our Emperor, against the impious Arius, and the gentile diversity of deity or rather (to speak accurately) multitude of gods taught by him, who by the unanimous acknowledgment of the faithful revealed and declared to us the consubstantiality of the Three Persons comprehended in the Divine Nature, not suffering this faith to lie hidden under the bushel of ignorance, but openly teaching the faithful to adore with one worship the Father, the Son, and the Holy Ghost, confuting and scattering to the winds the opinion of different grades, and demolishing and overturning the puerile toyings fabricated out of sand by the heretics against orthodoxy.

Likewise also we confirm that faith which was set forth by the one hundred and fifty fathers who in the time of Theodosius the Elder, our Emperor, assembled in this imperial city, accepting their decisions with regard to the Holy Ghost in assertion of his godhead, and expelling the profane Macedonius (together with all previous enemies of the truth) as one who dared to judge Him to be a servant who is Lord, and who wished to divide, like a robber, the inseparable unity, so that there might be no perfect mystery of our faith.

And together with this odious and detestable contender against the truth, we condemn Apollinaris, priest of the same iniquity, who impiously belched forth that the Lord assumed a body unendowed with a soul, thence also inferring that his salvation wrought for us was imperfect.

Moreover what things were set forth by the two hundred God-bearing fathers in the city of Ephesus in the days of Theodosius our Emperor, the son of Arcadius; these doctrines we assent to as the unbroken strength of piety, teaching that Christ the incarnate Son of God is one; and declaring that she who bare him without human seed was the immaculate Ever-Virgin, glorifying her as literally and in very truth the Mother of God. We condemn as foreign to the divine scheme the absurd division of Nestorius, who teaches that the one Christ consists of a man separately and of the Godhead separately and renews the Jewish impiety.

SEVEN ECUMENICAL COUNCILS OF THE CHURCH

Moreover we confirm that faith which at Chalcedon, the Metropolis, was set forth in accordance with orthodoxy by the six hundred and thirty God-approved fathers in the time of Marcian, who was our Emperor, which handed down with a great and mighty voice, even unto the ends of the earth, that the one Christ, the son of God, is of two natures, and must be glorified in these two natures, and which cast forth from the sacred precincts of the Church as a black pestilence to be avoided, Eutyches, babbling stupidly and inanely, and teaching that the great mystery of the incarnation (οἰκονωμίας) was perfected in thought only. And together with him also Nestorius and Dioscorus of whom the former was the defender and champion of the division, the latter of the confusion [of the two natures in the one Christ], both of whom fell away from the divergence of their impiety to a common depth of perdition and denial of God.

Also we recognize as inspired by the Spirit the pious voices of the one hundred and sixty-five God-bearing fathers who assembled in this imperial city in the time of our Emperor Justinian of blessed memory, and we teach them to those who come after us; for these synodically anathematized and execrated Theodore of Mopsuestia (the teacher of Nestorius), and Origen, and Didymus, and Evagrius, all of whom reintroduced feigned Greek myths, and brought back again the circlings of certain bodies and souls, and deranged turnings [or transmigrations] to the wanderings or dreamings of their minds, and impiously insulting the resurrection of the dead. Moreover [they condemned] what things were written by Theodoret against the right faith and against the Twelve Chapters of blessed Cyril, and that letter which is said to have been written by Ibas.

Also we agree to guard untouched the faith of the Sixth Holy Synod, which first assembled in this imperial city in the time of Constantine, our Emperor, of blessed memory, which faith received still greater confirmation from the fact that the pious Emperor ratified with his own signet that which was written for the security of future generations. This council taught that we should openly profess our faith that in the incarnation of Jesus Christ, our true God, there are two natural wills or volitions and two natural operations; and condemned by a just sentence those who adulterated the true doctrine and taught the people that in the one Lord Jesus Christ there is but one will and one operation; to wit, Theodore of Pharan, Cyrus of Alexandria, Honorius of Rome, Sergius, Pyrrhus, Paul and Peter, who were bishops of this God-preserved city; Macarius, who was bishop of Antioch; Stephen, who was his disciple, and the insane Polychronius, depriving them henceforth from the communion of the body of Christ our God.

And, to say so once for all, we decree that the faith shall stand firm and remain unsullied until the end of the world as well as the writings divinely handed down and the teachings of all those who have beautified and adorned the Church of God and were lights in the world, having embraced the word of life. And we reject and anathematize those whom they rejected and anathematized, as being enemies of the truth, and as insane ragers against God, and as lifters up of iniquity.

But if any one at all shall not observe and embrace the aforesaid pious decrees, and teach and preach in accordance therewith, but shall attempt to set himself in opposition thereto, let him be anathema, according to the decree already promulgated by the approved holy and blessed Fathers, and let him be cast out and stricken off as an alien from the number of Christians. For our decrees add nothing to the things previously defined, nor do they take anything away, nor have we any such power.

Canon 2

It has also seemed good to this holy Council, that the eighty-five canons, received and ratified by the holy and blessed Fathers before us, and also handed down to us in the name of the holy and glorious Apostles should from this time forth remain firm and unshaken for the cure of souls and the healing of disorders. And in these canons we are bidden to receive the Constitutions of the Holy Apostles [written] by Clement. But formerly through the agency of those who erred from the faith certain adulterous matter was introduced, clean contrary to piety, for the polluting of the Church, which obscures the elegance and beauty of the divine decrees in their present form. We therefore reject these Constitutions so as the better to make sure of the edification and security of the most Christian flock; by no means admitting the offspring of heretical error, and cleaving to the pure and perfect doctrine of the Apostles. But we set our seal likewise upon all the other holy canons set forth by our holy and blessed Fathers, that is, by the 318 holy God-bearing Fathers assembled at Nice, and those at Ancyra, further those at Neocæsarea and likewise those at Gangra, and besides, those at Antioch in Syria: those too at Laodicea in Phrygia: and likewise the 150 who assembled in this heaven-protected royal city: and the 200 who assembled the first time in the metropolis of the Ephesians, and the 630 holy and blessed Fathers at Chalcedon. In like manner those of Sardica, and those of Carthage: those also who again assembled in this heaven-protected royal city under its bishop Nectarius and Theophilus Archbishop of Alexandria. Likewise too the Canons [i.e. the decretal letters] of Dionysius, formerly Archbishop of the great city of Alexandria; and of Peter, Archbishop of Alexandria and Martyr; of Gregory the Wonder-worker, Bishop of Neocæsarea; of Athanasius, Archbishop of Alexandria; of Basil, Archbishop of Cæsarea in Cappadocia; of Gregory, Bishop of Nyssa; of Gregory Theologus; of Amphilochius of Iconium; of Timothy, Archbishop of Alexandria; of Theophilus, Archbishop of the same great city of Alexandria; of Cyril, Archbishop of the same Alexandria; of Gennadius, Patriarch of this heaven-protected royal city. Moreover the Canon set forth by Cyprian, Archbishop of the country of the Africans and Martyr, and by the Synod under him, which has been kept only in the country of the aforesaid Bishops, according to the custom delivered down to them. And that no one be allowed to transgress or disregard the aforesaid canons, or to receive others beside them, supposititiously set forth by certain who have attempted to make a traffic of the truth. But should any one be convicted of innovating upon, or attempting to overturn, any of the afore-mentioned canons, he shall be subject to receive the penalty which that canon imposes, and to be cured by it of his transgression.

Canon 3

Since our pious and Christian Emperor has addressed this holy and ecumenical council, in order that it might provide for the purity of those who are in the list of the clergy, and who transmit divine things to others, and that they may be blameless ministrants, and worthy of the sacrifice of the great God, who is both Offering and High Priest, a sacrifice apprehended by the intelligence: and that it might cleanse away the pollutions wherewith these have been branded by unlawful marriages: now whereas they of the most holy Roman Church purpose to keep the rule of exact perfection, but those who are under the throne of this heaven-protected and royal city keep that of kindness and consideration, so blending both together as our fathers have done, and as the love of God requires, that neither gentleness fall into licence, nor severity into harshness; especially as the fault of ignorance has reached no small number of men, we decree, that those who are involved in a second marriage, and have been slaves to sin up to the fifteenth of the past month of January, in the past fourth Indiction, the 6109th year, and have not resolved to repent of it, be subjected to canonical deposition: but that they who are involved in this disorder of a second marriage, but before our decree have acknowledged what is fitting, and have cut off their sin, and have put far from them this strange and illegitimate connection, or they whose wives by second marriage are already dead, or who have turned to repentance of their own accord, having learned continence, and having quickly forgotten their former iniquities, whether they be presbyters or deacons, these we have determined should cease from all priestly ministrations or exercise, being under punishment for a certain time, but should retain the honour of their seat and station, being satisfied with their seat before the laity and begging with tears from the Lord that the transgression of their ignorance be pardoned them: for unfitting it were that he should bless another who has to tend his own wounds. But those who have been married to one wife, if she was a widow, and likewise those who after their ordination have unlawfully entered into one marriage that is, presbyters, and deacons, and subdeacons, being debarred for some short time from sacred ministration, and censured, shall be restored again to their proper rank, never advancing to any further rank, their unlawful marriage being openly dissolved. This we decree to hold good only in the case of those that are involved in the aforesaid faults up to the fifteenth (as was said) of the month of January, of the fourth Indiction, decreeing from the present time, and renewing the Canon which declares, that he who has been joined in two marriages after his baptism, or has had a concubine, cannot be bishop, or presbyter, or deacon, or at all on the sacerdotal list; in like manner, that he who has taken a widow, or a divorced person, or a harlot, or a servant, or an actress, cannot be bishop, or presbyter, or deacon, or at all on the sacerdotal list.

Canon 4

If any bishop, presbyter, deacon, sub-deacon, lector, cantor, or door-keeper has had intercourse with a woman dedicated to God, let him be deposed, as one who has corrupted a spouse of Christ, but if a layman let him be cut off.

Canon 5

Let none of those who are on the priestly list possess any woman or maid servant, beyond those who are enumerated in the canon as being persons free from suspicion, preserving himself hereby from being implicated in any blame. But if anyone transgresses our decree let him be deposed. And let eunuchs also observe the same rule, that by foresight they may be free of censure. But those who transgress, let them be deposed, if indeed they are clerics; but if laymen let them be excommunicated.

Canon 6

Since it is declared in the apostolic canons that of those who are advanced to the clergy unmarried, only lectors and cantors are able to marry; we also, maintaining this, determine that henceforth it is in nowise lawful for any subdeacon, deacon or presbyter after his ordination to contract matrimony but if he shall have dared to do so, let him be deposed. And if any of those who enter the clergy, wishes to be joined to a wife in lawful marriage before he is ordained subdeacon, deacon, or presbyter, let it be done.

Canon 7

Since we have learned that in some churches deacons hold ecclesiastical offices, and that hereby some of them with arrogancy and license sit daringly before the presbyters: we have determined that a deacon, even if in an office of dignity, that is to say, in whatever ecclesiastical office he may be, is not to have his seat before a presbyter, except he is acting as representative of his own patriarch or metropolitan in another city under another superior, for then he shall be honoured as filling his place. But if anyone, possessed with a tyrannical audacity, shall have dared to do such a thing, let him be ejected from his peculiar rank and be last of all of the order in whose list he is in his own church; our Lord admonishing us that we are not to delight in taking the chief seats, according to the doctrine which is found in the holy Evangelist Luke, as put forth by our Lord and God himself. For to those who were called he taught this parable: "When you are bidden by anyone to a marriage sit not down in the highest room lest a more honourable man than you shall have been bidden by him; and he who bade you and him come and say to you: Give this man place, and you begin with shame to take the lowest room. But when you are bidden, sit down in the lowest place, so that when he who bade you comes he may say to you, Friend go up higher: then you shall have worship in the presence of them that sit with you. For whosoever exalts himself shall be abased, and he that humbles himself shall be exalted." But the same thing also shall be observed in the remaining sacred orders; seeing that we know that spiritual things are to be preferred to worldly dignity.

Canon 8

Since we desire that in every point the things which have been decreed by our holy fathers may also be established and confirmed, we hereby renew the canon which orders that synods of the bishops of each province be held every year where the bishop of the metropolis shall deem best. But since on account of the incursions of barbarians and certain other incidental causes, those who preside over the churches cannot hold synods twice a year, it seems right that by all means once a year— on account of ecclesiastical questions which are likely to arise— a synod of the aforesaid bishops should be holden in every province, between the holy feast of Easter and October, as has been said above, in the place which the Metropolitan shall have deemed most fitting. And let such bishops as do not attend, when they are at home in their own cities and are in good health, and free from all unavoidable and necessary business, be fraternally reproved.

Canon 9

Let no cleric be permitted to keep a "public house." For if it be not permitted to enter a tavern, much more is it forbidden to serve others in it and to carry on a trade which is unlawful for him. But if he shall have done any such thing, either let him desist or be deposed.

Canon 10

A bishop, or presbyter, or deacon who receives usury, or what is called hecatostæ, let him desist or be deposed.

Canon 11

Let no one in the priestly order nor any layman eat the unleavened bread of the Jews, nor have any familiar intercourse with them, nor summon them in illness, nor receive medicines from them, nor bathe with them; but if anyone shall take in hand to do so, if he is a cleric, let him be deposed, but if a layman let him be cut off.

Canon 12

Moreover this also has come to our knowledge, that in Africa and Libya and in other places the most God-beloved bishops in those parts do not refuse to live with their wives, even after consecration, thereby giving scandal and offense to the people. Since, therefore, it is our particular care that all things tend to the good of the flock placed in our hands and committed to us—it has seemed good that henceforth nothing of the kind shall in any way occur. And we say this, not to abolish and overthrow what things were established of old by Apostolic authority, but as caring for the health of the people and their advance to better things, and lest the ecclesiastical state should suffer any reproach. For the divine Apostle says: "Do all to the glory of God, give none offense, neither to the Jews, nor to the Greeks, nor to the Church of God, even as I please all men in all things, not seeking my own profit but the profit of many, that they may be saved. Be imitators of me even as I also am of Christ." But if any shall have been observed to do such a thing, let him be deposed.

Canon 13
Since we know it to be handed down as a rule of the Roman Church that those who are deemed worthy to be advanced to the diaconate or presbyterate should promise no longer to cohabit with their wives, we, preserving the ancient rule and apostolic perfection and order, will that the lawful marriages of men who are in holy orders be from this time forward firm, by no means dissolving their union with their wives nor depriving them of their mutual intercourse at a convenient time. Wherefore, if anyone shall have been found worthy to be ordained subdeacon, or deacon, or presbyter, he is by no means to be prohibited from admittance to such a rank, even if he shall live with a lawful wife. Nor shall it be demanded of him at the time of his ordination that he promise to abstain from lawful intercourse with his wife: lest we should affect injuriously marriage constituted by God and blessed by his presence, as the Gospel says: "What God has joined together let no man put asunder;" and the Apostle says, "Marriage is honourable and the bed undefiled;" and again, "Are you bound to a wife? Seek not to be loosed." But we know, as they who assembled at Carthage (with a care for the honest life of the clergy) said, that subdeacons, who handle the Holy Mysteries, and deacons, and presbyters should abstain from their consorts according to their own course [of ministration]. So that what has been handed down through the Apostles and preserved by ancient custom, we too likewise maintain, knowing that there is a time for all things and especially for fasting and prayer. For it is meet that they who assist at the divine altar should be absolutely continent when they are handling holy things, in order that they may be able to obtain from God what they ask in sincerity.

If therefore anyone shall have dared, contrary to the Apostolic Canons, to deprive any of those who are in holy orders, presbyter, or deacon, or subdeacon of cohabitation and intercourse with his lawful wife, let him be deposed. In like manner also if any presbyter or deacon on pretence of piety has dismissed his wife, let him be excluded from communion; and if he persevere in this let him be deposed.

Canon 14
Let the canon of our holy God-bearing Fathers be confirmed in this particular also; that a presbyter be not ordained before he is thirty years of age, even if he be a very worthy man, but let him be kept back. For our Lord Jesus Christ was baptized and began to teach when he was thirty. In like manner let no deacon be ordained before he is twenty-five, nor a deaconess before she is forty.

Canon 15
A subdeacon is not to be ordained under twenty years of age. And if any one in any grade of the priesthood shall have been ordained contrary to the prescribed time let him be deposed.

Canon 16

Since the book of the Acts tells us that seven deacons were appointed by the Apostles, and the synod of Neocæsarea in the canons which it put forth determined that there ought to be canonically only seven deacons, even if the city be very large, in accordance with the book of the Acts; we, having fitted the mind of the fathers to the Apostles' words, find that they spoke not of those men who ministered at the Mysteries but in the administration which pertains to the serving of tables. For the book of the Acts reads as follows: "In those days, when the number of the disciples was multiplied, there arose a murmuring dissension of the Grecians against the Hebrews, because their widows were neglected in the daily ministrations. And the Twelve called the multitude of the disciples with them and said, It is not meet for us to leave the word of God and serve tables. Look out therefore, brethren, from among you seven men of good report full of the Holy Ghost and of wisdom, whom we may appoint over this business. But we will give ourselves continually unto prayer and unto the ministry of the word. And the saying pleased the whole multitude: and they chose Stephen a man full of faith and of the Holy Ghost, and Philip, and Prochorus, and Nicanor, and Timon, and Parmenas, and Nicolas a proselyte of Antioch: whom they set before the Apostles."

John Chrysostom, a Doctor of the Church, interpreting these words, proceeds thus: "It is a remarkable fact that the multitude was not divided in its choice of the men, and that the Apostles were not rejected by them. But we must learn what sort of rank they had, and what ordination they received. Was it that of deacons? But this office did not yet exist in the churches. But was it the dispensation of a presbyter? But there was not as yet any bishop, but only Apostles, whence I think it is clear and manifest that neither of deacons nor of presbyters was there then the name."

But on this account therefore we also announce that the aforesaid seven deacons are not to be understood as deacons who served at the Mysteries, according to the teaching before set forth, but that they were those to whom a dispensation was entrusted for the common benefit of those that were gathered together, who to us in this also were a type of philanthropy and zeal towards those who are in need.

Canon 17

Since clerics of different churches have left their own churches in which they were ordained and betaken themselves to other bishops, and without the consent of their own bishop have been settled in other churches, and thus they have proved themselves to be insolent and disobedient; we decree that from the month of January of the past IVth Indiction no cleric, of whatsoever grade he be, shall have power, without letters dimissory of his own bishop, to be registered in the clergy list of another church. Whoever in future shall not have observed this rule, but shall have brought disgrace upon himself as well as on the bishop who ordained him, let him be deposed together with him who also received him.

Canon 18

Those clerics who in consequence of a barbaric incursion or on account of any other circumstance have gone abroad, we order to return again to their churches after the cause has passed away, or when the incursion of the barbarians is at an end. Nor are they to leave them for long without cause. If anyone shall not have returned according to the direction of this present canon— let him be cut off until he shall return to his own church. And the same shall be the punishment of the bishop who received him.

Canon 19

It behooves those who preside over the churches, every day but especially on Lord's days, to teach all the clergy and people words of piety and of right religion, gathering out of holy Scripture meditations and determinations of the truth, and not going beyond the limits now fixed, nor varying from the tradition of the God-bearing fathers. And if any controversy in regard to Scripture shall have been raised, let them not interpret it otherwise than as the lights and doctors of the church in their writings have expounded it, and in those let them glory rather than in composing things out of their own heads, lest through their lack of skill they may have departed from what was fitting. For through the doctrine of the aforesaid fathers, the people coming to the knowledge of what is good and desirable, as well as what is useless and to be rejected, will remodel their life for the better, and not be led by ignorance, but applying their minds to the doctrine, they will take heed that no evil befall them and work out their salvation in fear of impending punishment.

Canon 20

It shall not be lawful for a bishop to teach publicly in any city which does not belong to him. If any shall have been observed doing this, let him cease from his episcopate, but let him discharge the office of a presbyter.

Canon 21

Those who have become guilty of crimes against the canons, and on this account subject to complete and perpetual deposition, are degraded to the condition of layman. If, however, keeping conversion continually before their eyes, they willingly deplore the sin on account of which they fell from grace, and made themselves aliens therefrom, they may still cut their hair after the manner of clerics. But if they are not willing to submit themselves to this canon, they must wear their hair as laymen, as being those who have preferred the communion of the world to the celestial life.

Canon 22

Those who are ordained for money, whether bishops or of any rank whatever, and not by examination and choice of life, we order to be deposed as well as those also who ordained them.

Canon 23

That no one, whether bishop, presbyter, or deacon, when giving the immaculate Communion, shall exact from him who communicates fees of any kind. For grace is not to be sold, nor do we give the sanctification of the Holy Spirit for money; but to those who are worthy of the gift it is to be communicated in all simplicity. But if any of those enrolled among the clergy make demands on those he communicates let him be deposed, as an imitator of the error and wickedness of Simon.

Canon 24

No one who is on the priestly catalogue nor any monk is allowed to take part in horse-races or to assist at theatrical representations. But if any clergyman be called to a marriage, as soon as the games begin let him rise up and go out, for so it is ordered by the doctrine of our fathers. And if any one shall be convicted of such an offense let him cease therefrom or be deposed.

Canon 25

Moreover we renew the canon which orders that country (ἀγροικικὰς) parishes and those which are in the provinces (ἐγχωρίους) shall remain subject to the bishops who had possession of them; especially if for thirty years they had administered them without opposition. But if within thirty years there had been or should be any controversy on the point, it is lawful for those who think themselves injured to refer the matter to the provincial synod.

Canon 26

If a presbyter has through ignorance contracted an illegal marriage, while he still retains the right to his place, as we have defined in the sacred canons, yet he must abstain from all sacerdotal work. For it is sufficient if to such an one indulgence is granted. For he is unfit to bless another who needs to take care of his own wounds, for blessing is the imparting of sanctification. But how can he impart this to another who does not possess it himself through a sin of ignorance? Neither then in public nor in private can he bless nor distribute to others the body of Christ, [nor perform any other ministry]; but being content with his seat of honour let him lament to the Lord that his sin of ignorance may be remitted. For it is manifest that the nefarious marriage must be dissolved, neither can the man have any intercourse with her on account of whom he is deprived of the execution of his priesthood.

Canon 27

None of those who are in the catalogue of the clergy shall wear clothes unsuited to them, either while still living in town or when on a journey: but they shall wear such clothes as are assigned to those who belong to the clergy. And if any one shall violate this canon, he shall be cut off for one week.

Canon 28

Since we understand that in several churches grapes are brought to the altar, according to a custom which has long prevailed, and the ministers joined this with the unbloody sacrifice of the oblation, and distributed both to the people at the same time, we decree that no priest shall do this for the future, but shall administer the oblation alone to the people for the quickening of their souls and for the remission of their sins. But with regard to the offering of grapes as first fruits, the priests may bless them apart [from the offering of the oblation] and distribute them to such as seek them as an act of thanksgiving to him who is the Giver of the fruits by which our bodies are increased and fed according to his divine decree. And if any cleric shall violate this decree let him be deposed.

Canon 29

A canon of the Synod of Carthage says that the holy mysteries of the altar are not to be performed but by men who are fasting, except on one day in the year on which the Supper of the Lord is celebrated. At that time, on account perhaps of certain occasions in those places useful to the Church, even the holy Fathers themselves made use of this dispensation. But since nothing leads us to abandon exact observance, we decree that the Apostolic and Patristic tradition shall be followed; and define that it is not right to break the fast on the fifth feria of the last week of Lent, and thus to do dishonour to the whole of Lent.

Canon 30

Willing to do all things for the edification of the Church, we have determined to take care even of priests who are in barbarian churches. Wherefore if they think that they ought to exceed the Apostolic Canon concerning the not putting away of a wife on the pretext of piety and religion, and to do beyond that which is commanded, and therefore abstain by agreement with their wives from cohabitation, we decree they ought no longer to live with them in any way, so that hereby they may afford us a perfect demonstration of their promise. But we have conceded this to them on no other ground than their narrowness, and foreign and unsettled manners.

Canon 31

Clerics who in oratories which are in houses offer the Holy Mysteries or baptize, we decree ought to do this with the consent of the bishop of the place. Wherefore if any cleric shall not have so done, let him be deposed.

Canon 32

Since it has come to our knowledge that in the region of Armenia they offer wine only on the Holy Table, those who celebrate the unbloody sacrifice not mixing water with it, adducing, as authority thereof, John Chrysostom, a doctor of the Church, who says in his interpretation of the Gospel according to St. Matthew:

"And wherefore did he not drink water after he was risen again, but wine? To pluck up by the roots another wicked heresy. For since there are certain who use water in the Mysteries to show that both when he delivered the mysteries he had given wine and that when he had risen and was setting before them a mere meal without mysteries, he used wine, 'of the fruit,' says he, 'of the vine.' But a vine produces wine, not water." And from this they think the doctor overthrows the admixture of water in the holy sacrifice. Now, lest on the point from this time forward they be held in ignorance, we open out the orthodox opinion of the Father. For since there was an ancient and wicked heresy of the Hydroparastatæ; (i.e., of those who offered water), who instead of wine used water in their sacrifice, this divine, confuting the detestable teaching of such a heresy, and showing that it is directly opposed to Apostolic tradition, asserted that which has just been quoted. For to his own church, where the pastoral administration had been given him, he ordered that water mixed with wine should be used at the unbloody sacrifice, so as to show forth the mingling of the blood and water which for the life of the whole world and for the redemption of its sins, was poured forth from the precious side of Christ our Redeemer; and moreover in every church where spiritual light has shined this divinely given order is observed.

For also James, the brother, according to the flesh, of Christ our God, to whom the throne of the church of Jerusalem first was entrusted, and Basil, the Archbishop of the Church of Cæsarea, whose glory has spread through all the world, when they delivered to us directions for the mystical sacrifice in writing, declared that the holy chalice is consecrated in the Divine Liturgy with water and wine. And the holy Fathers who assembled at Carthage provided in these express terms: "That in the holy Mysteries nothing besides the body and blood of the Lord be offered, as the Lord himself laid down, that is bread and wine mixed with water." Therefore if any bishop or presbyter shall not perform the holy action according to what has been handed down by the Apostles, and shall not offer the sacrifice with wine mixed with water, let him be deposed, as imperfectly showing forth the mystery and innovating on the things which have been handed down.

Canon 33

Since we know that, in the region of the Armenians, only those are appointed to the clerical orders who are of priestly descent (following in this Jewish customs); and some of those who are even untonsured are appointed to succeed cantors and readers of the divine law, we decree that henceforth it shall not be lawful for those who wish to bring any one into the clergy, to pay regard to the descent of him who is to be ordained; but let them examine whether they are worthy (according to the decrees set forth in the holy canons) to be placed on the list of the clergy, so that they may be ecclesiastically promoted, whether they are of priestly descent or not; moreover, let them not permit any one at all to read in the ambo, according to the order of those enrolled in the clergy, unless such an one have received the priestly tonsure and the canonical benediction of his own pastor; but if any one shall have been observed to act contrary to these directions, let him be cut off.

Canon 34

But in future, since the priestly canon openly sets this forth, that the crime of conspiracy or secret society is forbidden by external laws, but much more ought it to be prohibited in the Church; we also hasten to observe that if any clerics or monks are found either conspiring or entering secret societies, or devising anything against bishops or clergymen, they shall be altogether deprived of their rank.

Canon 35

It shall be lawful for no Metropolitan on the death of a bishop of his province to appropriate or sell the private property of the deceased, or that of the widowed church: but these are to be in the custody of the clergy of the diocese over which he presided until the election of another bishop, unless in the said church there are no clergymen left. For then the Metropolitan shall protect the property without diminution, handing over everything to the bishop when he is appointed.

Canon 36

Renewing the enactments by the 150 Fathers assembled at the God-protected and imperial city, and those of the 630 who met at Chalcedon; we decree that the see of Constantinople shall have equal privileges with the see of Old Rome, and shall be highly regarded in ecclesiastical matters as that is, and shall be second after it. After Constantinople shall be ranked the See of Alexandria, then that of Antioch, and afterwards the See of Jerusalem.

Canon 37

Since at different times there have been invasions of barbarians, and therefore very many cities have been subjected to the infidels, so that the bishop of a city may not be able, after he has been ordained, to take possession of his see, and to be settled in it in sacerdotal order, and so to perform and manage for it the ordinations and all things which by custom appertain to the bishop: we, preserving honour and veneration for the priesthood, and in no wise wishing to employ the Gentile injury to the ruin of ecclesiastical rights, have decreed that those who have been ordained thus, and on account of the aforesaid cause have not been settled in their sees, without any prejudice from this thing may be kept [in good standing] and that they may canonically perform the ordination of the different clerics and use the authority of their office according to the defined limits, and that whatever administration proceeds from them may be valid and legitimate. For the exercise of his office shall not be circumscribed by a season of necessity when the exact observance of law is circumscribed.

Canon 38

The canon which was made by the Fathers we also observe, which thus decreed: If any city be renewed by imperial authority, or shall have been renewed, let the order of things ecclesiastical follow the civil and public models.

Canon 39

Since our brother and fellow-worker, John, bishop of the island of Cyprus, together with his people in the province of the Hellespont, both on account of barbarian incursions, and that they may be freed from servitude of the heathen, and may be subject alone to the sceptres of most Christian rule, have emigrated from the said island, by the providence of the philanthropic God, and the labour of our Christ-loving and pious Empress; we determine that the privileges which were conceded by the divine fathers who first at Ephesus assembled, are to be preserved without any innovations, viz.: that new Justinianopolis shall have the rights of Constantinople and whoever is constituted the pious and most religious bishop thereof shall take precedence of all the bishops of the province of the Hellespont, and be elected [?] by his own bishops according to ancient custom. For the customs which obtain in each church our divine Fathers also took pains should be maintained, the existing bishop of the city of Cyzicus being subject to the metropolitan of the aforesaid Justinianopolis, for the imitation of all the rest of the bishops who are under the aforesaid beloved of God metropolitan John, by whom, as custom demands, even the bishop of the very city of Cyzicus shall be ordained.

Canon 40

Since to cleave to God by retiring from the noise and turmoil of life is very beneficial, it behooves us not without examination to admit before the proper time those who choose the monastic life, but to observe respecting them the limit handed down by our fathers, in order that we may then admit a profession of the life according to God as for ever firm, and the result of knowledge and judgment after years of discretion have been reached. He therefore who is about to submit to the yoke of monastic life should not be less than ten years of age, the examination of the matter depending on the decision of the bishop, whether he considers a longer time more conducive for his entrance and establishment in the monastic life. For although the great Basil in his holy canons decreed that she who willingly offers to God and embraces virginity, if she has completed her seventeenth year, is to be entered in the order of virgins: nevertheless, having followed the example respecting widows and deaconesses, analogy and proportion being considered, we have admitted at the said time those who have chosen the monastic life. For it is written in the divine Apostle that a widow is to be elected in the church at sixty years old: but the sacred canons have decreed that a deaconess shall be ordained at forty, since they saw that the Church by divine grace had gone forth more powerful and robust and was advancing still further, and they saw the firmness and stability of the faithful in observing the divine commandments. Wherefore we also, since we most rightly comprehend the matter, appoint the benediction of grace to him who is about to enter the struggle according to God, even as impressing speedily a certain seal upon him, hereupon introducing him to the not-long-to-be-hesitated-over and declined, or rather inciting him even to the choice and determination of good.

Canon 41

Those who in town or in villages wish to go away into cloisters, and take heed for themselves apart, before they enter a monastery and practise the anchorite's life, should for the space of three years in the fear of God submit to the Superior of the house, and fulfil obedience in all things, as is right, thus showing forth their choice of this life and that they embrace it willingly and with their whole hearts; they are then to be examined by the superior (προέδρος) of the place; and then to bear bravely outside the cloister one year more, so that their purpose may be fully manifested. For by this they will show fully and perfectly that they are not catching at vain glory, but that they are pursuing the life of solitude because of its inherent beauty and honour. After the completion of such a period, if they remain in the same intention in their choice of the life, they are to be enclosed, and no longer is it lawful for them to go out of such a house when they so desire, unless they be induced to do so for the common advantage, or other pressing necessity urging on to death; and then only with the blessing of the bishop of that place.

And those who, without the above-mentioned causes, venture forth of their convents, are first of all to be shut up in the said convent even against their wills, and then are to cure themselves with fasting and other afflictions, knowing how it is written that "no one who has put his hand to the plough and has looked back, is fit for the kingdom of heaven."

Canon 42

Those who are called Eremites and are clothed in black robes, and with long hair go about cities and associate with the worldly both men and women and bring odium upon their profession— we decree that if they will receive the habit of other monks and wear their hair cut short, they may be shut up in a monastery and numbered among the brothers; but if they do not choose to do this, they are to be expelled from the cities and forced to live in the desert (ἐρήμους) from whence also they derive their name.

Canon 43

It is lawful for every Christian to choose the life of religious discipline, and setting aside the troublous surgings of the affairs of this life to enter a monastery, and to be shaven in the fashion of a monk, without regard to what faults he may have previously committed. For God our Saviour says: "Whoso comes to me, I will in no wise cast out."

As therefore the monastic method of life engraves upon us as on a tablet the life of penitence, we receive whoever approaches it sincerely; nor is any custom to be allowed to hinder him from fulfilling his intention.

Canon 44

A monk convicted of fornication, or who takes a wife for the communion of matrimony and for society, is to be subjected to the penalties of fornicators, according to the canons.

Canon 45

Whereas we understand that in some monasteries of women those who are about to be clothed with the sacred habit are first adorned in silks and garments of all kinds, and also with gold and jewels, by those who bring them there, and that they thus approach the altar and are there stripped of such a display of wealth, and that immediately thereafter the blessing of their habit takes place, and they are clothed with the black robe; we decree that henceforth this shall not be done. For it is not lawful for her who has already of her own free will put away every delight of life, and has embraced that method of life which is according to God, and has confirmed it with strong and stable reasons, and so has come to the monastery, to recall to memory the things which they had already forgotten, things of this world which perishes and passes away. For thus they raise in themselves doubts, and are disturbed in their souls, like the tossing waves, turning hither and there. Moreover, they should not give bodily evidence of heaviness of heart by weeping, but if a few tears drop from their eyes, as is like enough to be the case, they may be supposed by those who see them to have flowed μὴ μᾶλλον on account of their affection (διαθέσεως, affectionem) for the ascetic struggle rather than (ἢ) because they are quitting the world and worldly things.

Canon 46

Those women who choose the ascetic life and are settled in monasteries may by no means go forth of them. If, however, any inexorable necessity compels them, let them do so with the blessing and permission of her who is mother superior; and even then they must not go forth alone, but with some old women who are eminent in the monastery, and at the command of the lady superior. But it is not at all permitted that they should stop outside.

And men also who follow the monastic life let them on urgent necessity go forth with the blessing of him to whom the rule is entrusted.

Wherefore, those who transgress that which is now decreed by us, whether they be men or women, are to be subjected to suitable punishments.

Canon 47

No woman may sleep in a monastery of men, nor any man in a monastery of women. For it behooves the faithful to be without offense and to give no scandal, and to order their lives decorously and honestly and acceptably to God. But if any one shall have done this, whether he be cleric or layman, let him be cut off.

Canon 48

The wife of him who is advanced to the Episcopal dignity, shall be separated from her husband by their mutual consent, and after his ordination and consecration to the episcopate she shall enter a monastery situated at a distance from the abode of the bishop, and there let her enjoy the bishop's provision. And if she is deemed worthy she may be advanced to the dignity of a deaconess.

Canon 49

Renewing also the holy canon, we decree that the monasteries which have been once consecrated by the Episcopal will, are always to remain monasteries, and the things which belong to them are to be preserved to the monastery, and they cannot any more be secular abodes nor be given by any one to seculars. But if anything of this kind has been done already, we declare it to be null; and those who hereafter attempt to do so are to be subjected to canonical penalties.

Canon 50

No one at all, whether cleric or layman, is from this time forward to play at dice. And if any one hereafter shall be found doing so, if he be a cleric he is to be deposed, if a layman let him be cut off.

Canon 51

This holy and ecumenical synod altogether forbids those who are called "players," and their "spectacles," as well as the exhibition of hunts, and the theatrical dances. If any one despises the present canon, and gives himself to any of the things which are forbidden, if he be a cleric he shall be deposed, but if a layman let him be cut off.

Canon 52

On all days of the holy fast of Lent, except on the Sabbath, the Lord's day and the holy day of the Annunciation, the Liturgy of the Presanctified is to be said.

Canon 53

Whereas the spiritual relationship is greater than fleshly affinity; and since it has come to our knowledge that in some places certain persons who become sponsors to children in holy salvation-bearing baptism, afterwards contract matrimony with their mothers (being widows), we decree that for the future nothing of this sort is to be done. But if any, after the present canon, shall be observed to do this, they must, in the first place, desist from this unlawful marriage, and then be subjected to the penalties of fornicators.

Canon 54

The divine scriptures plainly teach us as follows, "You shall not approach to any that is near of kin to you to uncover their nakedness." Basil, the bearer-of-God, has enumerated in his canons some marriages which are prohibited and has passed over the greater part in silence, and in both these ways has done us good service. For by avoiding a number of disgraceful names (lest by such words he should pollute his discourse) he included impurities under general terms, by which course he showed to us in a general way the marriages which are forbidden. But since by such silence, and because of the difficulty of understanding what marriages are prohibited, the matter has become confused; it seemed good to us to set it forth a little more clearly, decreeing that from this time forth he who shall marry the daughter of his father's brother; or a father or son with a mother and daughter; or a father and son with two girls who are sisters; or a mother and daughter with two brothers; or two brothers with two sisters, fall under the canon of seven years, provided they openly separate from this unlawful union.

Canon 55

Since we understand that in the city of the Romans, in the holy fast of Lent they fast on the Saturdays, contrary to the ecclesiastical observance which is traditional, it seemed good to the holy synod that also in the Church of the Romans the canon shall immovably stands fast which says: "If any cleric shall be found to fast on a Sunday or Saturday (except on one occasion only) he is to be deposed; and if he is a layman he shall be cut off."

Canon 56

We have likewise learned that in the regions of Armenia and in other places certain people eat eggs and cheese on the Sabbaths and Lord's days of the holy lent. It seems good therefore that the whole Church of God which is in all the world should follow one rule and keep the fast perfectly, and as they abstain from everything which is killed, so also should they from eggs and cheese, which are the fruit and produce of those animals from which we abstain. But if any shall not observe this law, if they be clerics, let them be deposed; but if laymen, let them be cut off.

Canon 57

It is not right to offer honey and milk on the altar.

Canon 58

None of those who are in the order of laymen may distribute the Divine Mysteries to himself if a bishop, presbyter, or deacon be present. But whoso shall dare to do such a thing, as acting contrary to what has been determined shall be cut off for a week and thenceforth let him learn not to think of himself more highly than he ought to think.

Canon 59

Baptism is by no means to be administered in an oratory which is within a house; but they who are about to be held worthy of the spotless illumination are to go to a Catholic Church and there to enjoy this gift. But if any one shall be convicted of not observing what we have determined, if he be a cleric let him be deposed, if a layman let him be cut off.

Canon 60

Since the Apostle exclaims that he who cleaves to the Lord is one spirit, it is clear that he who is intimate with his [i.e. the Lord's] enemy becomes one by his affinity with him. Therefore, those who pretend they are possessed by a devil and by their depravity of manners feign to manifest their form and appearance; it seems good by all means that they should be punished and that they should be subjected to afflictions and hardships of the same kind as those to which they who are truly demoniacally possessed are justly subjected with the intent of delivering them from the [work or rather] energy of the devil.

Canon 61

Those who give themselves up to soothsayers or to those who are called hecatontarchs or to any such, in order that they may learn from them what things they wish to have revealed to them, let all such, according to the decrees lately made by the Fathers concerning them, be subjected to the canon of six years. And to this [penalty] they also should be subjected who carry about she-bears or animals of the kind for the diversion and injury of the simple; as well as those who tell fortunes and fates, and genealogy, and a multitude of words of this kind from the nonsense of deceit and imposture. Also those who are called expellers of clouds, enchanters, amulet-givers, and soothsayers.

Canon 62

The so-called Calends, and what are called Bota and Brumalia, and the full assembly which takes place on the first of March, we wish to be abolished from the life of the faithful. And also the public dances of women, which may do much harm and mischief. Moreover we drive away from the life of Christians the dances given in the names of those falsely called gods by the Greeks whether of men or women, and which are performed after an ancient and un-Christian fashion; decreeing that no man from this time forth shall be dressed as a woman, nor any woman in the garb suitable to men. Nor shall he assume comic, satyric, or tragic masks; nor may men invoke the name of the execrable Bacchus when they squeeze out the wine in the presses; nor when pouring out wine into jars [to cause a laugh], practising in ignorance and vanity the things which proceed from the deceit of insanity. Therefore those who in the future attempt any of these things which are written, having obtained a knowledge of them, if they be clerics we order them to be deposed, and if laymen to be cut off.

Canon 63

We forbid to be publicly read in Church, histories of the martyrs which have been falsely put together by the enemies of the truth, in order to dishonour the martyrs of Christ and induce unbelief among those who hear them, but we order that such books be given to the flames. But those who accept them or apply their mind to them as true we anathematize.

Canon 64

It does not befit a layman to dispute or teach publicly, thus claiming for himself authority to teach, but he should yield to the order appointed by the Lord, and to open his ears to those who have received the grace to teach, and be taught by them divine things; for in one Church God has made "different members," according to the word of the Apostle: and Gregory the Theologian, wisely interpreting this passage, commends the order in vogue with them saying: "This order brethren we revere, this we guard. Let this one be the ear; that one the tongue, the hand or any other member. Let this one teach, but let that one learn." And a little further on: "Learning in docility and abounding in cheerfulness, and ministering with alacrity, we shall not all be the tongue which is the more active member, not all of us Apostles, not all prophets, nor shall we all interpret." And again: "Why do you make yourself a shepherd when you are a sheep? Why become the head when you are a foot? Why do you try to be a commander when you are enrolled in the number of the soldiers?" And elsewhere: "Wisdom orders, Be not swift in words; nor compare yourself with the rich, being poor; nor seek to be wiser than the wise." But if any one be found weakening the present canon, he is to be cut off for forty days.

Canon 65

The fires which are lighted on the new moons by some before their shops and houses, upon which (according to a certain ancient custom) they are wont foolishly and crazily to leap, we order henceforth to cease. Therefore, whosoever shall do such a thing, if he be a cleric, let him be deposed; but if he be a layman, let him be cut off. For it is written in the Fourth Book of the Kings "And Manasses built an altar to the whole host of heaven, in the two courts of the Lord, and made his sons to pass through the fire, he used lots and augurs and divinations by birds and made ventriloquists [or pythons] and multiplied diviners, that he might do evil before the Lord and provoke him to anger."

Canon 66

From the holy day of the Resurrection of Christ our God until the next Lord's day, for a whole week, in the holy churches the faithful ought to be free from labour, rejoicing in Christ with psalms and hymns and spiritual songs; and celebrating the feast, and applying their minds to the reading of the holy Scriptures, and delighting in the Holy Mysteries; for thus shall we be exalted with Christ and together with him be raised up. Therefore, on the aforesaid days there must not be any horse races or any public spectacle.

Canon 67

The divine Scripture commands us to abstain from blood, from things strangled, and from fornication. Those therefore who on account of a dainty stomach prepare by any art for food the blood of any animal, and so eat it, we punish suitably. If anyone henceforth venture to eat in any way the blood of an animal, if he be a clergyman, let him be deposed; if a layman, let him be cut off.

Canon 68

It is unlawful for anyone to corrupt or cut up a book of the Old or New Testament or of our holy and approved preachers and teachers, or to give them up to the traders in books or to those who are called perfumers, or to hand it over for destruction to any other like persons: unless to be sure it has been rendered useless either by bookworms, or by water, or in some other way. He who henceforth shall be observed to do such a thing shall be cut off for one year. Likewise also he who buys such books (unless he keeps them for his own use, or gives them to another for his benefit to be preserved) and has attempted to corrupt them, let him be cut off.

Canon 69

It is not permitted to a layman to enter the sanctuary (Holy Altar, Gk.), though, in accordance with a certain ancient tradition, the imperial power and authority is by no means prohibited from this when he wishes to offer his gifts to the Creator.

Canon 70

Women are not permitted to speak at the time of the Divine Liturgy; but, according to the word of Paul the Apostle, "let them be silent. For it is not permitted to them to speak, but to be in subjection, as the law also says. But if they wish to learn anything let them ask their own husbands at home."

Canon 71

Those who are taught the civil laws must not adopt the customs of the Gentiles, nor be induced to go to the theatre, nor to keep what are called Cylestras, nor to wear clothing contrary to the general custom; and this holds good when they begin their training, when they reach its end, and, in short, all the time of its duration. If any one from this time shall dare to do contrary to this canon he is to be cut off.

Canon 72

An orthodox man is not permitted to marry an heretical woman, nor an orthodox woman to be joined to an heretical man. But if anything of this kind appear to have been done by any [we require them] to consider the marriage null, and that the marriage be dissolved. For it is not fitting to mingle together what should not be mingled, nor is it right that the sheep be joined with the wolf, nor the lot of sinners with the portion of Christ. But if any one shall transgress the things which we have decreed let him be cut off. But if any who up to this time are unbelievers and are not yet numbered in the flock of the orthodox have contracted lawful marriage between themselves, and if then, one choosing the right and coming to the light of truth and the other remaining still detained by the bond of error and not willing to behold with steady eye the divine rays, the unbelieving woman is pleased to cohabit with the believing man, or the unbelieving man with the believing woman, let them not be separated, according to the divine Apostle, "for the unbelieving husband is sanctified by the wife, and the unbelieving wife by her husband."

Canon 73

Since the life-giving cross has shown to us Salvation, we should be careful that we render due honour to that by which we were saved from the ancient fall. Wherefore, in mind, in word, in feeling giving veneration (προσκύνησιν) to it, we command that the figure of the cross, which some have placed on the floor, be entirely removed therefrom, lest the trophy of the victory won for us be desecrated by the trampling under foot of those who walk over it. Therefore those who from this present represent on the pavement the sign of the cross, we decree are to be cut off.

Canon 74
It is not permitted to hold what are called Agapæ, that is love-feasts, in the Lord's houses or churches, nor to eat within the house, nor to spread couches. If any dare to do so let him cease therefrom or be cut off.

Canon 75
We will that those whose office it is to sing in the churches do not use undisciplined vociferations, nor force nature to shouting, nor adopt any of those modes which are incongruous and unsuitable for the church: but that they offer the psalmody to God, who is the observer of secrets, with great attention and compunction. For the Sacred Oracle taught that the Sons of Israel were to be pious.

Canon 76
It is not right that those who are responsible for reverence to churches should place within the sacred bounds an eating place, nor offer food there, nor make other sales. For God our Saviour teaching us when he was tabernacling in the flesh commanded not to make his Father's house a house of merchandize. He also poured out the small coins of the money-changers, and drove out all those who made common the temple. If, therefore, anyone shall be taken in the aforesaid fault let him be cut off.

Canon 77
It is not right that those who are dedicated to religion, whether clerics or ascetics, should wash in the bath with women, nor should any Christian man or layman do so. For this is severely condemned by the heathens. But if any one is caught in this thing, if he is a cleric let him be deposed; if a layman, let him be cut off.

Canon 78
It behooves those who are illuminated to learn the Creed by heart and to recite it to the bishop or presbyters on the Fifth Feria of the Week.

Canon 79
As we confess the divine birth of the Virgin to be without any childbed, since it came to pass without seed, and as we preach this to the entire flock, so we subject to correction those who through ignorance do anything which is inconsistent therewith. Wherefore since some on the day after the holy Nativity of Christ our God are seen cooking σεμίδαλῖν, and distributing it to each other, on pretext of doing honour to the puerperia of the spotless Virgin Maternity, we decree that henceforth nothing of the kind be done by the faithful. For this is not honouring the Virgin (who above

thought and speech bare in the flesh the incomprehensible Word) when we define and describe, from ordinary things and from such as occur with ourselves, her ineffable parturition. If therefore anyone henceforth be discovered doing any such thing, if he be a cleric let him be deposed, but if a layman let him be cut off.

Canon 80

If any bishop, or presbyter, or deacon, or any of those who are enumerated in the list of the clergy, or a layman, has no very grave necessity nor difficult business so as to keep him from church for a very long time, but being in town does not go to church on three consecutive Sundays— three weeks— if he is a cleric let him be deposed, but if a layman let him be cut off.

Canon 81

Whereas we have heard that in some places in the hymn Trisagion there is added after "Holy and Immortal," "Who was crucified for us, have mercy upon us," and since this as being alien to piety was by the ancient and holy Fathers cast out of the hymn, as also the violent heretics who inserted these new words were cast out of the Church; we also, confirming the things which were formerly piously established by our holy Fathers, anathematize those who after this present decree allow in church this or any other addition to the most sacred hymn; but if indeed he who has transgressed is of the sacerdotal order, we command that he be deprived of his priestly dignity, but if he be a layman or monk let him be cut off.

Canon 82

In some pictures of the venerable icons, a lamb is painted to which the Precursor points his finger, which is received as a type of grace, indicating beforehand through the Law, our true Lamb, Christ our God. Embracing therefore the ancient types and shadows as symbols of the truth, and patterns given to the Church, we prefer "grace and truth," receiving it as the fulfilment of the Law. In order therefore that "that which is perfect" may be delineated to the eyes of all, at least in coloured expression, we decree that the figure in human form of the Lamb who takes away the sin of the world, Christ our God, be henceforth exhibited in images, instead of the ancient lamb, so that all may understand by means of it the depths of the humiliation of the Word of God, and that we may recall to our memory his conversation in the flesh, his passion and salutary death, and his redemption which was wrought for the whole world.

Canon 83

No one may give the Eucharist to the bodies of the dead; for it is written "Take and eat." But the bodies of the dead can neither "take" nor "eat."

Canon 84
Following the canonical laws of the Fathers, we decree concerning infants, as often as they are found without trusty witnesses who say that they are undoubtedly baptized; and as often as they are themselves unable on account of their age to answer satisfactorily in respect to the initiatory mystery given to them; that they ought without any offense to be baptized, lest such a doubt might deprive them of the sanctification of such a purification.

Canon 85
We have received from the Scriptures that in the mouth of two or three witnesses every word shall be established. Therefore we decree that slaves who are manumitted by their masters in the presence of three witnesses shall enjoy that honour; for they being present at the time will add strength and stability to the liberty given, and they will bring it to pass that faith will be kept in those things which they now witness were done in their presence.

Canon 86
Those who to the destruction of their own souls procure and bring up harlots, if they be clerics, they are to be [cut off and] deposed, if laymen to be cut off.

Canon 87
She who has left her husband is an adulteress if she has come to another, according to the holy and divine Basil, who has gathered this most excellently from the prophet Jeremiah: "If a woman has become another man's, her husband shall not return to her, but being defiled she shall remain defiled;" and again, "He who has an adulteress is senseless and impious." If therefore she appears to have departed from her husband without reason, he is deserving of pardon and she of punishment. And pardon shall be given to him that he may be in communion with the Church. But he who leaves the wife lawfully given him, and shall take another is guilty of adultery by the sentence of the Lord. And it has been decreed by our Fathers that they who are such must be "weepers" for a year, "hearers" for two years, "prostrators" for three years, and in the seventh year to stand with the faithful and thus be counted worthy of the Oblation [if with tears they do penance].

Canon 88
No one may drive any beast into a church except perchance a traveller, urged thereto by the greatest necessity, in default of a shed or resting-place, may have turned aside into said church. For unless the beast had been taken inside, it would have perished, and he, by the loss of his beast of burden, and thus without means of continuing his journey, would be in peril of death. And we are taught that the Sabbath was made for

man: wherefore also the safety and comfort of man are by all means to be placed first. But should anyone be detected without any necessity such as we have just mentioned, leading his beast into a church, if he be a cleric let him be deposed, and if a layman let him be cut off.

Canon 89

The faithful spending the days of the Salutatory Passion in fasting, praying and compunction of heart, ought to fast until the midnight of the Great Sabbath: since the divine Evangelists, Matthew and Luke, have shown us how late at night it was [that the resurrection took place], the one by using the words ὀψὲ σαββάτων, and the other by the words ὄρθρου βαθέος.

Canon 90

We have received from our divine Fathers the canon law that in honour of Christ's resurrection, we are not to kneel on Sundays. Lest therefore we should ignore the fullness of this observance we make it plain to the faithful that after the priests have gone to the Altar for Vespers on Saturdays (according to the prevailing custom) no one shall kneel in prayer until the evening of Sunday, at which time after the entrance for compline, again with bended knees we offer our prayers to the Lord. For taking the night after the Sabbath, which was the forerunner of our Lord's resurrection, we begin from it to sing in the spirit hymns to God, leading our feast out of darkness into light, and thus during an entire day and night, we celebrate the Resurrection.

Canon 91

Those who give drugs for procuring abortion, and those who receive poisons to kill the fœtus, are subjected to the penalty of murder.

Canon 92

The holy synod decrees that those who in the name of marriage carry off women and those who in any way assist the ravishers, if they be clerics, they shall lose their rank, but if they be laymen they shall be anathematized.

Canon 93

If the wife of a man who has gone away and does not appear, cohabit with another before she is assured of the death of the first, she is an adulteress. The wives of soldiers who have married husbands who do not appear are in the same case; as are also they who on account of the wanderings of their husbands do not wait for their return. But the circumstance here has some excuse, in that the suspicion of his death becomes very great. But she who in ignorance has married a man who at the time was deserted by his wife, and then is dismissed because his first wife returns to him, has indeed committed fornication, but through ignorance; therefore she is not prevented from marrying, but it is better if she remain as she is. If a soldier shall return after a long time, and find his wife on account of his long absence has been united to another man, if he so wishes, he may receive his own wife [back again], pardon being extended in consideration of their ignorance both to her and to the man who took her home in second marriage.

Canon 94

The canon subjects to penalties those who take heathen oaths, and we decree to them excommunication.

Canon 95

Those who from the heretics come over to orthodoxy, and to the number of those who should be saved, we receive according to the following order and custom. Arians, Macedonians, Novatians, who call themselves Cathari, Aristeri, and Testareskaidecatitæ, or Tetraditæ, and Apollinarians, we receive on their presentation of certificates and on their anathematizing every heresy which does not hold as does the holy Apostolic Church of God: then first of all we anoint them with the holy chrism on their foreheads, eyes, nostrils, mouth and ears; and as we seal them we say— "The seal of the gift of the Holy Ghost."

But concerning the Paulianists it has been determined by the Catholic Church that they shall by all means be rebaptized. The Eunomeans also, who baptize with one immersion; and the Montanists, who here are called Phrygians; and the Sabellians, who consider the Son to be the same as the Father, and are guilty in certain other grave matters, and all the other heresies— for there are many heretics here, especially those who come from the region of the Galatians— all of their number who are desirous of coming to the Orthodox faith, we receive as Gentiles. And on the first day we make them Christians, on the second Catechumens, then on the third day we exorcise them, at the same time also breathing thrice upon their faces and ears; and thus we initiate them, and we make them spend time in church and hear the Scriptures; and then we baptize them.

And the Manichæans, and Valentinians and Marcionites and all of similar heresies must give certificates and anathematize each his own heresy, and also Nestorius, Eutyches, Dioscorus, Severus, and the other chiefs of such heresies, and those who think with them, and all the aforesaid heresies; and so they become partakers of the holy Communion.

Canon 96

Those who by baptism have put on Christ have professed that they will copy his manner of life which he led in the flesh. Those therefore who adorn and arrange their hair to the detriment of those who see them, that is by cunningly devised intertwinings, and by this means put a bait in the way of unstable souls, we take in hand to cure paternally with a suitable punishment: training them and teaching them to live soberly, in order that having laid aside the deceit and vanity of material things, they may give their minds continually to a life which is blessed and free from mischief, and have their conversation in fear, pure, [and holy]; and thus come as near as possible to God through their purity of life; and adorn the inner man rather than the outer, and that with virtues, and good and blameless manners, so that they leave in themselves no remains of the left-handedness of the adversary. But if any shall act contrary to the present canon let him be cut off.

Canon 97

Those who have commerce with a wife or in any other manner without regard thereto make sacred places common, and treat them with contempt and thus remain in them, we order all such to be expelled, even from the dwellings of the catechumens which are in the venerable temples. And if any one shall not observe these directions, if he be a cleric let him be deposed, but if a layman let him be cut off.

Canon 98

He who brings to the intercourse of marriage a woman who is betrothed to another man who is still alive, is to lie under the charge of adultery.

Canon 99

We have further learned that, in the regions of the Armenians, certain persons boil joints of meat within the sanctuary and offer portions to the priests, distributing it after the Jewish fashion. Wherefore, that we may keep the church undefiled, we decree that it is not lawful for any priest to seize the separate portions of flesh meat from those who offer them, but they are to be content with what he that offers pleases to give them; and further we decree that such offering be made outside the church. And if any one does not thus, let him be cut off.

Canon 100

"Let your eyes behold the thing which is right," orders Wisdom, "and keep your heart with all care." For the bodily senses easily bring their own impressions into the soul. Therefore we order that henceforth there shall in no way be made pictures, whether they are in paintings or in what way so ever, which attract the eye and corrupt the mind, and incite it to the enkindling of base pleasures. And if any one shall attempt to do this he is to be cut off.

Canon 101

The great and divine Apostle Paul with loud voice calls man created in the image of God, the body and temple of Christ. Excelling, therefore, every sensible creature, he who by the saving Passion has attained to the celestial dignity, eating and drinking Christ, is fitted in all respects for eternal life, sanctifying his soul and body by the participation of divine grace. Wherefore, if any one wishes to be a participator of the immaculate Body in the time of the Synaxis, and to offer himself for the communion, let him draw near, arranging his hands in the form of a cross, and so let him receive the communion of grace. But such as, instead of their hands, make vessels of gold or other materials for the reception of the divine gift, and by these receive the immaculate communion, we by no means allow to come, as preferring inanimate and inferior matter to the image of God. But if any one shall be found imparting the immaculate Communion to those who bring vessels of this kind, let him be cut off as well as the one who brings them.

Canon 102

It behooves those who have received from God the power to loose and bind, to consider the quality of the sin and the readiness of the sinner for conversion, and to apply medicine suitable for the disease, lest if he is injudicious in each of these respects he should fail in regard to the healing of the sick man. For the disease of sin is not simple, but various and multiform, and it germinates many mischievous offshoots, from which much evil is diffused, and it proceeds further until it is checked by the power of the physician. Wherefore he who professes the science of spiritual medicine ought first of all to consider the disposition of him who has sinned, and to see whether he tends to health or (on the contrary) provokes to himself disease by his own behaviour, and to look how he can care for his manner of life during the interval. And if he does not resist the physician, and if the ulcer of the soul is increased by the application of the imposed medicaments, then let him mete out mercy to him according as he is worthy of it. For the whole account is between God and him to whom the pastoral rule has been delivered, to lead back the wandering sheep and to cure that which is wounded by the serpent; and that he may neither cast them down into the precipices of despair, nor loosen the bridle towards dissolution or contempt of life; but in some way or other, either by means of sternness and astringency, or by greater softness and mild medicines, to resist this sickness and exert himself for the healing of the ulcer, now examining the fruits of his repentance and wisely managing the man who is called to higher illumination. For we ought to know two things, to wit, the things which belong to strictness and those which belong to custom, and to follow the traditional form in the case of those who are not fitted for the highest things, as holy Basil teaches us.

SEVEN ECUMENICAL COUNCILS OF THE CHURCH

COUNCIL OF SECOND NICAEA

The Divine Sacra Sent by the Emperors Constantine and Irene to the Most Holy and Most Blessed Hadrian, Pope of Old Rome.

They who receive the dignity of the empire, or the honour of the principal priesthood from our Lord Jesus Christ, ought to provide and to care for those things which please him, and rule and govern the people committed to their care according to his will and good pleasure.

Therefore, O Most Holy Head [*Caput*], it is incumbent upon us and you, that irreprehensibly we know the things which be his, and that in these we exercise ourselves, since from him we have received the imperial dignity, and you the dignity of the chief priesthood.

But now to speak more to the point. Your paternal blessedness knows what has been done in times past in this our royal city against the venerable images, how those who reigned immediately before us destroyed them and subjected them to disgrace and injury: (O may it not be imputed to them, for it had been better for them had they not laid their hands upon the Church!)— and how they seduced and brought over to their own opinion all the people who live in these parts — yea, even the whole of the East, in like manner, up to the time in which God has exalted us to this kingdom, who seek his glory in truth, and hold that which has been handed down by his Apostles together with all other teachers. Whence now with pure heart and unfeigned religion we have, together with all our subjects and our most learned divines, had constant conferences respecting the things which relate to God, and by their advice have determined to summon a General Council. And we entreat your paternal blessedness, or rather the Lord God entreats, who will have all men to be saved and to come to the knowledge of the truth, that you will give yourself to us and make no delay, but come up hither to aid us in the confirmation and establishment of the ancient tradition of venerable images. It is, indeed, incumbent on your holiness to do this, since you know how it is written — Comfort, comfort my people, you priests, says the Lord, and the lips of the priest shall keep knowledge, and the law shall go forth out of his mouth, for he is the angel of the Lord of Hosts. And again, the divine Apostle, the preacher of the truth, who, from Jerusalem and round about unto Illyricum, preached the Gospel, has thus commanded — Feed with discipline the flock of Christ which he purchased with his own blood. As then you are the veritable chief priest (*primus sacerdos*) who presides in the place and in the see of the holy and superlaudable Apostle Peter, let your paternal blessedness come to us, as we have said before, and add your presence to all those other priests who shall be assembled together here, that thus the will of the Lord may be accomplished. For as we are taught in the Gospels our Lord says — When two or three are met together in my name, there am I in the midst of them— let your paternal and sacred blessedness be certified and confirmed by the great God and King of all, our Lord Jesus Christ, and by us his servants, that if you come up hither you shall be received with all honour and glory, and that everything necessary for you shall be granted. And again, when the definition (*capitulum*) shall be completed, which by the good pleasure of Christ our God we hope shall be done, we take upon us to provide for you every facility of returning with honour and distinction. If, however, your blessedness cannot attend upon us (which we can scarcely imagine, knowing what is your zeal about divine things), at least, pray select for us men of understanding, having with them letters from your holiness, that they may be present here in the person of your sacred and paternal blessedness. So, when they meet with the other priests who are here, the ancient tradition of our holy fathers may be synodically confirmed, and every evil plant of tares may be rooted out, and the words of our Lord and Saviour Jesus Christ may be fulfilled, that the gates of hell shall not prevail against her. And after this, may there be no further schism and separation in the one holy Catholic and Apostolic Church, of which Christ our true God is the Head.

We have had Constantine, beloved in Christ, most holy Bishop of Leontina in our beloved Sicily, with whom your paternal blessedness is well acquainted, into our presence; and, having spoken with him face to face, have sent him with this our present venerable jussio to you. Whom, after that he has seen you, immediately dismiss, that he may come back to us, and write us by him concerning your coming — what time we may expect will be spent in your journeying thence and coming to us. Moreover, he can retain with him the most holy Bishop of Naples, and come up hither together with him. And, as your journey will be by way of Naples and Sicily we have given orders to the Governor of Sicily about this, that he take due care to have every needful preparation made for your honour and rest, which is necessary in order that your paternal blessedness may come to us. Given on the ivth before the calends of September, the seventh indiction, from the Royal City.

The Imperial Sacra

Read at the First Session.

(Found in Labbe and Cossart, Concilia, Tom. *VII., col. 49.)*

Constantine and Irene — Sovereigns of the Romans in the Faith, to the most holy Bishops, who, by the grace of God and by the command of our pious Sovereignty, have met together in the Council of Nicaea.

The Wisdom which is truly according to the nature of God and the Father — our Lord Jesus Christ, our true God — who, by his most divine and wonderful dispensation in the flesh, has delivered us from all idolatrous error: and, by taking on him our nature, has renewed the same by the co-operation of the Spirit, which is of the same nature with himself; and having himself become the first High Priest, has counted you holy men, worthy of the same dignity.

He is that good Shepherd who, bearing on his own shoulders that wandering sheep — fallen man, has brought him back to his own peculiar folds — that is, the party of angelic and ministering powers Ephesians 2:14-15, and has reconciled us in himself and having taken away the wall of partition, has broken down the enmity through his flesh, and has bestowed upon us a rule of conduct tending to peace; wherefore, preaching to all, he says in the Gospel, Blessed are the peacemakers, for they shall be called the children of God Matthew 5:9. Of which blessedness, confirming as it does the exaltation of the adoption of sons, our pious Sovereignty desiring above all things to be made partakers, has ever applied the utmost diligence to direct all our Roman Commonwealth into the ways of unity and concord; and more especially have we been solicitous concerning the right regulation of the Church of God, and most anxious in every way to promote the unity of the priesthood. For which cause the Chiefs of the Sacerdotal Order of the East and of the North, of the West and of the South, are present in the person of their Representative Bishops, who have with them respectively the replies written in answers to the Synodical Epistle sent from the most holy Patriarch; for such was from the beginning the synodical regulation of the Church Catholic, which, from the one end of the earth to the other, has received the Gospel. On this account we have, by the good will and permission of God, caused you, his most holy Priests, to meet together — you who are accustomed to dispense his Testimony in the unbloody sacrifice— that your decision may be in accordance with the definitions of former councils who decreed rightly, and that the splendour of the Spirit may illumine you in all things, for, as our Lord teaches, No man lights a candle and puts it under a bushel, but on a candlestick, that it may give light to all that are in the house; even so, should you make such use of the various regulations which have been piously handed down to us of old by our Fathers, that all the Holy Churches of God may remain in peaceful order.

As for us, such was our zeal for the truth— such our earnest desire for the interests of religion, our care for ecclesiastical order, our anxiety that the ancient rules and orders should maintain their ground — that though fully engaged in military councils — though all our attention was occupied in political cares — yet, treating all these affairs as but of minor importance, we would allow nothing whatever to interfere with the convocation of your most holy council. To every one is given the utmost freedom of expressing his sentiments without the least hesitation, that thus the subject under enquiry may be most fully discussed and truth may be the more boldly spoken, that so all dissensions may be banished from the Church and we all may be united in the bonds of peace.

For, when the most holy Patriarch Paul, by the divine will, was about to be liberated from the bands of mortality and to exchange his earthly pilgrimage for a heavenly home with his Master Christ, he abdicated the Patriarchate and took upon him the monastic life, and when we asked him, Why have you done this? He answered, Because I fear that, if death should surprise me still in the episcopate of this royal and heaven-defended city, I should have to carry with me the anathema of the whole Catholic Church, which consigns me to that outer darkness which is prepared for the devil and his angels; for they say that a certain synod has been held here in order to the subversion of pictures and images which the Catholic Church holds, embraces, and receives, in memory of the persons whom they represent. This is that which distracts my soul— this is that which makes me anxiously to enquire how I may escape the judgment of God— since among such men I have been brought up and with such am I numbered. No sooner had he thus spoken in the presence of some of our most illustrious nobles than he expired.

When our Pious Sovereignty reflected on this awful declaration (and truly, even before this event, we had heard of similar questionings from many around), we took counsel with ourselves as to what ought to be done; and we determined, after mature deliberation, that when a new Patriarch had been elected, we should endeavour to bring this subject to some decisive conclusion. Wherefore, having summoned those whom we knew to be most experienced in ecclesiastical matters, and having called upon Christ our God, we consulted with them who was worthy to be exalted to the chair of the Priesthood of this Royal and God-preserved city; and they all with one heart and soul gave their vote in favour of Tarasius— he who now occupies the Pontifical Presidency. Having, therefore, sent for him, we laid before him our deliberations and our vote; but he would by no means consent, nor at all yield to that which had been determined. And when we enquired, Wherefore he thus refused his consent? — at first he answered evasively, That the yoke of the Chief Priesthood was too much for him. But we, knowing this to be a mere pretext coveting his unwillingness to obey us, would not desist from our importunity, but persisted in pressing the acceptance of the dignity of the Chief Priesthood upon him. When he found how urgent we were with him, he told us the cause of his refusal. It is (said he) because I perceive that the Church which has been founded on the rock, Christ our God, is rent and torn asunder by schisms, and that we are unstable in our confession, and that Christians in the East, of the same faith with ourselves, decline communion with us, and unite them with those of the West; and so we are estranged from all, and each day are anathematized by all: and, moreover, I should demand that an Ecumenical Council should be held, at which should be found Legates from the Pope of Rome and from the Chief Priests of the East. We, therefore, fully understanding these things, introduced him to the assembled company of the Priests — of our most illustrious Princes — and of all our Christian people; and then, in their presence, he repeated to them all that he had before said to us; which, when they heard, they received him joyfully, and earnestly entreated our peace-making and pious Sovereignty that an Ecumenical Council might be assembled. To this their request, we gave our hearty consent; for, to speak the truth, it is by the good will and under the direction of our God that we have assembled you together.

SEVEN ECUMENICAL COUNCILS OF THE CHURCH

Wherefore as God, willing to establish his own counsel, has for this purpose brought you together from all parts of the world, behold the Gospels now lying before you, and plainly crying aloud, Judge justly; stand firm as champions of religion, and be ready with unsparing hand to cut away all innovations and new fangled inventions. And, as Peter the Chief of the Apostolic College, struck the mad slave and cut off his Jewish ear with the sword, so in like manner do you wield the axe of the Spirit, and every tree which bears the fruit of contention, of strife, or newly-imported innovation, either renew by transplanting through the words of sound doctrine, or lay it low with canonical censure, and send it to the fires of the future Gehenna, so that the peace of the Spirit may evermore protect the whole body of the Church, compacted and united in one, and confirmed by the traditions of the Fathers; and so may all our Roman State enjoy peace as well as the Church.

We have received letters from Hadrian, most Holy Pope of old Rome, by his Legates — namely, Peter, the God-beloved Archpresbyter, and Peter, the God-beloved Presbyter and Abbot — who will be present in council with you; and we command that, according to synodical custom, these be read in the hearing of you all; and that, having heard these with becoming silence, and moreover the Epistles contained in two octavos sent by the Chief Priest and other Priests of the Eastern dioceses by John, most pious Monk and Chancellor of the Patriarchal throne of Antioch, and Thomas, Priest and Abbot, who also are present together with you, you may by these understand what are the sentiments of the Church Catholic on this point.

SEVEN ECUMENICAL COUNCILS OF THE CHURCH

Extracts from the Acts

Session 1

(Labbe and Cossart, *Concilia*, Tom. VII., col. 53.)

[Certain bishops who had been led astray by the Iconoclasts came, asking to be received back. The first of these was Basil of Ancyra.]

The bishop Basil of Ancyra read as follows from a book: Inasmuch as ecclesiastical legislation has canonically been handed down from past time, even from the beginning from the holy Apostles, and from their successors, who were our holy fathers and teachers, and also from the six holy and ecumenical synods, and from the local synods which were gathered in the interests of orthodoxy, that those returning from any heresy whatever to the orthodox faith and to the tradition of the Catholic Church, might deny their own heresy, and confess the orthodox faith.

Wherefore I, Basil, bishop of the city of Ancyra, proposing to be united to the Catholic Church, and to Hadrian the most holy Pope of Old Rome, and to Tarasius the most blessed Patriarch, and to the most holy apostolic sees, to wit, Alexandria, Antioch, and the Holy City, as well as to all orthodox high-priests and priests, make this written confession of my faith, and I offer it to you as to those who have received power by apostolic authority. And in this also I beg pardon from your divinely gathered holiness for my tardiness in this matter. For it was not right that I should have fallen behind in the confession of orthodoxy, but it arose from my entire lack of knowledge, and slothful and negligent mind in the matter. Wherefore the rather I ask your blessedness to grant me indulgence in God's sight.

I believe, therefore, and make my confession in one God, the Father Almighty, and in one Lord Jesus Christ, his only begotten Son, and in the Holy Ghost, the Lord and Giver of Life. The Trinity, one in essence and one in majesty, must be worshipped and glorified in one godhead, power, and authority. I confess all things pertaining to the incarnation of one of the Holy Trinity, our Lord and God, Jesus Christ, as the Saints and the six Ecumenical Synods have handed down. And I reject and anathematize every heretical babbling, as they also have rejected them. I ask for the intercessions (πρεσβείας) of our spotless Lady the Holy Mother of God, and those of the holy and heavenly powers, and those of all the Saints.

And receiving their holy and honourable relics with all honour (τιμῆς), I salute and venerate these with honour (τιμητικῶς προσκυνέω), hoping to have a share in their holiness. Likewise also the venerable images (εἰκόνας) of the incarnation of our Lord Jesus Christ, in the humanity he assumed for our salvation; and of our spotless Lady, the holy Mother of God; and of the angels like God; and of the holy Apostles, Prophets, Martyrs, and of all the Saints — the sacred images of all these, I salute and venerate — rejecting and anathematizing with my whole soul and mind the synod which was gathered together out of stubbornness and madness, and which styled itself the Seventh Synod, but which by those who think accurately was called lawfully and canonically a pseudo-synod, as being contrary to all truth and piety, and audaciously and temerariously against the divinely handed down ecclesiastical legislation, yea, even impiously having yelped at and scoffed at the holy and venerable images, and having ordered these to be taken away out of the holy churches of God; over which assembly presided Theodosius with the pseudonym of Ephesius, Sisinnius of Perga, with the surname Pastillas, Basilius of Pisidia, falsely called tricaccabus; with whom the wretched Constantine, the then Patriarch, was led (ἐματαιώθη) astray.

These things thus I confess and to these I assent, and therefore in simplicity of heart and in uprightness of mind, in the presence of God, I have made the subjoined anathematisms.

Anathema to the calumniators of the Christians, that is to the image breakers.

Anathema to those who apply the words of Holy Scripture which were spoken against idols, to the venerable images.

Anathema to those who do not salute the holy and venerable images.

Anathema to those who say that Christians have recourse to the images as to gods.

Anathema to those who call the sacred images idols.

Anathema to those who knowingly communicate with those who revile and dishonour the venerable images.

Anathema to those who say that another than Christ our Lord has delivered us from idols.

Anathema to those who spurn the teachings of the holy Fathers and the tradition of the Catholic Church, taking as a pretext and making their own the arguments of Arius, Nestorius, Eutyches, and Dioscorus, that unless we were evidently taught by the Old and New Testaments, we should not follow the teachings of the holy Fathers and of the holy Ecumenical Synods, and the tradition of the Catholic Church.

Anathema to those who dare to say that the Catholic Church has at any time sanctioned idols.

Anathema to those who say that the making of images is a diabolical invention and not a tradition of our holy Fathers.

This is my confession [of faith] and to these propositions I give my assent. And I pronounce this with my whole heart, and soul, and mind.

And if at any time by the fraud of the devil (which may God forbid!) I voluntarily or involuntarily shall be opposed to what I have now professed, may I be anathema from the Father, the Son and the Holy Ghost, and from the Catholic Church and every hierarchical order a stranger.

I will keep myself from every acceptance of a bribe and from filthy lucre in accordance with the divine canons of the holy Apostles and of the approved Fathers.

Tarasius, the most holy Patriarch, said: This whole sacred gathering yields glory and thanks to God for this confession of yours, which you have made to the Catholic Church.

The Holy Synod said: Glory to God which makes one that which was severed.

[*Theodore, bishop of Myra, then read the same confession, and was received. The next bishop who asked to be received read as follows:* (col. 60)]

SEVEN ECUMENICAL COUNCILS OF THE CHURCH

Theodosius, the humble Christian, to the holy and Ecumenical Synod: I confess and I agree to (συντίθεμαι) and I receive and I salute and I venerate in the first place the spotless image of our Lord Jesus Christ, our true God, and the holy image of her who bore him without seed, the holy Mother of God, and her help and protection and intercessions each day and night as a sinner to my aid I call for, since she has confidence with Christ our God, as he was born of her. Likewise also I receive and venerate the images of the holy and most laudable Apostles, prophets, and martyrs and the fathers and cultivators of the desert. Not indeed as gods (God forbid!) do I ask all these with my whole heart to pray for me to God, that he may grant me through their intercessions to find mercy at his hands at the day of judgment, for in this I am but showing forth more clearly the affection and love of my soul which I have borne them from the first. Likewise also I venerate and honour and salute the relics of the Saints as of those who fought for Christ and who have received grace from him for the healing of diseases and the curing of sicknesses and the casting out of devils, as the Christian Church has received from the holy Apostles and Fathers even down to us today.

Moreover, I am well pleased that there should be images in the churches of the faithful, especially the image of our Lord Jesus Christ and of the Holy Mother of God, of every kind of material, both gold and silver and of every color, so that his incarnation may be set forth to all men. Likewise there may be painted the lives of the Saints and Prophets and Martyrs, so that their struggles and agonies may be set forth in brief, for the stirring up and teaching of the people, especially of the unlearned.

For if the people go forth with lights and incense to meet the laurata and images of the Emperors when they are sent to cities or rural districts, they honour surely not the tablet covered over with wax, but the Emperor himself. How much more is it necessary that in the churches of Christ our God, the image of God our Saviour and of his spotless Mother and of all the holy and blessed fathers and ascetics should be painted? Even as also St. Basil says: Writers and painters set forth the great deeds of war; the one by word, the other by their pencils; and each stirs many to courage. And again the same author How much pains have you ever taken that you might find one of the Saints who was willing to be your importunate intercessor to the Lord?

And Chrysostom says, The charity of the Saints is not diminished by their death, nor does it come to an end with their exit from life, but after their death they are still more powerful than when they were alive, and many other things without measure. Therefore I ask you, O you Saints! I call out to you. I have sinned against heaven and in your sight. Receive me as God received the luxurious man, and the harlot, and the thief. Seek me out, as Christ sought out the sheep that was lost, which he carried on his shoulders; so that there may be joy in the presence of God and of his angels over my salvation and repentance, through your intervention, O all-holy lords! Let them who do not venerate the holy and venerable images be anathema! Anathema to those who blaspheme against the honourable and venerable images! To those who dare to attack and blaspheme the venerable images and call them idols, anathema! To the calumniators of Christianity, that is to say the Iconoclasts, anathema! To those who do not diligently teach all the Christ-loving people to venerate and salute the venerable and sacred and honourable images of all the Saints who pleased God in their several generations, anathema! To those who have a doubtful mind and do not confess with their whole hearts that they venerate the sacred images, anathema!

Sabbas, the most reverend *hegumenus* of the monastery of the Studium, said: According to the Apostolic precepts and the Ecumenical Synods he is worthy to be received back.

Tarasius, the most holy Patriarch, said: Those who formerly were the calumniators of orthodoxy, now have become the advocates of the truth.

[*Near the end of this session*, (col. 77)]

John, the most reverend bishop and legate of the Eastern high priests said: This heresy is the worst of all heresies. Woe to the iconoclasts! It is the worst of heresies, as it subverts the incarnation (οἰκονομίαν) of our Saviour.

Session 2

[*The Papal Letters were presented by the Legates. First was read that to Constantine and Irene, but not in its entirety, if we may trust Anastasius the Librarian, who gives what he says is the original Latin text. Here follows a* translation of this and of the Greek, also a translation of the Latin passage altogether omitted, (as we are told) with the consent of the Roman Legates.]

Part of Pope Hadrian's Letter.

[*As written by the Pope.*]

(Migne, *Pat. Lat.*, Tom. XCVI., col. 1217.)

If you persevere in that orthodox Faith in which you have begun, and the sacred and venerable images be by your means erected again in those parts, as by the lord, the Emperor Constantine of pious memory, and the blessed Helen, who promulgated the orthodox Faith, and exalted the holy Catholic and Apostolic Roman Church your spiritual mother, and with the other orthodox Emperors venerated it as the head of all Churches, so will your Clemency, that is protected of God, receive the name of another Constantine, and another Helen, through whom at the beginning the holy Catholic and Apostolic Church derived strength, and like whom your own imperial fame is spread abroad by triumphs, so as to be brilliant and deeply fixed in the whole world. But the more, if following the traditions of the orthodox Faith, you embrace the judgment of the Church of blessed Peter, chief of the Apostles, and, as of old your predecessors the holy Emperors acted, so you, too, venerating it with honour, love with all your heart his Vicar, and if your sacred majesty follow by preference their orthodox Faith, according to our holy Roman Church. May the chief of the Apostles himself, to whom the power was given by our Lord God to bind and remit sins in heaven and earth, be often your protector, and trample all barbarous nations under your feet, and everywhere make you conquerors. For let sacred authority lay open the marks of his dignity, and how great veneration ought to be shown to his, the highest See, by all the faithful in the world. For the Lord set him who bears the keys of the kingdom of heaven as chief over all, and by Him is he honoured with this privilege, by which the keys of the kingdom of heaven are entrusted to him. He, therefore, that was preferred with so exalted an honour was thought worthy to confess that Faith on which the Church of Christ is founded. A blessed reward followed that blessed confession, by the preaching of which the holy universal Church was illumined, and from it the other Churches of God have derived the proofs of Faith. For the blessed Peter himself, the chief of the Apostles, who first sat in the Apostolic See, left the chiefship of his

Apostolate, and pastoral care, to his successors, who are to sit in his most holy seat forever. And that power of authority, which he received from the Lord God our Saviour, he too bestowed and delivered by divine command to the Pontiffs, his successors, etc.

[*As read in Greek to the Council.*]

(Migne, *Pat. Lat.*, Tom. XCVI., col. 1218.)

If the ancient orthodoxy be perfected and restored by your means in those regions, and the venerable icons be placed in their original state, you will be partakers with the Lord Constantine, Emperor of old, now in the Divine keeping, and the Empress Helena, who made conspicuous and confirmed the orthodox Faith, and exalted still more your holy mother, the Catholic and Roman and spiritual Church, and with the orthodox Emperors who ruled after them, and so your most pious and heaven-protected name likewise will be set forth as that of another Constantine and another Helena, being renowned and praised through the whole world, by whom the holy Catholic and Apostolic Church is restored. And especially if you follow the tradition of the orthodox Faith of the Church of the holy Peter and Paul, the chief Apostles, and embrace their Vicar, as the Emperors who reigned before you of old both honoured their Vicar, and loved him with all their heart: and if your sacred majesty honour the most holy Roman Church of the chief Apostles, to whom was given power by God the Word himself to loose and to bind sins in heaven and earth. For they will extend their shield over your power, and all barbarous nations shall be put under your feet: and wherever you go they will make you conquerors. For the holy and chief Apostles themselves, who set up the Catholic and orthodox Faith, have laid it down as a written law that all who after them are to be successors of their seats, should hold their Faith and remain in it to the end.

[*The part which was never read to the Council at all.*]

(Found in L. and C., *Concilia*, Tom. VII., col. 117.)

We greatly wondered that in your imperial commands, directed for the Patriarch of the royal city, Tarasius, we find him there called Universal: but we know not whether this was written through ignorance or schism, or the heresy of the wicked. But henceforth we advise your most merciful and imperial majesty, that he be by no means called Universal in your writings, because it appears to be contrary to the institutions of the holy Canons and the decrees of the traditions of the holy Fathers. For he never could have ranked second, save for the authority of our holy Catholic and Apostolic Church, as is plain to all. Because if he be named Universal, above the holy Roman Church which has a prior rank, which is the head of all the Churches of God, it is certain that he shows himself as a rebel against the holy Councils, and a heretic. For, if he is Universal, he is recognized to have the Primacy even over the Church of our See, which appears ridiculous to all faithful Christians: because in the whole world the chief rank and power was given to the blessed Apostle Peter by the Redeemer of the world himself; and through the same Apostle, whose place we unworthily hold, the holy Catholic and Apostolic Roman Church holds the first rank, and the authority of power, now and for ever, so that if any one, which we believe not, has called him, or assents to his being called Universal, let him know that he is estranged from the orthodox Faith, and a rebel against our holy Catholic and Apostolic Church.

[*After the reading was ended* (col. 120)]

Tarasius the most holy patriarch said: Did you yourselves receive these letters from the most holy Pope, and did you carry them to our pious Emperor?

Peter and Peter the most beloved-of-God presbyters who held the place of Hadrian, the most holy pope of Rome, said: We ourselves received such letters from our apostolic father and delivered them to the pious lords.

John, the most magnificent Logothete, said: That this is the case is also known to the Sicilians, the beloved of God Theodore, the bishop of Catanea, and the most revered deacon Epiphanius who is with him, who holds the place of the archbishop of Sardinia. For both of these at the bidding of our pious Emperors, went to Rome with the most reverend apocrisarius of our most holy patriarch.

Theodore the God-beloved bishop of Catanea, standing in the midst, said: The pious emperor, by his honourable jussio, bid send Leo, the most god-beloved presbyter (who together with myself is a slave of your holiness), with the precious letter of his most sacred majesty; and he who reveres our [*sic* in Greek, your, in Latin] holiness, being the governor (στρατηγὸς) of my province of Sicily, sent me to Rome with the pious jussio of our orthodox Emperors.

And when we had gone, we announced the orthodox faith of the pious emperors.

And when the most blessed Pope heard it, he said: Since this has come to pass in the days of their reign, God has magnified their pious rule above all former reigns. And this suggestion (ἀναφορὰν) which has been read he sent to our most pious kings together with a letter to your holiness and with his vicars who are here present and presiding.

Cosmas, the deacon, notary, and chamberlain (*Cubuclesius*) said: And another letter was sent by the most holy Pope of Old Rome to Tarasius, our most holy and œcumenical Patriarch. Let it be disposed of as your holy assembly shall direct.

The Holy Synod said, Let it be read.

[*Then was read Hadrian's letter to Tarasius of Constantinople, which ends by saying that,* our dearly-loved proto-presbyter of the Holy Church of Rome, and Peter, a monk, a presbyter, and an abbot, who have been sent by us to the most tranquil and pious emperors, we beg you will deem them worthy of all kindness and humane amenity for the sake of St. Peter, coropheus of the Apostles, and for our sakes, so that for this we may be able to offer you our sincere thanks. *The letter being ended* (col. 128),]

Peter and Peter, the most reverend presbyters and representatives of the most holy Pope of Old Rome said: Let the most holy Tarasius, Patriarch of the royal city, say whether he agrees (στοιχεῖ) with the letters of the most holy Pope of Old Rome or not.

Tarasius the most holy patriarch said: The divine Apostle Paul, who was filled with the light of Christ, and who has begotten us through the gospel, in writing to the Romans, commending their zeal for the true faith which they had in Christ our true God, thus said: Your faith has gone forth into all the world. It is necessary to follow out this witness, and he that would contradict it is without good sense. Wherefore Hadrian, the ruler of Old Rome, since he was a sharer of these things, thus borne witness to, wrote expressly and truly to our religious Emperors, and to our humility, confirming admirably and beautifully the ancient tradition of the Catholic Church. And we also ourselves, having examined both in writing, and by inquisition, and syllogistically and by demonstration, and having been taught by the teachings of the Fathers, so have confessed, so do confess, and so will confess; and shall be fast, and shall remain, and shall stand firm in the sense of the letters which have just been read, receiving the imaged representations according to the ancient tradition of our holy fathers; and these we venerate with firmly-attached affection, as made in the name of Christ our God, and of our Spotless Lady the Holy Mother of God, and of the Holy Angels, and of all the Saints, most clearly giving our adoration and faith to the one only true God.

And the holy Synod said: The whole holy Synod thus teaches.

Peter and Peter, the God-loved presbyters and legates of the Apostolic See, said: Let the holy Synod say whether it receives the letters of the most holy Pope of Old Rome.

The holy Synod said: We follow, we receive, we admit them.

[*The bishops then give one by one their votes all in the same sense.*]

Session 3

(Labbe and Cossart, *Concilia*, Tom. VII., col. 188.)

Constantine, the most holy bishop of Constantia in Cyprus, said: Since I, unworthy that I am, find that the letter which has just been read, which was sent from the East to Tarasius the most holy archbishop and ecumenical patriarch, is in no sense changed from that confession of faith which he himself had before made, to these I consent and become of one mind, receiving and saluting with honour the holy and venerable images. But the worship of adoration I reserve alone to the supersubstantial and life-giving Trinity. And those who are not so minded, and do not so teach I cast out of the holy Catholic and Apostolic Church, and I smite them with anathema, and I deliver them over to the lot of those who deny the incarnation and the bodily economy of Christ our true God.

Session 4

[Among numerous passages of the Fathers one was read from a sermon by St. Gregory Nyssen in which he describes a painting representing the sacrifice of Isaac and tells how he could not pass it without tears.]

The most glorious princes said: See how our father grieved at the depicted history, even so that he wept.

Basil, the most holy bishop of Ancyra, said: Many times the father had read the story, but perchance he had not wept; but when once he saw it painted, he wept.

John the most reverend monk and presbyter and representative of the Eastern high priests, said: If to such a doctor the picture was helpful and drew forth tears, how much more in the case of the ignorant and simple will it bring compunction and benefit.

The holy Synod said: We have seen in several places the history of Abraham painted as the father says.

Theodore the most holy bishop of Catanea, said: If the holy Gregory, vigilant in divine cogitation, was moved to tears at the sight of the story of Abraham, how much more shall a painting of the incarnation of our Lord Christ, who for us was made man, move the beholders to their profit and to tears?

Tarasius the most holy Patriarch said: Shall we not weep when we see an image of our crucified Lord?

The holy Synod said: We shall indeed — for in that shall be found perfectly the profundity of the abasement of the incarnate God for our sakes.

[Post nonnulla a passage is read from St. Athanasius in which he describes the miracles worked at Berytus, after which there is found the following (col. 224),]

Tarasius, the most holy Patriarch, said: But perhaps someone will say, Why do not the images which we have work miracles? To which we answer, that as the Apostle has said, signs are for those who do not believe, not for believers. For they who approached that image were unbelievers. Therefore God gave them a sign through the image, to draw them to our Christian faith. But an evil and adulterous generation that seeks after a sign and no sign shall be given it.

[After a number of other quotations, was read the Canon of the Council in Trullo as a canon of the Sixth Synod (col. 233).]

Tarasius, the most holy Patriarch said: There are certain affected with the sickness of ignorance who are scandalized by these canons [viz. of the Trullan Synod] and say, And do you really think they were adopted at the Sixth Synod? Now let all such know that the holy great Sixth Synod was assembled at Constantinople concerning those who said that there was but one energy and will in Christ. These anathematized the heretics, and having expounded the orthodox faith, they went to their homes in the fourteenth year of Constantine. But after four or five years the same fathers came together under Justinian, the son of Constantine, and set forth the before-mentioned canons. And let no one doubt concerning them. For they who subscribed under Constantine were the same as they who under Justinian signed the present chart, as can manifestly be established from the unchangeable similarity of their own handwriting. For it was right that they who had appeared at an ecumenical synod should also set forth ecclesiastical canons. They said that we should be led as (by the hand) by the venerable images to the recollection of the incarnation of Christ and of his saving death, and if by them we are led to the realization of the incarnation of Christ our God, what sort of an opinion shall we have of them who break down the venerable images?

[At the close of the Session, after a number of anathematisms had been pronounced, the following was read, to which all the bishops subscribed (col. 317).]

Fulfilling the divine precept of our God and Saviour Jesus Christ, our holy Fathers did not hide the light of the divine knowledge given by him to them under a bushel, but they set it upon the candlestick of most useful teaching, so that it might give light to all in the house — that is to say, to those who are born in the Catholic Church; lest perchance anyone of those who piously confess the Lord might strike his foot against the stone of heretical evil doctrine. For they expelled every error of heretics and they cut off the rotten member if it was incurably sick. And with a fan they purged the floor. And the good wheat, that is to say the word which nourishes and which makes strong the heart of man, they laid up in the granary of the Catholic Church;

SEVEN ECUMENICAL COUNCILS OF THE CHURCH

but throwing outside the chaff of heretical evil opinion they burned it with unquenchable fire. Therefore also this holy and ecumenical Synod, met together for the second time in this illustrious metropolis of Nice, by the will of God and at the bidding of our pious and most faithful Emperors, Irene a new Helena, and a new Constantine, her God-protected offspring, having considered by their perusal the teachings of our approved and blessed Fathers, has glorified God himself, from whom there was given to them wisdom for our instruction, and for the perfecting of the Catholic and Apostolic Church: and against those who do not believe as they did, but have attempted to overshadow the truth through their novelty, they have chanted the words of the psalm: Oh how much evil have your enemies done in your sanctuary; and have glorified themselves, saying, There is not a teacher any more, and they shall not know that we treated with guile the word of truth. But we, in all things holding the doctrines and precepts of the same our God-bearing Fathers, make proclamation with one mouth and one heart, neither adding anything, nor taking anything away from those things which have been delivered to us by them. But in these things we are strengthened, in these things we are confirmed. Thus we confess, thus we teach, just as the holy and ecumenical six Synods have decreed and ratified. We believe in one God the Father Almighty, maker of all things visible and invisible; and in one Lord Jesus Christ, his only-begotten Son and Word, through whom all things were made, and in the Holy Ghost, the Lord and giver of life, consubstantial and coeternal with the same Father and with his Son who has had no beginning. The unbuilt-up, indivisible, incomprehensible, and non-circumscribed Trinity; he, wholly and alone, is to be worshipped and revered with adoration; one Godhead, one Lordship, one dominion, one realm and dynasty, which without division is apportioned to the Persons, and is fitted to the essence severally. For we confess that one of the same holy and consubstantial Trinity, our Lord Jesus Christ the true God, in these last days was incarnate and made man for our salvation, and having saved our race through his saving incarnation, and passion, and resurrection, and ascension into heaven; and having delivered us from the error of idols; as also the prophet says, Not an ambassador, not an angel, but the Lord himself has saved us. Him we also follow, and adopt his voice, and cry aloud; No Synod, no power of kings, no God-hated agreement has delivered the Church from the error of the idols, as the Judaizing conciliabulum has madly dreamed, which raved against the venerable images; but the Lord of glory himself, the incarnate God, has saved us and has snatched us from idolatrous deceit. To him therefore be glory, to him be thanks, to him be eucharists, to him be praise, to him be magnificence. For his redemption and his salvation alone can perfectly save, and not that of other men who come of the earth. For he himself has fulfilled for us, upon whom the ends of the earth have come through the economy of his incarnation, the words spoken beforehand by his prophets, for he dwelt among us, and went in and out among us, and cast out the names of idols from the earth, as it was written. But we salute the voices of the Lord and of his Apostles through which we have been taught to honour in the first place her who is properly and truly the Mother of God and exalted above all the heavenly powers; also the holy and angelic powers; and the blessed and altogether lauded Apostles, and the glorious Prophets and the triumphant Martyrs which fought for Christ, and the holy and God-bearing Doctors, and all holy men; and to seek for their intercessions, as able to render us at home with the all-royal God of all, so long as we keep his commandments, and strive to live virtuously. Moreover we salute the image of the honourable and life-giving Cross, and the holy relics of the Saints; and we receive the holy and venerable images: and we salute them, and we embrace them, according to the ancient traditions of the holy Catholic Church of God, that is to say of our holy Fathers, who also received these things and established them in all the most holy Churches of God, and in every place of his dominion. These honourable and venerable images, as has been said, we honour and salute and reverently venerate: to wit, the image of the incarnation of our great God and Saviour Jesus Christ, and that of our spotless Lady the all-holy Mother of God, from whom he pleased to take flesh, and to save and deliver us from all impious idolatry; also the images of the holy and incorporeal Angels, who as men appeared to the just. Likewise also the figures and effigies of the divine and all-lauded Apostles, also of the God-speaking Prophets, and of the struggling Martyrs and of holy men. So that through their representations we may be able to be led back in memory and recollection to the prototype, and have a share in the holiness of some one of them.

Thus we have learned to think of these things, and we have been strengthened by our holy Fathers, and we have been strengthened by their divinely handed down teaching. And thanks be to God for his ineffable gift, that he has not deserted us at the end nor has the rod of the ungodly come into the lot of the righteous, lest the righteous put their hands, that is to say their actual deeds, unto wickedness. But he does well unto those who are good and true of heart, as the psalmist David melodiously has sung; with whom also we sing the rest of the psalm: As for such as turn back unto their own wickedness, the Lord shall lead them forth with the evil doers; and peace shall be upon the Israel of God.

[*The subscriptions follow immediately and close the acts of this session* (col. 321-346).]

Session 6

(Labbe and Cossart, *Concilia*, Tom. VII., col. 389.)

Leo the most renowned secretary said: The holy and blessed Synod know how at the last session we examined various sayings of the God-forsaken heretics, who had brought charges against the holy and spotless Church of the Christians for the setting up of the holy images. But today we have in our hands the written blasphemy of those calumniators of the Christians, that is to say, the absurd, and easily answered, and self-convicting definition (ὅρον) of the pseudosyllogus, in all respects agreeing with the impious opinion of the God-hated heretics. But not only have we this, but also the artful and most drastic refutation thereof, which the Holy Spirit had supervised. For it was right that this definition should be made a triumph by wise contradictions, and should be torn to pieces with strong refutations. This also we submit so as to know your pleasure with regard to it.

The holy Synod said: Let it be read.

John, the deacon and chancellor [of the most holy great Church of Constantinople, *in Lat. only*] read.

[*John, the deacon, then read the orthodox refutation, and Gregory, the bishop of Neocæsarea, the Definition of the Mock Council, the one reading the heretical statement and the other the orthodox answer.*]

SEVEN ECUMENICAL COUNCILS OF THE CHURCH

The Definition

The holy and Ecumenical synod, which by the grace of God and most pious command of the God-beloved and orthodox Emperors, Constantine and Leo, now assembled in the imperial residence city, in the temple of the holy and inviolate Mother of God and Virgin Mary, surnamed in Blachernæ, have decreed as follows.

Satan misguided men, so that they worshipped the creature instead of the Creator. The Mosaic law and the prophets cooperated to undo this ruin; but in order to save mankind thoroughly, God sent his own Son, who turned us away from error and the worshipping of idols, and taught us the worshipping of God in spirit and in truth. As messengers of his saving doctrine, he left us his Apostles and disciples, and these adorned the Church, his Bride, with his glorious doctrines. This ornament of the Church the holy Fathers and the six Ecumenical Councils have preserved inviolate. But the before-mentioned demi-urgos of wickedness could not endure the sight of this adornment, and gradually brought back idolatry under the appearance of Christianity. As then Christ armed his Apostles against the ancient idolatry with the power of the Holy Spirit, and sent them out into all the world, so has he awakened against the new idolatry his servants our faithful Emperors, and endowed them with the same wisdom of the Holy Spirit. Impelled by the Holy Spirit they could no longer be witnesses of the Church being laid waste by the deception of demons, and summoned the sanctified assembly of the God-beloved bishops, that they might institute at a synod a scriptural examination into the deceitful coloring of the pictures (ὁμοιωμάτων) which draws down the spirit of man from the lofty adoration (λατρείας) of God to the low and material adoration (λατρείαν) of the creature, and that they, under divine guidance, might express their view on the subject.

Our holy synod therefore assembled, and we, its 338 members, follow the older synodal decrees, and accept and proclaim joyfully the dogmas handed down, principally those of the six holy Ecumenical Synods. In the first place the holy and ecumenical great synod assembled at Nice, etc.

After we had carefully examined their decrees under the guidance of the Holy Spirit, we found that the unlawful art of painting living creatures blasphemed the fundamental doctrine of our salvation—namely, the Incarnation of Christ, and contradicted the six holy synods. These condemned Nestorius because he divided the one Son and Word of God into two sons, and on the other side, Arius, Dioscorus, Eutyches, and Severus, because they maintained a mingling of the two natures of the one Christ.

Wherefore we thought it right, to show forth with all accuracy, in our present definition the error of such as make and venerate these, for it is the unanimous doctrine of all the holy Fathers and of the six Ecumenical Synods, that no one may imagine any kind of separation or mingling in opposition to the unsearchable, unspeakable, and incomprehensible union of the two natures in the one hypostasis or person. What avails, then, the folly of the painter, who from sinful love of gain depicts that which should not be depicted — that is, with his polluted hands he tries to fashion that which should only be believed in the heart and confessed with the mouth? He makes an image and calls it Christ. The name Christ signifies God and man. Consequently it is an image of God and man, and consequently he has in his foolish mind, in his representation of the created flesh, depicted the Godhead which cannot be represented, and thus mingled what should not be mingled. Thus he is guilty of a double blasphemy— the one in making an image of the Godhead, and the other by mingling the Godhead and manhood. Those fall into the same blasphemy who venerate the image, and the same woe rests upon both, because they err with Arius, Dioscorus, and Eutyches, and with the heresy of the Acephali. When, however, they are blamed for undertaking to depict the divine nature of Christ, which should not be depicted, they take refuge in the excuse: We represent only the flesh of Christ which we have seen and handled. But that is a Nestorian error. For it should be considered that that flesh was also the flesh of God the Word, without any separation, perfectly assumed by the divine nature and made wholly divine. How could it now be separated and represented apart? So is it with the human soul of Christ which mediates between the Godhead of the Son and the dulness of the flesh. As the human flesh is at the same time flesh of God the Word, so is the human soul also soul of God the Word, and both at the same time, the soul being deified as well as the body, and the Godhead remained undivided even in the separation of the soul from the body in his voluntary passion. For where the soul of Christ is, there is also his Godhead; and where the body of Christ is, there too is his Godhead. If then in his passion the divinity remained inseparable from these, how do the fools venture to separate the flesh from the Godhead, and represent it by itself as the image of a mere man? They fall into the abyss of impiety, since they separate the flesh from the Godhead, ascribe to it a subsistence of its own, a personality of its own, which they depict, and thus introduce a fourth person into the Trinity. Moreover, they represent as not being made divine, that which has been made divine by being assumed by the Godhead. Whoever, then, makes an image of Christ, either depicts the Godhead which cannot be depicted, and mingles it with the manhood (like the Monophysites), or he represents the body of Christ as not made divine and separate and as a person apart, like the Nestorians.

The only admissible figure of the humanity of Christ, however, is bread and wine in the holy Supper. This and no other form, this and no other type, has he chosen to represent his incarnation. Bread he ordered to be brought, but not a representation of the human form, so that idolatry might not arise. And as the body of Christ is made divine, so also this figure of the body of Christ, the bread, is made divine by the descent of the Holy Spirit; it becomes the divine body of Christ by the mediation of the priest who, separating the oblation from that which is common, sanctifies it.

The evil custom of assigning names to the images does not come down from Christ and the Apostles and the holy Fathers; nor have these left behind them any prayer by which an image should be hallowed or made anything else than ordinary matter.

If, however, some say, we might be right in regard to the images of Christ, on account of the mysterious union of the two natures, but it is not right for us to forbid also the images of the altogether spotless and ever-glorious Mother of God, of the prophets, apostles, and martyrs, who were mere men and did not consist of two natures; we may reply, first of all: If those fall away, there is no longer need of these. But we will also consider what may be said against these in particular. Christianity has rejected the *whole* of heathenism, and so not merely heathen sacrifices, but also the heathen worship of images. The Saints live on eternally with God, although they have died. If anyone thinks to call them back again to life by a dead art, discovered by the heathen, he makes himself guilty of blasphemy. Who dares attempt with heathenish

SEVEN ECUMENICAL COUNCILS OF THE CHURCH

art to paint the Mother of God, who is exalted above all heavens and the Saints? It is not permitted to Christians, who have the hope of the resurrection, to imitate the customs of demon-worshippers, and to insult the Saints, who shine in so great glory, by common dead matter.

Moreover, we can prove our view by Holy Scripture and the Fathers. In the former it is said: God is a Spirit: and they that worship him must worship him in spirit and in truth; and: You shall not make you any graven image, or any likeness of anything that is in heaven above, or that is in the earth beneath; on which account God spoke to the Israelites on the Mount, from the midst of the fire, but showed them no image. Further: They changed the glory of the incorruptible God into an image made like to corruptible man,...and served the creature more than the Creator. [*Several other passages, even less to the point, are cited.*]

The same is taught also by the holy Fathers. [*The Synod appeals to a spurious passage from Epiphanius and to one inserted into the writings of Theodotus of Ancyra, a friend of St. Cyril's; to utterances — in no way striking — of Gregory of Nazianzum, of SS. Chrysostom, Basil, Athanasius of Amphilochius and of Eusebius Pamphili, from his* Letter to the Empress Constantia, *who had asked him for a picture of Christ.*]

Supported by the Holy Scriptures and the Fathers, we declare unanimously, in the name of the Holy Trinity, that there shall be rejected and removed and cursed out of the Christian Church every likeness which is made out of any material and color whatever by the evil art of painters.

Whoever in future dares to make such a thing, or to venerate it, or set it up in a church, or in a private house, or possesses it in secret, shall, if bishop, presbyter, or deacon, be deposed; if monk or layman, be anathematised, and become liable to be tried by the secular laws as an adversary of God and an enemy of the doctrines handed down by the Fathers. At the same time we ordain that no incumbent of a church shall venture, under pretext of destroying the error in regard to images, to lay his hands on the holy vessels in order to have them altered, because they are adorned with figures. The same is provided in regard to the vestments of churches, cloths, and all that is dedicated to divine service. If, however, the incumbent of a church wishes to have such church vessels and vestments altered, he must do this only with the assent of the holy Ecumenical patriarch and at the bidding of our pious

Emperors. So also no prince or secular official shall rob the churches, as some have done in former times, under the pretext of destroying images. All this we ordain, believing that we speak as does the Apostle, for we also believe that we have the spirit of Christ; and as our predecessors who believed the same thing spoke what they had synodically defined, so we believe and therefore do we speak, and set forth a definition of what has seemed good to us following and in accordance with the definitions of our Fathers.

(1) If anyone shall not confess, according to the tradition of the Apostles and Fathers, in the Father, the Son and the Holy Ghost one godhead, nature and substance, will and operation, virtue and dominion, kingdom and power in three subsistences, that is in their most glorious Persons, let him be anathema.

(2) If anyone does not confess that one of the Trinity was made flesh, let him be anathema.

(3) If anyone does not confess that the holy Virgin is truly the Mother of God, let him be anathema.

(4) If anyone does not confess one Christ both God and man, let him be anathema.

(5) If anyone does not confess that the flesh of the Lord is life-giving because it is the flesh of the Word of God, let him be anathema.

(6) If anyone does not confess two natures in Christ, let him be anathema.

(7) If anyone does not confess that Christ is seated with God the Father in body and soul, and so will come to judge, and that he will remain God forever without any grossness, let him be anathema.

(8) If anyone ventures to represent the divine image (χαρακτήρ) of the Word after the Incarnation with material colors, let him be anathema!

(9) If anyone ventures to represent in human figures, by means of material colors, by reason of the incarnation, the substance or person (*ousia* or *hypostasis*) of the Word, which cannot be depicted, and does not rather confess that even after the Incarnation he [i.e., the Word] cannot be depicted, let him be anathema!

(10) If anyone ventures to represent the hypostatic union of the two natures in a picture, and calls it Christ, and thus falsely represents a union of the two natures, let him be anathema!

(11) If anyone separates the flesh united with the person of the Word from it, and endeavours to represent it separately in a picture, let him be anathema!

(12) If anyone separates the one Christ into two persons, and endeavours to represent Him who was born of the Virgin separately, and thus accepts only a relative (σχετική) union of the natures, let him be anathema.

(13) If anyone represents in a picture the flesh deified by its union with the Word, and thus separates it from the Godhead, let him be anathema.

(14) If anyone endeavours to represent by material colors, God the Word as a mere man, who, although bearing the form of God, yet has assumed the form of a servant in his own person, and thus endeavours to separate him from his inseparable Godhead, so that he thereby introduces a quaternity into the Holy Trinity, let him be anathema.

(15) If anyone shall not confess the Holy Ever-Virgin Mary, truly and properly the Mother of God, to be higher than every creature whether visible or invisible, and does not with sincere faith seek her intercessions as of one having confidence in her access to our God, since she bore him, let him be anathema.

(16) If anyone shall endeavour to represent the forms of the Saints in lifeless pictures with material colors which are of no value (for this notion is vain and introduced by the devil), and does not rather represent their virtues as living images in himself, let him be anathema.

(17) If anyone denies the profit of the invocation of Saints, let him be anathema.

(18) If anyone denies the resurrection of the dead, and the judgment, and the condign retribution to everyone, endless torment and endless bliss, let him be anathema.

(19) If anyone does not accept this our Holy and Ecumenical Seventh Synod, let him be anathema from the Father and the Son and the Holy Ghost, and from the seven holy Ecumenical Synods!

[*Then follows the prohibition of the making or teaching any other faith, and the penalties for disobedience. After this follow the acclamations.*]

The divine Kings Constantine and Leo said: Let the holy and ecumenical synod say, if with the consent of all the most holy bishops the definition just read has been set forth.

The holy synod cried out: Thus we all believe, we all are of the same mind. We have all with one voice and voluntarily subscribed. This is the faith of the Apostles. Many years to the Emperors! They are the light of orthodoxy! Many years to the orthodox Emperors! God preserve your Empire! You have now more firmly proclaimed the inseparability of the two natures of Christ! You have banished all idolatry! You have destroyed the heresies of Germanus [of Constantinople], George and Mansur [μανσουρ, John Damascene]. Anathema to Germanus, the double-minded, and worshipper of wood! Anathema to George, his associate, to the falsifier of the doctrine of the Fathers! Anathema to Mansur, who has an evil name and Saracen opinions! To the betrayer of Christ and the enemy of the Empire, to the teacher of impiety, the perverter of Scripture, Mansur, anathema! The Trinity has deposed these three!

SEVEN ECUMENICAL COUNCILS OF THE CHURCH

The Decree

(*Found in Labbe and Cossart,* Concilia. *Tom. VII., col. 552.*)

The holy, great, and Ecumenical Synod which by the grace of God and the will of the pious and Christ-loving Emperors, Constantine and Irene, his mother, was gathered together for the second time at Nice, the illustrious metropolis of Bithynia, in the holy church of God which is named Sophia, having followed the tradition of the Catholic Church, has defined as follows:

Christ our Lord, who has bestowed upon us the light of the knowledge of himself, and has redeemed us from the darkness of idolatrous madness, having espoused to himself the Holy Catholic Church without spot or defect, promised that he would so preserve her: and gave his word to this effect to his holy disciples when he said: Lo! I am with you always, even unto the end of the world, which promise he made, not only to them, but to us also who should believe in his name through their word. But some, not considering of this gift, and having become fickle through the temptation of the wily enemy, have fallen from the right faith; for, withdrawing from the traditions of the Catholic Church, they have erred from the truth and as the proverb says: The husbandmen have gone astray in their own husbandry and have gathered in their hands nothingness, because certain priests, priests in name only, not in fact, had dared to speak against the God-approved ornament of the sacred monuments, of whom God cries aloud through the prophet, Many pastors have corrupted my vineyard, they have polluted my portion.

And, forsooth, following profane men, led astray by their carnal sense, they have calumniated the Church of Christ our God, which he has espoused to himself, and have failed to distinguish between holy and profane, styling the images of our Lord and of his Saints by the same name as the statues of diabolical idols. Seeing which things, our Lord God (not willing to behold his people corrupted by such manner of plague) has of his good pleasure called us together, the chief of his priests, from every quarter, moved with a divine zeal and brought hither by the will of our princes, Constantine and Irene, to the end that the traditions of the Catholic Church may receive stability by our common decree. Therefore, with all diligence, making a thorough

SEVEN ECUMENICAL COUNCILS OF THE CHURCH

examination and analysis, and following the trend of the truth, we diminish nought, we add nought, but we preserve unchanged all things which pertain to the Catholic Church, and following the Six Ecumenical Synods, especially that which met in this illustrious metropolis of Nice, as also that which was afterwards gathered together in the God-protected Royal City.

We believe...life of the world to come. Amen.

We detest and anathematize Arius and all the sharers of his absurd opinion; also Macedonius and those who following him are well styled Foes of the Spirit (Pneumatomachi). We confess that our Lady, St. Mary, is properly and truly the Mother of God, because she was the Mother after the flesh of One Person of the Holy Trinity, to wit, Christ our God, as the Council of Ephesus has already defined when it cast out of the Church the impious Nestorius with his colleagues, because he taught that there were two Persons [in Christ]. With the Fathers of this synod we confess that he who was incarnate of the immaculate Mother of God and Ever-Virgin Mary has two natures, recognizing him as perfect God and perfect man, as also the Council of Chalcedon has promulgated, expelling from the divine Atrium [αὐλῆς] as blasphemers, Eutyches and Dioscorus; and placing in the same category Severus, Peter and a number of others, blaspheming in various fashions. Moreover, with these we anathematize the fables of Origen, Evagrius, and Didymus, in accordance with the decision of the Fifth Council held at Constantinople. We affirm that in Christ there be two wills and two operations according to the reality of each nature, as also the Sixth Synod, held at Constantinople, taught, casting out Sergius, Honorius, Cyrus, Pyrrhus, Macarius, and those who agree with them, and all those who are unwilling to be reverent.

To make our confession short, we keep unchanged all the ecclesiastical traditions handed down to us, whether in writing or verbally, one of which is the making of pictorial representations, agreeable to the history of the preaching of the Gospel, a tradition useful in many respects, but especially in this, that so the incarnation of the Word of God is shown forth as real and not merely phantastic, for these have mutual indications and without doubt have also mutual significations.

We, therefore, following the royal pathway and the divinely inspired authority of our Holy Fathers and the traditions of the Catholic Church

SEVEN ECUMENICAL COUNCILS OF THE CHURCH

(for, as we all know, the Holy Spirit indwells her), define with all certitude and accuracy that just as the figure of the precious and life-giving Cross, so also the venerable and holy images, as well in painting and mosaic as of other fit materials, should be set forth in the holy churches of God, and on the sacred vessels and on the vestments and on hangings and in pictures both in houses and by the wayside, to wit, the figure of our Lord God and Saviour Jesus Christ, of our spotless Lady, the Mother of God, of the honourable Angels, of all Saints and of all pious people. For by so much more frequently as they are seen in artistic representation, by so much more readily are men lifted up to the memory of their prototypes, and to a longing after them; and to these should be given due salutation and honourable reverence (ἀσπασμὸν καὶ τιμητικὴν προσκύνησιν), not indeed that true worship of faith (λατρείαν) which pertains alone to the divine nature; but to these, as to the figure of the precious and life-giving Cross and to the Book of the Gospels and to the other holy objects, incense and lights may be offered according to ancient pious custom. For the honour which is paid to the image passes on to that which the image represents, and he who reveres the image reveres in it the subject represented. For thus the teaching of our holy Fathers, that is the tradition of the Catholic Church, which from one end of the earth to the other has received the Gospel, is strengthened. Thus we follow Paul, who spoke in Christ, and the whole divine Apostolic company and the holy Fathers, holding fast the traditions which we have received. So we sing prophetically the triumphal hymns of the Church, Rejoice greatly, O daughter of Sion; Shout, O daughter of Jerusalem. Rejoice and be glad with all your heart. The Lord has taken away from you the oppression of your adversaries; you are redeemed from the hand of your enemies. The Lord is a King in the midst of you; you shall not see evil any more, and peace be unto you forever.

Those, therefore who dare to think or teach otherwise, or as wicked heretics to spurn the traditions of the Church and to invent some novelty, or else to reject some of those things which the Church has received (*e.g.*, the Book of the Gospels, or the image of the cross, or the pictorial icons, or the holy relics of a martyr), or evilly and sharply to devise anything subversive of the lawful traditions of the Catholic Church or to turn to common uses the sacred vessels or the venerable monasteries, if they be Bishops or Clerics, we command that they be deposed; if religious or laics, that they be cut off from communion.

[After all had signed, the acclamations began (col. 576).]

The holy Synod cried out: So we all believe, we all are so minded, we all give our consent and have signed. This is the faith of the Apostles, this is the faith of the orthodox, this is the faith which has made firm the whole world. Believing in one God, to be celebrated in Trinity, we salute the honourable images! Those who do not so hold, let them be anathema. Those who do not thus think, let them be driven far away from the Church. For we follow the most ancient legislation of the Catholic Church. We keep the laws of the Fathers. We anathematize those who add anything to or take anything away from the Catholic Church. We anathematize the introduced novelty of the revilers of Christians. We salute the venerable images. We place under anathema those who do not do this. Anathema to them who presume to apply to the venerable images the things said in Holy Scripture about idols. Anathema to those who do not salute the holy and venerable images. Anathema to those who call the sacred images idols. Anathema to those who say that Christians resort to the sacred images as to gods. Anathema to those who say that any other delivered us from idols except Christ our God. Anathema to those who dare to say that at any time the Catholic Church received idols.

Many years to the Emperors, etc., etc.

SEVEN ECUMENICAL COUNCILS OF THE CHURCH

The Canons

Canon 1

That the sacred Canons are in all things to be observed.

The pattern for those who have received the sacerdotal dignity is found in the testimonies and instructions laid down in the canonical constitutions, which we receiving with a glad mind, sing unto the Lord God in the words of the God-inspired David, saying: I have had as great delight in the way of your testimonies as in all manner of riches. You have commanded righteousness as your testimonies forever. Grant me understanding and I shall live. Now if the word of prophesy bids us keep the testimonies of God forever and to live by them, it is evident that they must abide unshaken and without change. Therefore Moses, the prophet of God, speaks after this manner: To them nothing is to be added, and from them nothing is to be taken away. And the divine Apostle glorying in them cries out, which things the angels desire to look into, and, if an angel preach to you anything besides that which you have received, let him be anathema. Seeing these things are so, being thus well-testified unto us, we rejoice over them as he that has found great spoil, and press to our bosom with gladness the divine canons, holding fast all the precepts of the same, complete and without change, whether they have been set forth by the holy trumpets of the Spirit, the renowned Apostles, or by the Six Ecumenical Councils, or by Councils locally assembled for promulgating the decrees of the said Ecumenical Councils, or by our holy Fathers. For all these, being illumined by the same Spirit, defined such things as were expedient. Accordingly those whom they placed under anathema, we likewise anathematize; those whom they deposed, we also depose; those whom they excommunicated, we also excommunicate; and those whom they delivered over to punishment, we subject to the same penalty. And now let your conversation be without covetousness, cries out Paul the divine Apostle, who was caught up into the third heaven and heard unspeakable words.

Ancient Epitome: We gladly embrace the Divine Canons, viz.: those of the Holy Apostles, of the Six Ecumenical Synods, as also of the local synods and of our Holy Fathers, as inspired by one and the same Holy Spirit. Whom they anathematize we also anathematize; whom they depose, we depose; whom they cut off, we cut off; and whom they subject to penalties, we also so subject.

Canon 2

That he who is to be ordained a Bishop must be steadfastly resolved to observe the canons, otherwise he shall not be ordained.

When we recite the psalter, we promise God: I will meditate upon your statutes, and will not forget your words. It is a salutary thing for all Christians to observe this, but it is especially incumbent upon those who have received the sacerdotal dignity. Therefore we decree, that every one who is raised to the rank of the episcopate shall know the psalter by heart, so that from it he may admonish and instruct all the clergy who are subject to him. And diligent examination shall be made by the metropolitan whether he be zealously inclined to read diligently, and not merely now and then, the sacred canons, the holy Gospel, and the book of the divine Apostle, and all other divine Scripture; and whether he lives according to God's commandments, and also teaches the same to his people. For the special treasure (οὐσία) of our high priesthood is the oracles which have been divinely delivered to us, that is the true science of the Divine Scriptures, as says Dionysius the Great. And if his mind be not set, and even glad, so to do and teach, let him not be ordained. For says God by the prophet, You have rejected knowledge, I will also reject you, that you shall be no priest to me.

Ancient Epitome: Whoever is to be a bishop must know the Psalter by heart: he must thoroughly understand what he reads, and not merely superficially, but with diligent care, that is to say the Sacred Canons, the Holy Gospel, the book of the Apostle, and the whole of the Divine Scripture. And should he not have such knowledge, he is not to be ordained.

Canon 3

That it does not pertain to princes to choose a Bishop.

Let every election of a bishop, presbyter, or deacon, made by princes stand null, according to the canon which says: If any bishop making use of the secular powers shall by their means obtain jurisdiction over any church, he shall be deposed, and also excommunicated, together with all who remain in communion with him. For he who is raised to the episcopate must be chosen by bishops, as was decreed by the holy fathers of Nice in the canon which says: It is most fitting that a bishop be ordained by all the bishops in the province; but if this is difficult to arrange, either on account of urgent necessity, or because of the length of the journey, three bishops at least having met together and given their votes, those also who are absent having signified their assent by letters, the ordination shall take place. The confirmation of what is thus done, shall in each province be given by the metropolitan thereof.

Ancient Epitome: Every election made by a secular magistrate is null.

Canon 4

That Bishops are to abstain from all receiving of gifts.

The Church's herald, Paul the divine Apostle, laying down a rule (κανόνα) not only for the presbyters of Ephesus but for the whole company of the priesthood, speaks thus explicitly, saying, I have coveted no man's silver or gold, or apparel. I have showed you all things, how that so labouring you ought to support the weak; for he accounted it more blessed to give. Therefore we being taught by him do decree, that under no circumstances, shall a Bishop for the sake of filthy lucre invent feigned excuses for sins, and exact gold or silver or other gifts from the bishops, clergy, or monks who are subject to him. For says the Apostle, The unrighteous shall not possess the kingdom of God, and, The children ought not to lay up for the parents, but the parents for the children. If then any is found, who for the sake of exacting gold or any other gift, or who from personal feeling, has suspended from the ministry, or even excommunicated, any of the clergy subject to his jurisdiction, or who has closed any of the venerable temples, so that the service of God may not be celebrated in it, pouring out his madness even upon things insensible, and thus showing himself to be without understanding, he shall be subjected to the same punishment he devised for others, and his trouble shall return on his own head, as a transgressor of God's commandment and of the apostolic precepts. For Peter the supreme head (ἡ κερυφαία ἀκρότης) of the Apostles commands, Feed the flock of God which is among you, taking the oversight thereof, not by constraint, but willingly; not for filthy lucre but of a ready mind; neither as being lords over the clergy (τῶν κλήρων [A.V. God's heritage]); but being ensamples to the flock. And when the chief shepherd shall appear, you shall receive a crown of glory that fades not away.

Ancient Epitome: We decree that no bishop shall extort gold or silver, or anything else from bishops, clerics, or monks subject to his jurisdiction. And if anyone through the power of gold or of any other thing or through his own whims, shall be found to have prevented any one of the clergy who are subject to him, from the celebration of the holy offices, or shall have shut up a venerable temple so that the sacred worship of God could not be performed in it, he shall be subject to the lex talionis. For Peter the Apostle says: Feed the flock of God, not of necessity but willingly, and according to God; not for filthy lucre's sake, but with a prompt mind; not exercising lordship over the clergy, but being an example to the flock.

Canon 5

That they who cast contumely upon clerics because they have been ordained in the church without bringing a gift with them, are to be published with a fine.

It is a sin unto death when men incorrigibly continue in their sin, but they sin more deeply, who proudly lifting themselves up oppose piety and sincerity, accounting mammon of more worth than obedience to God, and caring nothing for his canonical precepts. The Lord God is not found among such, unless, perchance, having been humbled by their own fall, they return to a sober mind. It behooves them the rather to turn to God with a contrite heart and to pray for forgiveness and pardon of so grave a sin, and no longer to boast in an unholy gift. For the Lord is near unto them that are of a contrite heart. With regard, therefore, to those who pride themselves that because of their benefactions of gold they were ordained in the Church, and resting confidently in this evil custom (so alien from God and inconsistent with the whole priesthood), with a proud look and open mouth vilify with abusive words those who on account of the strictness of their life were chosen by the Holy Ghost and have been ordained without any gift of money, we decree in the first place that they take the lowest place in their order; but if they do not amend let them be subjected to a fine. But if it appear that any one has done this [i.e., given money], at any time as a price for ordination, let him be dealt with according to the Apostolic Canon which says: If a bishop has obtained possession of his dignity by means of money (the same rule applies also to a presbyter or deacon) let him be deposed and also the one who ordained him, and let him also be altogether cut off from communion, even as Simon Magus was by me Peter. To the same effect is the second canon of our holy fathers of Chalcedon, which says: If any bishop gives ordination in return for money, and puts up for sale that which cannot be sold, and ordains for money a bishop or chorepiscopus, or presbyter, or deacon, or any other of those who are reckoned among the clergy; or who for money shall appoint anyone to the office of œconomus, advocate, or paramonarius; or, in a word, who has done anything else contrary to the canon, for the sake of filthy lucre — he who has undertaken to do anything of this sort, having been convicted, shall be in danger of losing his degree. And he who has been ordained shall derive no advantage from the ordination or promotion thus negotiated; but let him remain a stranger to the dignity and responsibility which he attained by means of money. And if any one shall appear to have acted as a go-between in so shameful and godless a traffic, he also, if he be a cleric, shall be removed from his degree; if he be a layman or a monk, let him be excommunicated.

Ancient Epitome: It seems that such as glory in the fact that they owe their position to their liberality in gold to the Church, and who contemn those who were chosen because of their virtue and were appointed without any largess, should receive the lowest place in their order. And should they continue in their ways, let them be punished. But those who made such gifts so as to get ordinations, let such be cast forth from communion, as Simon Magus was by Peter.

Canon 6

Concerning the holding of a local Synod at the time appointed.

Since there is a canon which says, twice a year in each province, the canonical enquiries shall be made in the gatherings of the bishops; but because of the inconveniences which those who thus came together had to undergo in travelling, the holy fathers of the Sixth Council decreed that once each year, without regard to place or excuse which might be urged, a council should be held and the things which are amiss corrected. This canon we now renew. And if any prince be found hindering this being carried out, let him be excommunicated. But if any of the metropolitans shall take no care that this be done, he being free from constraint or fear or other reasonable excuse, let him be subjected to the canonical penalties. While the council is engaged in considering the canons or matters which have regard to the Gospel, it behooves the assembled Bishops, with all attention and grave thought to guard the divine and life-giving commandments of God, for in keeping of them there is great reward; because our lamp is the commandment, and our light is the law, and trial and discipline are the way of life, and the commandment of the Lord shining afar gives light to the eyes. It is not permitted to a metropolitan to demand any of those things which the bishops bring with them, whether it be a horse or any other gift. If he be convicted of doing anything of this sort, he shall restore fourfold.

Ancient Epitome: Whenever it is not possible for a synod to meet according to the decree formulated long ago, twice in each year, at least let it be held once, as seemed good to the Sixth Synod. Should any magistrate forbid such meeting, let him be cast out: and a bishop who shall take no pains to assemble it, shall be subject to punishment. And when the synod is held, should it appear that the Metropolitan has taken anything away from any bishop, let him restore four-fold.

Canon 7

That to churches consecrated without any deposit of the relics of the Saints, the defect should be made good.

Paul the divine Apostle says: The sins of some are open beforehand, and some they follow after. These are their primary sins, and other sins follow these. Accordingly upon the heels of the heresy of the traducers of the Christians, there followed close other ungodliness. For as they took out of the churches the presence of the venerable images, so likewise they cast aside other customs which we must now revive and maintain in accordance with the written and unwritten law. We decree therefore that relics shall be placed with the accustomed service in as many of the sacred temples as have been consecrated without the relics of the Martyrs. And if any bishop from this time forward is found consecrating a temple without holy relics, he shall be deposed, as a transgressor of the ecclesiastical traditions.

Ancient Epitome: Let relics of the Holy Martyrs be placed in such churches as have been consecrated without them, and this with the accustomed prayers. But whoever shall consecrate a church without these shall be deposed as a transgressor of the traditions of the Church.

Canon 8

That Hebrews ought not to be received unless they have been converted in sincerity of heart.

Since certain, erring in the superstitions of the Hebrews, have thought to mock at Christ our God, and feigning to be converted to the religion of Christ do deny him, and in private and secretly keep the Sabbath and observe other Jewish customs, we decree that such persons be not received to communion, nor to prayers, nor into the Church; but let them be openly Hebrews according to their religion, and let them not bring their children to baptism, nor purchase or possess a slave. But if any of them, out of a sincere heart and in faith, is converted and makes profession with his whole heart, setting at naught their customs and observances, and so that others may be convinced and converted, such an one is to be received and baptized, and his children likewise; and let them be taught to take care to hold aloof from the ordinances of the Hebrews. But if they will not do this, let them in no way be received.

Ancient Epitome: Hebrews must not be received unless they are manifestly converted with sincerity of heart.

Canon 9

That none of the books containing the heresy of the traducers of the Christians are to be hid.

All the childish devices and mad ravings which have been falsely written against the venerable images, must be delivered up to the Episcopium of Constantinople, that they may be locked away with other heretical books. And if anyone is found hiding such books, if he be a bishop or presbyter or deacon, let him be deposed; but if he be a monk or layman, let him be anathema.

Ancient Epitome: If any one is found to have concealed a book written against the venerable images, if he is on the clergy list let him be deposed; if a layman or monk let him be cut off.

Canon 10

That no cleric ought to leave his diocese and go into another without the knowledge of the Bishop.

Since certain of the clergy, misinterpreting the canonical constitutions, leave their own diocese and run into other dioceses, especially into this God-protected royal city, and take up their abode with princes, celebrating liturgies in their oratories, it is not permitted to receive such persons into any house or church without the license of their own Bishop and also that of the Bishop of Constantinople. And if any clerk shall do this without such license, and shall so continue, let him be deposed. With regard to those who have done this with the knowledge of the aforesaid Bishops, it is not lawful for them to undertake mundane and secular responsibilities, since this is forbidden by the sacred canons. And if anyone is discovered holding the office of those who are called Meizoteroi; let him either lay it down, or be deposed from the priesthood. Let him rather be the instructor of the children and others of the household, reading to them the Divine Scriptures, for to this end he received the priesthood.

Ancient Epitome: A clergyman who after leaving his own parish has settled in another far off from his own bishop and from the bishop of Constantinople, shall be received neither into house nor church. And if he shall persevere in his course, he shall be deposed. But if they shall do this with a knowledge of what we have said, they shall not receive a secular position; or should they have received them, they shall cease from them. And if they refuse they shall be deposed.

Canon 11

That Œconomi ought to be in the Episcopal palaces and in the Monasteries.

Since we are under obligation to guard all the divine canons, we ought by all means to maintain in its integrity that one which says œconomi are to be in each church. If the metropolitan appoints in his Church an œconomus, he does well; but if he does not, it is permitted to the Bishop of Constantinople by his own (ἰδίας) authority to choose an œconomus for the Church of the Metropolitan. A like authority belongs to the metropolitans, if the Bishops who are subject to them do not wish to appoint œconomi in their churches. The same rule is also to be observed with respect to monasteries.

Ancient Epitome: If the Metropolitan does not elect an œconomus of the metropolis, the patriarch shall do so. If the bishop shall not do so, the Metropolitan shall; for so it seemed good to the fathers assembled at Chalcedon. The same law shall hold in monasteries.

Canon 12

That a Bishop or Hegumenos ought not to alienate any part of the suburban estate of the church.

If bishop or *hegumenos* is found alienating any part of the farm lands of the bishoprick or monastery into the hands of secular princes, or surrendering them to any other person, such act is null according to the canon of the holy Apostles, which says: Let the bishop take care of all the Church's goods, and let him administer the same according as in the sight of God. It is not lawful for him to appropriate any part himself, or to confer upon his relations the things which belong to God. If they are poor let them be helped among the poor; but let them not be used as a pretext for smuggling away the Church's property. And if it be urged that the land is only a loss and yields no profit, the place is not on that account to be given to the secular rulers, who are in the neighbourhood; but let it be given to clergymen or husbandmen. And if they have resorted to dishonest craft, so that the ruler has bought the land from the husbandman or cleric, such transaction shall likewise be null, and the land shall be restored to the bishoprick or monastery. And the bishop or *hegumenos* doing this shall be turned out, the bishop from his bishoprick and the *hegumenos* from his monastery, as those who wasted what they did not gather.

Ancient Epitome: According to what seemed good to the Holy Apostles, any act of alienation of the goods of a diocese or of a monastery made by the bishop, or by the superior of the monastery, shall be null. And the Bishop or Superior who shall have done this shall be expelled.

Canon 13

That they are worthy of special condemnation who turn the monasteries into public houses.

During the calamity which was brought to pass in the Churches, because of our sins, some of the sacred houses, for example, bishops' palaces and monasteries, were seized by certain men and became public inns. If those who now hold them choose to give them back, so that they may be restored to their original use, well and good; but if not, and these persons are on the sacerdotal list, we command that they be deposed; if they be monks or laymen, that they be excommunicated, as those who have been condemned from the Father, and the Son, and the Holy Ghost, and assigned their place where the worm dies not and the fire is not quenched, because they set themselves against the voice of the Lord, which says: Make not my Father's house a house of merchandise.

Ancient Epitome: Those who make common diocesan or monastic goods, unless they restore to the bishop or superior the things belonging to the diocese or monastery, the whole proceeding shall be null. If they are persons in Holy Orders they shall be deposed, but if laymen or monks they shall be cast out.

Canon 14

That no one without ordination ought to read in the ambo during the synaxis.

That there is a certain order established in the priesthood is very evident to all, and to guard diligently the promotions of the priesthood is well pleasing to God. Since therefore we see certain youths who have received the clerical tonsure, but who have not yet received ordination from the bishop, reading in the ambo during the Synaxis, and in doing this violating the canons, we forbid this to be done (from henceforth,) and let this prohibition be observed also among the monks. It is permitted to each *hegumenos* in his own monastery to ordain a reader, if he himself had received the laying on of hands by a bishop to the dignity of *hegumenos*, and is known to be a presbyter. Chorepiscopi may likewise, according to ancient custom and with the bishop's authorization, appoint readers.

Ancient Epitome: No one shall read from the ambon unless he has been ordained by the bishop. And this shall be in force also among monks. The superior of a monastery, if he has been ordained by the bishop, may ordain a lector but only in his own monastery. A chorepiscopus also can make a lector.

Canon 15

That a clerk ought not to be set over two churches.

From henceforth no clergyman shall be appointed over two churches, for this savours of merchandise and filthy lucre, and is altogether alien from ecclesiastical custom. We have heard by the very voice of the Lord that, No man can serve two masters, for either he will hate the one and love the other, or else he will hold to the one and despise the other. Each one, therefore, as says the Apostle, in the calling wherein he was called, in the same he ought to abide, and in one only church to give attendance. For in the affairs of the Church, what is gained through filthy lucre is altogether separate from God. To meet the necessities of this life, there are various occupations, by means of which, if one so desire, let him procure the things needful for the body. For says the Apostle, These hands have ministered unto my necessities, and to them that were with me. Occupations of this sort may be obtained in the God-protected city. But in the country places outside, because of the small number of people, let a dispensation be granted.

Ancient Epitome: Hereafter at Constantinople a cleric may not serve two churches. But in the outskirts this may be permitted on account of the scarcity of men.

Canon 16

That it does not become one in holy orders to be clad in costly apparel.

All buffoonery and decking of the body ill becomes the priestly rank. Therefore those bishops and clerics who array themselves in gay and showy clothing ought to correct themselves, and if they do not amend they ought to be subjected to punishment. So likewise they who anoint themselves with perfumes. When the root of bitterness sprang up, there was poured into the Catholic Church the pollution of the heresy of the traducers of the Christians. And such as were defiled by it, not only detested the pictured images, but also set at naught all decorum, being exceedingly mad against those who lived gravely and religiously; so that in them was fulfilled that which is written, The service of God is abominable to the sinner. If therefore, any are found deriding those who are clad in poor and grave raiment, let them be corrected by punishment. For from early times every man in holy orders wore modest and grave clothing; and verily whatever is worn, not so much because of necessity, as for the sake of outward show, savours of dandyism, as says Basil the Great. Nor did anyone array himself in raiment embroidered with silk, nor put many colored ornaments on the border of his garments; for they had heard from the lips of God that They that wear soft clothing are in kings' houses.

SEVEN ECUMENICAL COUNCILS OF THE CHURCH

Ancient Epitome: Bishops and clergymen arraying themselves in splendid clothes and anointed with perfumes must be corrected. Should they persist, they must be punished.

Canon 17

That he shall not be allowed to begin the building of an oratory, who has not the means wherewith to finish it.

Certain monks having left their monasteries because they desired to rule, and, unwilling to obey, are undertaking to build oratories, but have not the means to finish them. Now whoever shall undertake to do anything of this sort, let him be forbidden by the bishop of the place. But if he have the means wherewith to finish, let what he has designed be carried on to completion. The same rule is to be observed with regard to laymen and clerics.

Ancient Epitome: Whoever wishes to build a monastery, if he has the wherewithal to finish it, let him begin the work, and let him bring it to a conclusion. But if not, let him be prohibited by the bishop of the place. The same law shall apply to laymen and monks.

Canon 18

That women ought not to live in bishops' houses, nor in monasteries of men.

Be without offense to those who are without, says the divine Apostle. Now for women to live in Bishops' houses or in monasteries is ground for grave offense. Whoever therefore is known to have a female slave or freewoman in the episcopal palace or in a monastery for the discharge of some service, let him be rebuked. And if he still continue to retain her, let him be deposed. If it happens that women are on the suburban estates, and the bishop or *hegumenos* desires to go there, so long as the bishop or *hegumenos* is present, let no woman at that time continue her work, but let her betake herself to some other place until the bishop [or *hegumenos*] has departed, so that there be no occasion of complaint.

Ancient Epitome: It is not fitting that women should be kept in episcopal houses or in monasteries. If anyone shall dare to do so, he shall be reproved; but if he persists, he shall be deposed. No woman is allowed to serve or even to appear where a bishop or a superior of a monastery is present, but let her keep herself apart until he be gone.

Canon 19

That the vows of those in holy orders and of monks, and of nuns are to be made without the exaction of gifts.

The abomination of filthy lucre has made such inroads among the rulers of the churches, that certain of those who call themselves religious men and women, forgetting the commandments of the Lord have been altogether led astray, and for the sake of money have received those presenting themselves for the sacerdotal order and the monastic life. And hence the first step of those so received being unlawful, the whole proceeding is rendered null, as says Basil the Great. For it is not possible that God should be served by means of mammon. If therefore, anyone is found doing anything of this kind, if he be a bishop or *hegumenos*, or one of the priesthood, either let him cease to do so any longer or else let him be deposed, according to the second canon of the Holy Council of Chalcedon. If the offender be an abbess, let her be sent away from her monastery, and placed in another in a subordinate position. In like manner is a *hegumenos* to be dealt with, who has not the ordination of a presbyter. With regard to what has been given by parents as a dowry for their children, or which persons themselves have contributed out of their own property, with the declaration that such gifts were made to God, we have decreed, that whether the persons in whose behalf the gifts were made, continue to live in the monastery or not, the gifts are to remain with the monastery in accordance with their first determination; unless indeed there be ground for complaint against the superior.

Ancient Epitome: Whoever for money admits those coming to Holy Orders or to the monastic life, if he be bishop, or superior of a monastery or any other in sacred orders, shall either cease or be deposed. And the Superior of a monastery of women shall be expelled [if she have done so] and shall be given over to subjection. The same shall be the case with a superior of monks, if he be not a priest. But the possessions brought by those who come in, let them remain, whether the persons remain or not, provided the superior be not to blame.

Canon 20

That from henceforth, no double monastery shall be erected; and concerning the double monasteries already in existence.

We decree that from henceforth, no double monastery shall be erected; because this has become an offense and cause of complaint to many. In the case of those persons who with the members of their family propose to leave the world and follow the monastic life, let the men go into a monastery for men, and the women into a monastery for women; for this is well-pleasing to God. The double monasteries which are already in existence, shall observe the rule of our holy Father Basil, and shall be ordered by his precepts, monks and nuns shall not dwell together in the same monastery, for in thus living together adultery finds its occasion. No monk shall have access to a nunnery; nor shall a nun be permitted to enter a monastery for the sake of conversing with anyone therein. No monk shall sleep in a monastery for women, nor eat alone with a nun. When food is brought by men to the canonesses, let the abbess accompanied by some one of the aged nuns, receive it outside the gates of the women's monastery. When a monk desires to see one of his kinswomen, who may be in the nunnery, let him converse with her in the presence of the abbess, and that in a very few words, and then let him speedily take his departure.

Ancient Epitome: Monasteries shall not be double, neither shall monks and nuns live in the same building, nor shall they talk together apart. Moreover if a man takes anything to a canoness, let him wait without and hand it to her, and let him see his relative in the presence of her superior.

Canon 21

That monks are not to leave their monasteries and go into others.

A monk or nun ought not to leave the monastery to which he or she is attached, and betake themselves to others. But if one do this, he ought to be received as a . It is not however proper that he be made a member of the monastery, without the consent of his *hegumenos*.

Ancient Epitome: It is not allowed to a monk or a nun to leave her own house and enter another; but if he (or she) enters let (him or her) be received as a ; but let him (or her) not be admitted at all nor given hospitality contrary to the will of the superior.

Canon 22

That when it happens that monks have to eat with women they ought to observe giving of thanks, and abstemiousness, and discretion.

To surrender all things to God, and not to serve our own wills, is great gain. For says the divine Apostle, whether you eat or drink, do all to the glory of God. And Christ our God has bidden us in his Gospels, to cut off the beginning of sins; for not only is adultery rebuked by him, but even the movement of the mind towards the act of adultery when he says, Whosoever looks on a woman to lust after her, has committed adultery with her already in his heart. We who have been thus taught ought therefore to purify our minds. Now although all things are lawful, all things are not expedient, as we have been taught by the mouth of the Apostle. It is needful that all men should eat in order that they may live. And for those to whom life consists of marrying, and bringing forth children, and of the condition of the lay state, there is nothing unbecoming in men and women eating together, only let them give thanks to the giver of the food; but if there be the entertainments of the theatre, that is, Satanic songs accompanied with the meretricious inflections of harps, there come upon them, through these things, the curse of the prophet, who thus speaks: Woe to them who drink wine with harp and psaltery, but they regard not the works of the Lord, and consider not the works of his hands. Whenever persons of this sort are found among Christians, let them amend their ways; but if they will not do so, let there overtake them the penalties which have been enacted in the canons by our predecessors. With regard to those whose life is free from care and apart from men, that is, those who have resolved before the Lord God to carry the solitary yoke, they should sit down alone and in silence. Moreover it is also altogether unlawful for those who have chosen the priestly life to eat in private with women, unless it be with God-fearing and discreet men and women, so that even their feast may be turned to spiritual edification. The same rule is to be observed with relatives. Again, if it happen that a monk or priest while on a journey does not have with him what is absolutely necessary for him, and, because of his pressing needs, thinks well to turn aside into an inn or into someone's house, this he is permitted to do, seeing that need compels.

Ancient Epitome: There is no objection to laywomen eating with men: it is not right however for men who have chosen the lonely life, to eat privately with women; unless perchance together with them that fear God and with religious men and women. But when travelling, a monk or anyone in sacred orders, not carrying necessary provisions with him, may enter a public house.

The Letter of the Synod to the Emperor and Empress

(Labbe and Cossart, *Concilia*, Tom. VII., col. 577.)

To our most religious and most serene princes, Constantine and Irene his mother. Tarasius, the unworthy bishop of your God-protected royal city, new Rome, and all the holy Council which met at the good pleasure of God and upon the command of your Christ-loving majesty in the renowned metropolis of Nice, the second council to assemble in this city.

Christ our God (who is the head of the Church) was glorified, most noble princes, when your heart, which he holds in his hands, gave forth that good word bidding us to assemble in his name, in order that we might strengthen our hold on the sure, immovable, and God-given truth contained in the Church's dogmas. As your heads were crowned with gold and most brilliant stones, so likewise were your minds adorned with the precepts of the Gospel and the teachings of the Fathers. And being the disciples and companions, as it were, of those whose sounds went forth into all the earth, you became the leaders in the way of piety of all who bore the name of Christ, setting forth clearly the word of truth, and giving a brilliant example of orthodoxy and piety; so that you were to the faithful as so many burning lamps. The Church which was ready to fall, you upheld with your hands, strengthening it with sound doctrine, and bringing into the unity of a right judgment those who were at variance. We may therefore well say with boldness that it was through you that the good pleasure of God brought about the triumph of godliness, and filled our mouth with joy and our tongue with gladness. And these things our lips utter with a formal decree. For what is more glorious than to maintain the Church's interests; and what else is more calculated to provoke our gladness?

SEVEN ECUMENICAL COUNCILS OF THE CHURCH

Certain men rose up, having the form of godliness, inasmuch as they were clothed with the dignity of the priesthood, but denying the power thereof; and thus deserving for themselves the charge of being but priests of Babylon. Of such the word of prophecy had before declared that lawlessness went forth from the priests of Babylon. Nay more, they banded themselves together in a sanhedrim, like to that which Caiaphas held, and became the propagators of ungodly doctrines. And having a mouth full of cursing and bitterness, they thought to win the mastery by means of abusive words. With a slanderous tongue and a pen of a like character, and objecting to the very terms used by God himself, they devised marvellous tales, and then proceeded to stigmatise as idolaters the royal priesthood and the holy nation, even those who had put on Christ, and by his grace had been kept safe from the folly of idols. And having a mind set upon evil, they took in hand unlawful deeds, thinking to suppress altogether the depicting of the venerable images. Accordingly, as many icons as were set in mosaic work they dug out, and those which were in painted waxwork, they scraped away; thus turning the comely beauty of the sacred temples into complete disorder. Among doings of this sort, it is to be specially noted that the pictures set up on tablets in memory of Christ our God and of his Saints, they gave over to the flames. Finally, in a word, having desecrated our churches, they reduced them to utter confusion. Then some bishops became the leaders of this heresy and where before was peace, they fomented strife among the people; and instead of wheat sowed tares in the Church's fields. They mingled wine with water, and gave the foul draught to those about them. Although but Arabian wolves, they hid themselves under sheeps' clothing, and by specious reasoning against the truth sought to commend their lie. But all the while they hatched asps' eggs and wove a spider's web, as says the prophet; and he that would eat of their eggs, having crushed one, found it to be addled, with a basilisk within it, and giving forth a deadly stench.

In such a state of affairs, with a lie busy destroying the truth, you, most gracious and most noble princes, did not idly allow so grave a plague, and such soul-destroying error long to continue in your day. But moved by the divine Spirit which abides in you, you set yourselves with all your strength utterly to exterminate it, and thus preserve the stability of the Church's government, and likewise concord among your subjects; so that your whole empire might be established in peace agreeably with the name [Irene] you bear. You rightly reasoned, that it was not to be patiently endured, that while in other matters we could be of one mind and live in concord, yet in what ought to be the chief concern of our life, the peace of the Churches, there was among us strife and division. And that too, when Christ being our head, we ought to be members one of another, and one body, by our mutual agreement and faith. Accordingly, you commanded our holy and numerously-attended council to assemble in the metropolis of Nice, in order that after having rid the Church of division, we might restore to unity the separated members, and might be careful to rend and utterly destroy the coarse cloak of false doctrine, which they had woven of thorn fibre, and unfold again the fair robe of orthodoxy.

And now having carefully traced the traditions of the Apostles and Fathers, we are bold to speak. Having but one mind by the inbreathing of the most Holy Spirit, and being all knit together in one, and understanding the harmonious tradition of the Catholic Church, we are in perfect harmony with the symphonies set forth by the six, holy and ecumenical councils; and accordingly we have anathematised the madness of Arius, the frenzy of Macedonius, the senseless understanding of Appolinarius, the man-worship of Nestorius, the irreverent mingling of the natures devised by Eutyches and Dioscorus, and the many-headed hydra which is their companion. We have also anathematised the idle tales of Origen, Didymus, and Evagrius; and the doctrine of one will held by Sergius, Honorius, Cyrus, and Pyrrhus, or rather, we have anathematised their own evil will. Finally, taught by the Spirit, from whom we have drawn pure water, we have with one accord and one soul, altogether wiped out with the sponge of the divine dogmas the newly devised heresy, well-worthy to be classed with those just mentioned, which springing up after them, uttered such empty nonsense about the sacred icons. And the contrivers of this vain, but revolutionary babbling we have cast forth far from the Church's precincts.

And as the hands and feet are moved in accordance with the directions of the mind, so likewise, we, having received the grace and strength of the Spirit, and having also the assistance and co-operation of your royal authority, have with one voice declared as piety and proclaimed as truth: that the sacred icons of our Lord Jesus Christ are to be had and retained, inasmuch as he was very man; also those which set forth what is historically narrated in the Gospels; and those which represent our undefiled Lady, the holy Mother of God; and likewise those of the Holy Angels (for they have manifested themselves in human form to those who were counted worthy of the vision of them), or of any of the Saints. [We have also decreed] that the brave deeds of the Saints be portrayed on tablets and on the walls, and upon the sacred vessels and vestments, as has been the custom of the holy Catholic Church of God from ancient times; which custom was regarded as having the force of law in the teaching both of those holy leaders who lived in the first ages of the Church, and also of their successors our reverend Fathers. [We have likewise decreed] that these images are to be reverenced (προσκυνεῖν), that is, salutations are to be offered to them. The reason for using the word is, that it has a two-fold signification. For κυνεῖν in the old Greek tongue signifies both to salute and to kiss. And the preposition προς gives to it the additional idea of strong desire towards the subject; as for example, we have φέρω and προσφέρω, κυρῶ and προσκυρῶ, and so also we have κυνέω and προσκυνέω. Which last word implies salutation and strong love; for that which one loves he also reverences (προσκυνεῖ) and what he reverences that he greatly loves, as the everyday custom, which we observe towards those we love, bears witness, and in which both ideas are practically illustrated when two friends meet together. The word is not only made use of by us, but we also find it set down in the Divine Scriptures by the ancients. For it is written in the histories of the Kings, And David rose up and fell upon his face and did reverence to (προσεκυνήσε) Jonathan three times and kissed him 1 Kings 20:41. And what is it that the Lord in the Gospel says concerning the Pharisees? They love the uppermost rooms at feasts and greetings (ἀσπασμοὺς) in the markets. It is evident that by greetings here, he means reverence (προσκύνησιν) for the Pharisees being very high-minded and thinking themselves to be righteous were eager to be reverenced by all, but not [merely] to be kissed. For to receive salutations of this latter sort savoured too much of lowly humility, and this was not to the Pharisees' liking. We have also the example of Paul the divine Apostle, as Luke in the Acts of the Apostles relates: When we had come to Jerusalem, the brethren received us gladly, and the day following Paul went in with us unto James, and all the presbyters were present. And when he had saluted (ἀσπασάμενος) them, he declared particularly what things God had wrought among the Gentiles by his ministry Acts 21:17-19. By the salutation here mentioned, the Apostle evidently intended to render that reverence of honour (τιμητικὴν προσκύνησιν) which we show to one another, and of which he speaks when he says concerning Jacob, that he reverenced (προσεκύνησεν) the top of his staff Hebrews 11:21. With these examples agrees what Gregory surnamed Theologus says: Honour Bethlehem, and reverence (προσκυνήσον) the manger.

Now who of those rightly and sincerely understanding the Divine Scriptures, has ever supposed that these examples which we have cited speak of the worship in spirit (τῆς ἐν πνεύματι λατρείας)? [Certainly no one has ever thought so] except perhaps some persons utterly bereft of sense and ignorant of all knowledge of the Scriptures and of the teaching of the Fathers. Surely Jacob did not adore (ἐλάτρευσεν) the top of his staff; and surely Gregory Theologus does not bid us to adore (λατρεύειν) the manger? By no means.

Again, when offering salutations to the life-giving Cross, we together sing: We reverence (προσκυνῶμεν), your cross, O Lord, and we also reverence (προσκυνῶμεν) the spear which opened the life-giving side of your goodness. This is clearly but a salutation, and is so called, and its character is evinced by our touching the things mentioned with our lips. We grant that the word προσκύνησις is frequently found in the Divine Scriptures and in the writings of our learned and holy Fathers for the worship in spirit (ἐπὶ της ἐν πνεύματι λατρείας), since, being a word of many significations, it may be used to express that kind of reverence which is service. As there is also the veneration of honour, love and fear. In this sense it is, that we venerate your glorious and most noble majesty. So also there is another veneration which comes of fear alone, thus Jacob venerated Esau. Then there is the veneration of gratitude, as Abraham reverenced the sons of Heth, for the field which he received from them for a burying place for Sarah his wife. And finally, those looking to obtain some gift, venerate those who are above them, as Jacob venerated Pharaoh. Therefore because this term has these many significations, the Divine Scriptures teaching us, You shall venerate the Lord your God, and him only shall you serve, says simply that veneration is to be given to God, but does not add the word only; for veneration being a word of wide meaning is an ambiguous term; but it goes on to say you shall serve (λατρεύσεις) him only, for to God alone do we render *latria*.

SEVEN ECUMENICAL COUNCILS OF THE CHURCH

The things which we have decreed, being thus well supported, it is confessedly and beyond all question acceptable and well-pleasing before God, that the images of our Lord Jesus Christ as man, and those of the undefiled Mother of God, the ever-virgin Mary, and of the honourable Angels and of all Saints, should be venerated and saluted. And if anyone does not so believe, but undertakes to debate the matter further and is evil affected with regard to the veneration due the sacred images, such an one our holy ecumenical council (fortified by the inward working of the Spirit of God, and by the traditions of the Fathers and of the Church) anathematises. Now anathema is nothing less than complete separation from God. For if any are quarrelsome and will not obediently accept what has now been decreed, they but kick against the pricks, and injure their own souls in their fighting against Christ. And in taking pleasure at the insults which are offered to the Church, they clearly show themselves to be of those who madly make war upon piety, and are therefore to be regarded as in the same category with the heretics of old times, and their companions and brethren in ungodliness.

We have sent our brethren and fellow priests, God-beloved Bishops, together with certain of the Hegumenoi and clergy, that they may give a full report of our proceedings to your godly-hearing ears. In proof and confirmation of what we have decreed, and also for the assurance of your most religious majesty, we have submitted proofs from the Fathers, a few of the many we have gathered together in illustration of the brightly shining truth.

And now may the Saviour of us all, who reigns with you (συμβασιλεύων ὑμῖν) and who was pleased to vouchsafe his peace to the Churches through you, preserve your kingdom for many years, and also your council, princes, and faithful army, and the whole estate of the empire; and may he also give you victory over all your enemies. For he it is, who says: As I live, says the Lord, they that glorify me, I will glorify. He it is also who has girded you with strength, and will smite all your enemies, and make your people to rejoice.

And do, O city, the new Sion, rejoice and be glad; you that are the wonder of the whole world. For although David has not reigned in you, nevertheless your pious princes here preside over your affairs as

SEVEN ECUMENICAL COUNCILS OF THE CHURCH

David would have done. The Lord is in the midst of you; may his name be blessed forever and ever. Amen.

www.ingramcontent.com/pod-product-compliance
Lightning Source LLC
Chambersburg PA
CBHW050253010526
44107CB00003B/298